Clay Pigeon Shooting:
A History

Clay Pigeon Shooting:
A History

by

Michael Yardley
© 2005

Clay Pigeon Shooting: A History
Text © Michael Yardley
Additional text © Mike Barnes, Philip Barker, Wesley Stanton & Charlie Jacoby
Illustrations/photographs © see credits
First published in 2005 by Blaze Publishing, UK
Edited by Charlie Jacoby http://users.tinyonline.co.uk/jacoby
Cover design by Chris Haddon
Printed in England by Imagery

ISBN 0-9549597-0-1

Frontispiece: wind and rain at Harrogate, shortly after the Second World War

FOR MY YOUNG GUNS
HARRY and JAMIE and possibly ELIZABETH, not to mention ALEXANDRA
WHO HAS THE STRENGTH OF SPIRIT TO PREFER TENNIS

Contents

Percy Stanbury (left) talking guns with ET Peacock at the Skeet Championship meeting, Northolt, Middlesex, in September 1949

Preface

by George Digweed

CLAY PIGEON shooting has had a long history. It may be called a minor sport but there is nothing minor about how it has come to be what it is today, with up to a million Brits a year giving it a go and some of them shooting pretty well!

First there were the live bird shoots with their big money wagers in the nineteenth century, then the development of the glass ball and then the clay itself. It was an early Olympic sport, then dropped by the Olympics before the Second World War, restarted afterwards and is now 100% on song.

Clay pigeon shooting has had a history that's closely intertwined with gameshooting—and I'm glad to say that that theme continues today. I'm best known for clay shooting but I also run two game shoots and I enjoy pigeon shooting in a hide. In 1996 in Berkshire, I broke the then world pigeon shooting record.

Clay shooting does not, however, get the media recognition that it should. The top shooters of the nineteenth century were regarded much as Michael Schumacher and David Beckham are today. I hope they will be again. It goes to show that I was born in the wrong century!

Clay pigeon shooting is a fluid sport: clay grounds have come and gone—some of them as well-known and important to the world of sport in their day as Wembley Stadium is today. Great shooters have played and won and occasionally lost—and have been consigned to this history book. Techniques and equipment have changed over the years with, as now, the latest kit hailed as great technological advances—and then left to rust as new and greater kit supplants it.

Writing this book has been a monumental piece of work by Michael Yardley. He has gone through all the major and most of the minor sources for historical snippets about clay pigeon shooting and put them all together to make a fascinating narrative about our sport. You will see in this book just how good a shot some of the early target shooters must have been. I won't say shooting is easy. But the careful design of clay guns like my own Perazzi has made the job less difficult. The shooters of the nineteenth century had quite different guns—and still a few of them straighted 100s.

I also share with Michael a great sense of hope for the sport, as long as all of us shooters pull together and work towards a better future. There is no doubt that shooting has never been so popular. Even though Britain is becoming more and more crowded, especially my part of it in the South-East, there is demand by people and companies to open clay pigeon clubs just as there was great demand to open golf clubs in the 1980s. People want to go shooting.

The London Olympics in 2012 is going to be the ideal expo for our sport. It's a show that we can really benefit from. I said before that clay pigeon shooting doesn't get the media recognition that it should—but I think it will. It is becoming so much more popular. And, in the meantime, shooters and the shooting press know all about it.

George Digweed in action at West Kent Shooting School, 2004. George Digweed has won 14 Sporting world championships, including the FITASC World Championship and World Cup and the World Sporting Championship. He runs the George Digweed sporting agency. Visit www.georgedigweed.com

Early reference to a 'clay' pigeon

REPORT OF a performance by Miss Annie Oakley (pictured) at the Gun Club, Notting Hill, London, in *The Field* in 1887:

Saturday, June 11. The invitations sent out to witness a private performance by Miss Annie Oakley (of the Wild West Show) brought a large and distinguished company of ladies and gentlemen to the Gun Club and at half-past one o'clock a neatly printed card was handed round to the visitors and the following programme was expeditiously got through: Short exhibition of small rifle shooting.

Clay pigeon shooting—two shots straight, Miss Oakley pulling trap herself; standing back to trap, turning and firing; the snap shot; a double rise; picking gun from ground after trap was sprung and same with double rise.

Holding gun with one hand and throwing away ball with other; throwing up two balls and breaking both; throwing ball backwards, picking up gun and breaking it; six balls thrown up by assistant and all broken in four seconds; breaking five balls in five seconds, first with rifle, others with shotguns, changing gun three times.

The several difficult feats were skilfully performed. The entertainment concluded by Miss Annie Oakley shooting at twenty-five blue rocks, 23 yards rise.

'Little Sure Shot' proved herself no mean adept at shooting flying, for no less than eighteen pigeons were brought down in fine style, several of the birds falling at a long distance to the second barrel. It is needless to say that the different feats were loudly applauded.

Lord Stormont, the president of the club, now came forward and, in an excellent speech, thanked Miss Annie Oakley, on behalf of the ladies and gentlemen present for the entertainment she had afforded them. The proceedings terminated by his lordship handing to Miss Oakley a souvenir of her visit in the shape of a handsome gold medal. Beautifully engraved on the face was the pavilion and shooting enclosure and on the clasps were the words 'Presented to Miss Annie Oakley by the members of the London Gun Club, June 11, 1887'. The little American, in reply, declared she should always look back with pleasure to her visit to England, where she had met with the greatest kindness and with pride she should wear the Gun Club medal at all entertainments of any importance.

The gun used by Miss Oakley for the pigeon shooting was built expressly for her by C Lancaster and weighed 6lb 14oz. The charge was 1 1/8oz shot, both EC and black powder being used. For the artistic part of the entertainment Schultze powder was used. An excellent substitute for glass ball shooting is the sphere used at the Wild West Show. It is cast in pitch, breaks easily and will not cut anything that it comes in contact with, like glass.[1]

Thanks

THIS BOOK—a rather eccentric history of live pigeon and clayshooting—was written as a labour of love and occasional desperation. It has taken more than half a dozen years to come this far, so the forbearance of family is a given. It would not have seen the light of day at all without the input and friendly pressure of publisher Wes Stanton, my eldest son Jamie—who is always urging me to finish books so that I can start *Have Guns Will Travel*—and my editor and world's most amusing lunch companion, Charlie Jacoby. There are many others whose help has been invaluable:

John Hargreaves, who has a unique working collection of pigeon and early inanimate target shooting paraphernalia and who has been extraordinarily generous of his time and knowledge in more areas than I can list; Philip Barker, whose contribution to the Olympic sections has been critical; Ian Peel, winner of the silver medal for Trap at Sydney in 2000 and who kindly read through the modern Olympic material in this work; Andy Rivas, Peter Jackson, Paul Roberts, Paul Payne, Jack Montgomery, Pat Farey and Dig Hadoke, for being stalwart friends as ever; Alan Rhone; Terry Blaney; Richard Rawlingson, editor of *Clay Shooting*; Tim Woodhouse, Peter Boden and Mick Shepherd; Richard Horton, for turning detective; Justin Hardwicke; Bob Pitcher of the London Proof House; Bill Harding of the Birmingham Proof House; Charlotte Lubert, *chargée du patrimoine historique*, Société des Bains de Mer; Robin Chute, author of the excellent bibliographic works *Shooting Flying* and *Shooting Sitting* for confirming certain details relating to Victorian sporting literature; Alastair Balmain, deputy editor of *Shooting Times*; Linda Tubbs, for information relating to turkey shoots in the USA; Kevin Gill, one of our best internationals, for his comments on the Olympic section; Nigella Baskerville, for kindly researching points relating to the first, 1881, edition of *The Gun and Its Development*; Professor Mike Cooley, director of Cogswell & Harrison, for his kindness at an early stage in this project; Bob Brister; Paul Lester, a research officer at House of Commons Information, for providing detail concerning George Anderson MP; Charles Birchall, for explaining the origins of *The Iliad* and *The Aeneid*; Bob Bigwood, who once owned a gun shop in Botley Hampshire, for confirming certain details about the Botley Clay Pigeon Club, the earliest recorded regional club in Britain; Jonathan Young, editor of *The Field*, for access to *The Field*'s archives; David Baker, for stimulating my interest with his articles on pigeon guns; Joel Etchen, son of Rudy and grandson of Fred for information about his family and modern Trap shooting; Karl Waktare, Bjorn Waktare and Robert Frampton; Grant Dorrall of the CPSA, for his help with information relating to modern shooting organisations; David Penn, Imperial War Museum, London; Ralph Finch, editor and publisher of *On Target!*, 'the international newsletter for collectors of target balls', for providing information on the great exhibition shooters Paine, Bogardus and Carver; Morlin Ellis MA; Gavin Gardiner of Sotheby's for his comments on pigeon shooting guns; Bill Harriman, head of firearms at the British Association for Shooting & Conservation; Gerald Quinn, formerly of Remington and one of those in at the very start of Sporting clays in the USA, for taking the trouble to timeline the early history of Sporting in the USA; Chris Potter and Pat Lynch, who have done so much to promote Hélice in the UK; Nick Holt and Andrew Orr of Holt & Co; Peter Croft, former Olympian and 'Mr Memory' when it comes to clayshooting facts; And, not least, the late and much missed and much loved Chris Cradock. Without them, there would have been far more gaps.

I would also like to acknowledge certain books here that have inspired or informed (a more comprehensive bibliography appears in the appendix). My select bibliography includes: Hawker's *Instructions to Young Sportsmen*; WW Greener's *The Gun and Its Development*; and Basil '20-bore' Tozer's *Practical Hints on Shooting*, an encyclopaedia that deserves to be reprinted in the same manner as the 1910 (ninth) edition of Greener's masterpiece—all the more because it has become so scarce. *Holt's Shooting Calendar*, sporting almanacs for 1882 and 1883, have been important sources too, as has Captain Albert Money's little book *Pigeon Shooting*; William Leffingwell's *The Art of Wingshooting*; Courtney Ryley Cooper's *Annie Oakley*; and DH Eaton's *Trapshooting: The Patriotic Sport*, another candidate for facsimile reprinting.

I must also cite Teasdale-Buckell's *Experts on Guns and Shooting* and Bogardus's *Field Cover and Trap Shooting*. Both are important works, but Teasdale-Buckell can be pompous and 'Captain' Bogardus was a blowhard as well a great shot. Archibald Stuart-Wortley who wrote the informative pigeon shooting section in the Badminton Library's *Shooting: Field and Covert* must also be mildly chastised, not least for his snobbery concerning Bogardus. Similarly, *'Wild West' Doc Carver: Spirit Gun of the West* by Raymond Thorp has been a useful source and one that enlightens on many topics — not least Buffalo Bill Cody's drinking habits—but is outrageously partisan.

Post-Second World War works that have proven indispensable include FM McFarland's *Clay Pigeon Shooting* from the *Shooting Times* series; Bob Hinman's *The Golden Age of Shotgunning*; Colonel Jim Crossman's *Olympic Shooting*; and Don Masters' excellent *The House of Churchill*, a work far more comprehensive than its title might suggest. Donald Dallas has contributed to the history of pigeon shooting significantly with his excellent work on *Holland & Holland*. I should also note the critical importance of the long-forgotten magazine *Clay Target Shooting* (later *Clay Pigeon Shooting Monthly*) once issued by the Imperial Chemical Industries. I have a complete proof set—January 1925 to December 1929—that came to me from Chris Cradock. Without it, much of the British history in the key post-First World War and pre-Second World War era would have been lost. Finally, no work on this subject could be completed without reference to back issues of *Bell's Life* and those still great institutions *Shooting Times* and *The Field*.

MY

Editor's credits

I would like to thank James Marchington, editor of *Sporting Shooter*, for answering queries late into the night. I would also like to thank popinjay shooter Neil Morris, Lewis Drake & Associates, John Iverson of Earlham College, Hélice specialist Wells Equipment, Calvin Hedgeman of the United States Olympic Association, Andrew Orr (again), Moira Anderson of the CPSA, Louisa Horton of the Imperial War Museum, The Govnor's granddaughter Sue Hartman of West Country Guns in Somerset, Luke Piper for scanning, Glyn Jones, Ashley Vellacott and Mike Barnes.

CJ

A very personal introduction

JUST AS you must build a clay bird score one target at a time, so you build a book—one fact at a time. There must be a plan, you must have a form in mind but it is a big mistake to think too far ahead or ponder on the enormity of the task you are undertaking. At times, this project has certainly appeared too big to its author. Nevertheless, there is something addictive about the material. It just sucks you in.

This tome actually began as two chapters for another work—a broader historical treatise on guns and shooting (which may yet see the light of day). The chapters on live pigeon and inanimate target shooting grew and grew until they demanded a separate existence.

The resultant history of Trap shooting—as you might collectively call live pigeon, glass ball and clayshooting—might seem just a bit obsessive to those not interested in the subject. But the delight, as well as the devil, are in the detail. You might not be able to write a thousand words on the inside of a ping pong ball as sadistic schoolmasters once used to demand but you could certainly write tens of thousands words on ball targets and what went inside them (wood shavings, confetti and explosives among other things). Indeed there is already a magazine devoted to this marvellously esoteric subject—Ralph Finch's *On Target!*—and a dedicated book is also in the works.

If one problem has been knowing when to stop, then another has been deciding where to begin this sporting genealogy. You will find significant amount of material on live pigeon shooting here, not to mention references to popinjay or 'papingo' competition. The inclusion of so much material on pigeon shooting—as, henceforth captive bird shooting will be called—may prompt comment and warrants explanation.

Clayshooting might wish to distance itself from its disreputable relation, but it cannot. Pigeon shooting, in some aspects so familiar and in others so alien, is the missing link between the modern competitor and his sporting forebears. It not only gives clay busting much of its terminology—trap, pull!, no bird etc—but also provides the basic model upon which glass ball, clay target and ZZ/Hélice shooting are still organised. In addition, if it were not for pigeon shooting, the science of sporting gunnery would have advanced far more slowly.

Specialist pigeon guns profoundly influenced modern clay and game guns. Much the same may be said of the ammunition developed for use in them. Shot cups, smokeless powder and the long-case 'magnum' 12-bore cartridge owe much of their development to the quest to drop one more bird on the pigeon field. Shooters of the 1860, 1870s and 1880s no doubt reacted to the arrival of the breechloader, choke and the terracotta discus target much as we have reacted to semi-automatics, multi-chokes and electric traps.

Technology is not the only issue. The development of 'aristocratic' clubs, following the era of peripatetic matches and pub shoots, is a fascinating window on British society and its class and club systems. The history of pigeon shooting is unusually contained, moreover. It provides an insight into the development of sport generally. The fastidious rules of the pre-eminent Victorian clubs, Hurlingham and the Gun Club, the obsession with competition itself, with statistics and with fair play, explain why founder of the modern Olympics Baron de Coubertin came to England to see how sport really should be organised. Pigeon shooting may not have survived to prosper on these shores, Britannia may no longer rule the waves, but Rules Britannia are still much in evidence across the globe embedded in the regulations of a dozen or more major sports—not least clayshooting, golf, tennis, and football.

Pigeon shooting was also one of the first activities to get the serious attention of organised antis. In its most despicable form, sparrow shooting, it even merits a quote from Dickens (in *Martin Chuzzlewit*). The oft-expressed disdain for live bird trapshooting within the shooting community and the way it is sometimes capriciously described by influential writers such as Teasdale-Buckell cast a long and significant shadow. Clayshooting was guilty from birth by association. Though gambling was banned and dishonesty less prevalent, it shared the same terminology and organisation, it favoured specialist guns and encouraged the 'unsporting' desire to win.

The conspicuous consumption and complex social codes of the game bird battue, meantime, were in direct contrast to the relative economy and egalitarianism of clayshooting (although the new sport quickly became obsessed with its own rules as noted). The gameshooters might justify their prejudice by pronouncements on the flying characteristics of clays; the deeper truth was social. Clayshooting—at least in its competitive form— was, until quite recently, a poor relation to gameshooting in Britain. And, as a consequence, some clay shots fostered an inverted snobbery towards gameshooters.

Happily, the intrinsic challenge and excitement of clayshooting ensured its eventual success. By the time you get to the twentieth century—when inanimate target shooting had, by and large, supplanted box trap birdshooting—the overwhelming impression is that things were much the same at a clay club as they are today. In the words of a friend rummaging through some of my research materials 'not much seems to have changed'. That continuity is comforting. The sense of it, however, begins about 1890.

It is always fun to meet the ancestors and find them recognisable.

It is in trawling through the detritus of lost worlds, though, that the most fun and the real revelation is to be had. There is so much that is novel, bizarre or simply unexpected in this story: pigeon shooting as a kind of Formula 1 circus from 1870 to 1900; the hard fought but long forgotten battles between Carver and Bogardus; the role of Annie Oakley and the Western myth in promoting inanimate target shooting; the musician and composer John Philip Sousa's obsession with breaking pitch disks; ICI's paternalistic but positive patronage of British clayshooting; Winchester's wonderful Wingo—a sophisticated shooting game designed to compete with bowling in the 1960s.

In sorting and enjoying the trivia, the broader picture becomes clearer. Issues of the 'Shakespeare was a Russian' kind are easily resolved. The glass ball target was perfected in America in the 1860s and 1870s from a British concept. Essentially American developments included the terracotta clay—the seminal idea for a disc target that spawned the sport, the clay trap, the improved composition clay, introduced in about 1884, and the dedicated clay gun. Americans, moreover, made clayshooting a mass-participation activity that was consuming 30 million targets a year by 1892. Skeet—developed circa 1915—and Trap shooting are quintessentially American games.

The British, however, perfected the double shotgun (both side-by-side and over-and-under), pigeon shooting, smokeless powder for shotguns and Sporting clays—not to mention the driven gameshooting that inspired it. The Brits also developed methods of formal instruction for game and clayshooting and have provided shotgun marksmen with much stylistic theory, not least the Lancaster, Churchill and Stanbury shooting methods. The laurels for the *development* of choke boring—and muzzle constriction was a requirement for effective shooting at clays, in particular the early hard-baked variety—are evenly split.

Lest I be accused of an Anglo-American bias at this early stage, let me also note that Canadians, Belgians, Danes, Swedes, Dutch, Germans, Finns, Greeks,

French and Russians were keen clayshooters pre First World War. Greener's *Modern Shotgun* notes two clubs in Sweden and one in Denmark in 1891. The Italian contribution to clayshooting post Second World War is worthy of a book in itself. The sport has become bigger and more international than clayshooting pioneer George Ligowsky might have dreamed. The annual, world-wide consumption of clays is now close to two billion.

There is satisfaction in collating so much information. There is also some frustration as this project comes to an end. This history is not as complete as might be desired by black-belt anoraks (or, in truth, by its time-challenged author). Small, but important facts have proved evasive. I have not, for example, been able to find much on pigeon shooting in the eighteenth century, nor a pre-1866 mention of glass ball shooting with guns, though I came up with an intriguing reference to archery. It would

The Govnor, Albert Browning

also be interesting to know more about the training role of clayshooting during the First World War (there is a brief reference to it in Robert Churchill's *How to Shoot*) and between the wars in Germany, to which Major Northover draws attention. The baton must be passed on, now. Time has simply run out.

Let me slip in a few more excuses and in doing so, point out some other areas that deserve more research. There is great material waiting to be mined on the period 1930-1965 and, in particular, on characters such as Albert 'The Govnor' Browning and Joe Wheater. The latter definitely does not feature in this book as much as he should. In small compensation, let me note here that he was the George Digweed of his day—an all-round shot of the highest ability and a man who refused to suffer fools and could appear rude to rivals. Wheater won the British Open Sporting Championship 1961,1962, 1964, 1971 and 1972 and, unofficially, recorded 199 ex 200 at Olympic Trench in Germany in 1961. He also shot 100 straight at English Skeet on 14 June 1958, 200 straight at DTL on 29 and 30 May 1958 and won the European OT Championship in 1959.

Great Britain has only won this event four times. Wheater's was the first success, then Teddy Fear in 1961, Peter Croft in 1980 and Ian Peel in 1996.

The Commonwealth Games is not especially well served in this work either. This, however, was the author's deliberate choice as he began to drown under the weight of Olympic facts and made a 'command decision' not to get too distracted by the Commonwealth material as well. The internet, at least, speeded my Olympic fact checking and also brought me into contact with the excellent American Amateur Trapshooting Association Hall of Fame website www.shootata.com. Readers who want to pursue the history of pigeon and

The author calls 'pull!'

inanimate target shooting further will find excellent articles there posted by Alex Kerr, Richard Hamilton, director of the ATA Hall of Fame Dick Baldwin and others. Having discovered their work at the last minute, I have been impressed with its depth and detail. I was also surprised to find so many other modern researchers engaged in this area.

What is presented in this book is certainly not intended to be the last word. The aim is to entertain and stimulate interest. It has certainly stimulated the author. When you look at a subject in real detail, it is amazing where it takes you and what else it illuminates. Connections are made that increase your understanding of many aspects of the world in which we live. The eighteenth and nineteenth centuries may look very different to ours but, in the motivation and aspiration of individuals and in their creative and competitive spirit, little has changed. That fraternity with those long dead is rather moving.

Now, to put what follows in to a personal context, to explain the writer's motivation and to bore my kids (and their kids) in years to come when they happen upon this volume, it is now appropriate—and fun—to add some autobiographical information. My apologies for transgressing the normal inside back-flap allocation, but I am trying to get into the habit of personal disclosure so that all may soon be revealed in *Have Guns Will Travel* (promised to my son Jamie before the end of 2005).

I have used and studied guns and shooting all my life—as I write this, for something more than forty years. My ballistic odyssey began on my grandmother's farm Greystones in Kent with a bow and arrow in about 1960; various air-weapons and a homemade crossbow soon supplemented my armoury. Shotgunning began—sometime after experiments with gunpowder and petrol bombs—with a 9mm Webley garden gun and Jacob's cream crackers used as (static) targets. I graduated to a Canadian Cooey .410 and a hand trap, after encounters with a sparrow and a swallow (of which I am especially and still ashamed). The hand trap, at least, was a step in the right direction, save for the fact that I had to be my own flinger.

My interest in shooting has always been combined with an interest in the history and technology of arms. I started collecting books in about 1965. My favourite volumes were the thick, large-format, *Gun Digest* paperbacks that contained well-researched historical pieces, wide-ranging general features and—joy of joys—a catalogue section. This contained all the illicit and wonderful things a kid in London (to where my family moved) might not be able to possess—Sheridan pneumatic air rifles (then subject to Firearms Certificates in Britain), Crossman CO2-powered pistols (ditto) not to mention really exotic marvels like Remington's Fireball .221 bolt-action hand cannon.

The evolution of the gun was the subject for my first academic dissertation at Westminster School at the age of fourteen. My membership of the CPSA— no 4431—dates from 1970 (a year later). By this time I was already a long-standing member of the 11th County of London Home Guard Battalion Rifle Club—which met on Wednesday evenings at the TA hall at Vauxhall—and the Kensington Rifle & Pistol Club. The Army happened at eighteen, then university, then the Army again at twenty-five, after a few romantic and sporting digressions on the Continent.

I found myself a student officer at the Royal Military Academy Sandhurst in 1980 and won RMAS Colours for shooting. This remains a source of some pride, as I believe I was the first in the modern era to achieve it. It was also the start of a more serious approach to competitive marksmanship and historical research. I was brought into contact with world class experts like QMSI Jim Cairns—who would become a double Commonwealth Games pistol medallist—and the late David Chandler, the Napoleonic scholar who would later commission me to write the concluding chapter of the *Oxford History of the British Army* as well as other sections of that work.

When I left the military, I began working as a conflict photographer and journalist and, when time allowed, as a shooting instructor. Three wars (Lebanon, Afghanistan and Kosovo), three marriages, a revolution (Poland) and four kids later, I have retained the interest in history. I have kept buying (and writing) books. And I am still shooting and teaching people how to shoot. My output of shooting articles usually exceeds ten a month. As Chris Cradock used to say: 'It beats a proper job.'

Now, lest I depress myself too much by considering just how long ago some of the above sounds, I might cheer myself up—and end this autobiographical digression—by noting that age is no barrier to effective shotgun marksmanship. This point was delightfully confirmed by ninety-three-year-old Jim Snow when he shot his first registered 100 straight at a San Diego gun club in the spring of 2004. He did it in spite of the impediment of having only one and a half fingers on his right hand (he lost the others during an accident in the Navy in 1944). Mr Snow's 100 came after 83 years of shotgunning. It prompted him to comment:

'Everybody made such a big deal about it. I think they were surprised… I knew I could do it… I knew someday I would do it… if I lived long enough. I don't really know what took me so long, except I wasn't hittin' 'em…'[2]

Let us hope Jim Snow is still hittin' a few on his hundredth birthday. If the author manages a mere ninety, it still gives another forty-one sporting years at the time of writing—an encouraging calculation. Meantime, Mr Snow's long experience not only stands as a wonderful and optimistic example to all clayshooters, it also makes the point that shooting is a way of life as well as a sport. It is a means by which to enjoy the company of friends, a way to challenge and test yourself competitively, a way to get fresh air and exercise and, not least important, a means by which to explore and understand the past.

In spite of all the good things that it offers—and my apologies for a change of tone now—shooting remains a curiously hidden sport in modern Britain. It has become the sport that dare not speak its name. Happily, this is not yet the case in the United States. Nevertheless, it is worthy of note that a hundred years ago, shooting ranked as one of the most important and glamorous activities in Britain. It made the news pages of the mainstream press for positive reasons often eclipsing what might now be called 'popular' sports. Shooting is rarely given positive mention in this country today, save by its participants.

Yet there are still almost a million private citizens who use firearms legitimately in Britain and many more if you include

Jim Snow, 93

airgunners. Britain has about 700,000 shotgun certificate holders and you would guess about half of them have shot clays at some time, perhaps 100,000 on a fairly regular basis. Whether on the media blacklist or not, shooting is only beaten by golf and fishing in terms of individual participation. In other words, it not only was popular, it is popular.

There has been a decline—most notably over the last generation—and, there has legislative persecution. The Shepherd's Bush police murders in 1966 involved illegal handguns but led—via the Criminal Justice Act 1967 and the Firearms Act 1968 * —to new restrictions on sporting shotguns in Britain. Prior to this you could get a gun licence at the post-office for ten shillings. Similarly, Michael Ryan's murderous rampage 1987 at Hungerford involved a semi-automatic rifle and a pistol but led to more legislation on shotguns as well as a ban on semi-automatic rifles. It need hardly be added that all these measures, like the sporting pistol ban after the Dunblane tragedy, entirely missed their stated target: criminals. Handgun crime, for example, has more or less doubled in the decade to 2004. The burden of legislation in modern Britain may be viewed as a deliberate sickener. The logic, or lack of it, is immaterial to the unstated, arguably primary purpose of attrition and curtailment of individual firearms ownership. Lest you might think this danger overstated, note that British pistol shooting teams now train in Switzerland and had to import their guns to their own country under special licence for the duration of the last Commonwealth Games. Let us hope that clayshooters never suffer the same home-government-imposed humiliation.

It has certainly seemed as if there has been an increasingly unhidden agenda operating against shooting in Britain. It has been aided by outrageously biased media reporting. The tabloid and tele hacks typically confusing the apples of gun crime with the oranges of shooting sports. There is also a refusal to give our sport fair coverage. As former minister of sport Kate Hoey has pointed out, blind bowls received more TV coverage than clayshooting at the last Commonwealth Games.

However—and most happily—in spite of the misinformation and malice concerning shooting in general, clayshooting in particular appears to be growing again. Sporting clays in the USA is positively booming. On the other side of the Atlantic, there are more than eighty million gun owners and recent figures suggest that more than three million have tried Sporting. It was only introduced to the other side of the great pond circa 1980. Sporting is also on the rise in France, Belgium, Holland, Germany, the Czech Republic, Portugal, Spain, Italy, Greece and Cyprus, Scandinavia, South Africa, Namibia, Australia, New Zealand, Canada, Russia and no doubt half a dozen other countries that have not yet come to my attention. In Bahrain—where the King is a keen shot and from where I have just returned as I write this—a sporting layout is about to be built. Hélice (ZZ) also seems to be doing well globally. Even Skeet seems to have had a renaissance in Britain, partly as a result of the efforts of my publisher, Wes Stanton.

Because our sport is expanding again and because Sporting clays is becoming such a major activity, it is all the more timely that we should understand and become familiar with our roots. Knowledge of this heritage—which is surprisingly scant in the UK—is not only entertaining but it may help to defend an increasingly unpredictable future. The writer's enthusiasm for the history of 'mud saucers and gyro pigeons' meantime is apparent by the fact of this volume. If it prompts readers to the occasional 'I never realised that' or 'so that's why...' it will have succeeded in its purpose.

Michael Yardley, Colchester, October 2005

---

* Oddly paralleling the US Gun Control Act 1968—that nation's prime firearms statute

Part I

Popping at the popinjay

IF WW Greener is to believed, the spirit which moves us to break pitch disks today and which motivated our sporting ancestors to shoot at glass spheres and pigeons released from box traps, may be traced to the far older and rather curious practice of shooting at the popinjay. Initially, this was a live and tethered bird—typically a pigeon—later, a colourful stuffed one that was placed at the top of a mast or pole * (see opposite and below).

It is certainly an ancient practice. In Homer's epic *The Iliad*—written about 750BC—a dove is set atop a ship's mast as a target for the archers of Achilles during funeral games for his friend Patroclus, who had been killed by Hector with divine help from Apollo:

> He set a mast up... at the sand's edge and tethered by a cord around one foot a rock-dove. 'Shoot at that!'
> The man who hits the fluttering dove may carry all the double-axes home. If someone cuts the cord he'll miss the bird. Call it a poor shot! Second prize for him![3]

Virgil's fifth book of *The Aeneid*—as quoted by Sir Ralph Payne-Gallwey in his book *The Crossbow*—also includes a classical reference to popinjay-style shooting, funeral games and ships masts in the mythic age of Greek heroes.

> This done, Aeneas orders for the close
> The strife of Archers with contending bows
> The mast, Sergestus' shattered galley bore
> With his own hands he raises on the shore
> A fluttering dove upon the top they tie
> The living mark at which their arrows fly.[4]

Popinjay shooting was subsequently seen in many cultures, across many centuries. Competitions involving the use of bow, crossbow or gun were common in medieval and renaissance Europe and are depicted in many old prints and pictures. Wooden or stuffed birds usually replaced the live tethered ones. The activity took various local forms and dedicated weapons were developed for it. In the firearms era, these included long-barrelled wheel-lock rifles. As well as tethered and stuffed birds, the target might be a weathercock on a church spire. Occasionally, 'birds' were attached to the moving sails of a windmill. Circular aiming marks, much like the modern bulls-eye target, were also put on tall posts.

Popinjay aloft

Popinjay events were popular in England where 'The Festival of the Popinjay' was traditionally held on the first Sunday in May. The decline of martial archery may have affected it. Nevertheless, the Toxophilite Society ** created as part of the resurgence of interest in archery as sport in the eighteenth century is said to have held frequent matches. WW Greener suggests the last of these was in 1792. Colonel Walrond, however, notes that there were popinjay matches with bows in England as late as the 1840s, again connected with the resurgence of interest in sporting archery. They appear to have been abandoned soon after[5].

Sir Walter Scott mentions Popinjay shoots with guns in

---

* The English 'popinjay' is a corruption of the old French word *papegai*—parrot
** Toxophilite is a student or lover of archery

The Tale of Old Mortality[6]. He writes in chapter two that: 'The festival of the Popinjay is still, I believe, practised at Maybole in Ayrshire' and describes it in an accompanying note:

Setting up the popinjay

> The young men, as was usual, were to mix in various sports, of which the chief was to shoot at the popinjay, an ancient game formerly practised with archery but at this period with firearms. This was the figure of a bird, decked with parti-coloured feathers, so as to resemble a popinjay or parrot. It was suspended to a pole and served for a mark, at which the competitors discharged their fuses and carabines in rotation, at the distance of sixty or seventy paces. He whose ball brought down the mark held the proud title of Captain of the Popinjay for the remainder of the day and was usually escorted in triumph to the most reputable change-house in the neighbourhood, where the evening was closed with conviviality...

The Kilwinning Archers of Ayrshire still have an annual popinjay or 'papingo' shoot conducted along ancient lines with bows. It takes place on the first Saturday of June. A wooden bird is mounted on a pole and suspended from the clock tower of the old Kilwinning Abbey. Archers attempt to dislodge the wings and then the bird itself. The winner of the papingo contest used to become Captain of Archers for the next twelve months. Today, that office is decided by another event, but the papingo tradition lives on in the annual competition.

Although the society pre-dates its annals, the records of the Kilwinning Archers commence in 1688. An administrative meeting in 1870 recorded:

> Shooting with bow and arrow at butts and papingo has been used and practised at Kilwinning by the inhabitants thereof for the space of two hundred years and upwards. The prize shot for at the game of papingo in former times was a piece of fine Persian taffetie, three ells long and three-quarters broad [about 8ft x 2ft], of several colours—red, blue, green, scarlet, &c—to the value of twenty pounds at least, which they termed a Benn. The person who gained the same by shooting down the Papingo on the day appointed for that effect had the said Benn tyed about his waist as a badge of honour and was thereupon denominated Captain; and, making a parade through the town attended by the former Captains, each wearing about their waists the Benns they had gained and accompanied by the rest of the Archers, each changekeeper brought forth to them ale and other liquors to drink the Captain's health, &c. The said antient game turning into disuetude for some years, was restored and again renewed at Kilwinning on the 4th day of September, 1688[7]

The Irvine Toxophilites, who are not quite as ancient as their Kiliwinning brothers in arms, also developed an interesting popinjay-inspired event in the early decades of the nineteenth century. They shot at an 'elevated target' from a range of 40 yards. Their mark was 18in across and fixed at the top a 30ft pole.

In Flanders, popinjay shooting is still a significant sport and it featured in the 1920 Antwerp Olympics. Events today take place with both bows and crossbows. A 'cock' has pride of place at the top of a 30m pole; shooting usually takes place within 4m of it. The target is covered in feathers and floats to the ground when knocked off its perch. Blunt arrows are used. Lower down the mast, there are two 'hens'. They are smaller and have less elaborate plumage. There are also variants of the classical form where archers or crossbowmen shoot in the *horizontal* plane at shuttlecocks with coloured feathers, called 'chickens' and 'chicks' in this context. All things considered, popinjay shooting is an amazing survival. The Continental clubs, some of which can trace their existence to the fourteenth and fifteenth centuries must rank as the oldest sports clubs in existence, although the merry men of Kiliwinning cannot be far behind.

Pigeon shooting

PIGEON SHOOTING—typically the practice of shooting captive birds released from traps—is the father of clayshooting. It probably began in the second half of the eighteenth century but its precise origins are unclear. Greener speculates that it might have originated as a means by which gamekeepers and poachers might test their skill without breaking the law[8]. He cites no evidence to back this up, however.

The term 'pigeon shooting' is ambiguous. It is rather more inclusive than you might imagine. What is discussed in sporting literature under this general heading commonly involved the shooting of starlings, sparrows and larks as well as members of the family *Columbidae*. In later contests, birds were released from purpose-built traps—hence trapshooting. In the early days, though, much cruder means were adopted: hats over holes in the ground (allegedly), buckets, baskets, or boxes. Sometimes, birds were simply thrown up by hand, a practice that survives in a form of shooting known as *columbaire*.

Early references are scarce. The first date that might be attached to pigeon shooting is 1777. It was a difficult year for the British in their American colonies. It may have also seen the establishment of the first pigeon shooting club near London. The source is tenuous, however. In *Squire Osbaldeston: His Autobiography*, a book created from a long-forgotten manuscript by ED Cuming and published by Bodley Head in 1926, sixty years after Osbaldeston's death, the sporting squire notes that '[Captain] Ross and I were both members [of the Old Hats]'. In his commentary to this work, Cuming elucidates:

> The Old Hats was the oldest [pigeon shooting club]. Founded in the year 1777, the members had no ground of their own, but met at various places on the outskirts of London; Ealing was a favourite resort; Islington, Highbury and North Cheam were also patronised.[9]

Cuming does not mention his sources but it might be added that the Old Hats at Ealing appears to have been the first fashionable pigeon shooting venue and continued as such until the 1820s when many of its punters moved on to the Red House at Battersea which became the next well-known London venue.

The first contemporary reference to pigeon shooting and the one most often cited by authors of shooting books, relates to a feature in *The Sporting Magazine* of February 1793. The article is of historical significance and worth quoting at some length because of it:

> The great celebrity of this sport, in which some of the first shots in England are so frequently engaged, encourages us to communicate an account of its fashionable influence and increasing prevalence… Matches coming under this denomination are of two kinds: the first are supported by private subscription, among such gentlemen only as members of their distinct and separate clubs. Others of an inferior complexion come on, or take place, by public contribution from candidates of every subscription and are generally excited and brought about by the landlords of inns, who offer prizes of plate, purses of gold, &c, &c, to be shot for.

The periodical goes on to report that this is type of shooting was common 'in almost every part of the kingdom' but nowhere were matches 'so frequently repeated or so fashionably followed as in and around London'. The order of shooting between 'gentlemen from different clubs opposed to each other or members of the same club' was decided by tossing a coin. It continued in a tone more applicable to the bloody events then unfolding in revolutionary France where Louis had been beheaded by guillotine the previous month:

Pigeon shooting at Hornsey Wood

Several dozens of pigeons having been provided for the purpose, are disposed in baskets behind the company, there to wait the destructive crisis, the 'deadly level' that dooms them to instant death, or gives them liberty. A shallow box of about 1ft long and 8 or 10in wide, is sunk in the ground parallel with the surface and just 21 yards from the footmark at which each gunner is bound to take aim. The box has a sliding lid, to which is affixed a string held by one, appointed to the office, who is placed next the person going to shoot, from whom he takes the word of command for drawing the string whenever he is ready to take his aim, another pigeon being so expeditiously placed in the box for the succeeding shots stands ready (by the runners that furnish the pigeons), that ten, twelve, or fifteen dozen of pigeons are deposited in the box, flown and shot, in much less time than it is possible to conceive. The gunner is not permitted to put his gun to his shoulder till the bird is on the wing [the first known reference to a gun-down rule]; and the bird must fall within one hundred yards of the box, or is deemed a lost shot.

During this rapid succession (one of each side shooting alternately), the arbiter [scorer] is employed in pencilling opposite to each name the success of every individual, by A 1, or A 0; this, at the end of the match, denotes the superiority, by demonstrating which party has killed most pigeons at the least number of shots. Exclusive of the general betting upon the match, there is a variety among individuals—the shots of some against others and the field betting of the bird against the gun, as fancy may prompt, or the reputation of the gunner dictate. He that kills most pigeons in the match, at an equal number of shots with the rest, is by such pre-eminence the captain of the day [note the similar terminology to that used in British popinjay and papingo shoots], stands elected as chairman for the meeting and does the offices of the table accordingly.

Matches of an inferior description are still more numerous and generally come under the denomination of a help-all or make-feast, at the instigation of those industrious, liberal landlords who advertise three pieces of plate to be given to three best shots! But at the moment of entering the list, it becomes a collateral part of the contract that each adventurer is to contribute his proportion towards the gifts of the plate, to pay for his pigeons and to dine at the ordinary. These matters properly adjusted, the shooting is carried on in precisely the same manner as before described, with this exception only that every individual shoots for himself alone, without any connection with party. The candidate killing most pigeons at the least number of lots becomes entitled to the piece of plate highest in value and so in proportion; but in so great a number of candidates there is frequently an equality of success; in such cases they are called ties and are shot off at the remaining pigeons till the superiority is ascertained and the victor proclaimed. This done, the day concludes with the same degree of festivity and superabundance as before described, but in a style of inferiority, necessarily regulated by the pecuniary resources of the parties concerned.

Looking, however, to its attraction as a matter of sport, little or nothing can be said in its favour when put in competition with more noble and manly enjoyment of the sports of the field. The liberal mind finds a temporary repugnance at the idea of first confining and then liberating from that containment, hundreds of domestic animals doomed to instant death, with a very slender possibility in their favour, when a moderate shot will bring down fourteen or fifteen and some nineteen out of twenty [which sounds like very good shooting for the cylinder or near cylinder bored guns of the day]… it is the most infatuating and expensive amusement the juvenile sportsman can possibly engage in; for one day very seldom terminates without the appointment of a second; one extravagance constantly engenders another, to the utter exclusion of economy, which is upon all similar occasions generally laughed out of countenance. Experience has also convinced us, that eight, nine and ten pounds for pigeons, in addition to a bill for fashionable exorbitances for the day, amounting to… two or three guineas each, has sent many a pigeon-shooter to his bed and awakened him to the pillow of reflection.[10]

The article implies an activity that has been in existence for some time, that has become fashionable in and around London and which has spread nationally. The form of trapping, with boxes sunk into the ground, is relatively sophisticated. The rules are evolved too: shooting from 21 yards rise; a gun-down stipulation; and a 100-yard boundary.

For our next, even more scathing reference we may turn to Volume II of *Rural Sports*, written by the Rev William Daniel[11]. This interesting but rare encyclopaedia of fieldsports has a short but important section on pigeon shooting. It expounds:

As a mode of shooting to bet large sums of money upon, it is perhaps the least objectionable, since every shooter has an equal chance as to the distance from whence the bird is sprung, but it is certainly not the exact shooting that a sportsman will ever try or fancy as an amusement; besides the mind that thinks at all must feel a repugnance as the idea of first confining and then setting at liberty, hundreds of domestic animals doomed to instant death, or, what is worse, to languish under wounds that in the end prove mortal. This representation and it is by no means over-charged, peremptorily checks any opinion of that man's humanity, who indulges largely with his gun in this species of slaughter; there is no excuse for the wanton barbarity of it; for the shooting of pigeon and of game is so widely different, that a person may almost always strike his bird from the box, that scarcely ever makes shift to hit it when rising from the bush… .

Having put the boot in rather comprehensively, Daniel changes tone and tells readers that 'the most extraordinary performance' was by Tupor, gamekeeper to Sir H Mildmay 'the same person who broke the sow to stand game' who shot six pigeons of ten with single ball 'for a considerable wager'. We also learn from the sporting cleric of a Mr Elliot of Sussex who managed to shoot 45 ex 50 on a windy day near Petworth and of a match for a thousand guineas (more like a £1 million today) that was shot at Wrotham in Kent in March 1801.

The protagonists in this great contest were 'Messrs Barton and Myers against the Hon W Coventry and Robinson the Cricketter'. Each man shot at twelve birds and the traps or boxes were at 18 yards, the first official distance for clayshooting in Britain, though 3 yards shorter than the yet-to-be-established norm for pigeons. Barton and Myers won with the rather average score of 12 ex 24. Robinson was high gun with seven birds, but unlucky in his partner who only managed three.

The book *Rural Sports* finishes its section on pigeon shooting with the following remarks:

The Gun Club, Notting Hill

> At one of the best attended and oldest established pigeon clubs [it might well be the Old Hats] the first marksmen, who perhaps one day will bring down every bird they fire at, yet, upon an average of three years' shooting, do not (except in very few instances indeed) kill more shots than they miss. It is to be remembered, that for the shot to be entered in the club book, the pigeon must drop within a certain space.

This text suggests that there are a number of pigeon clubs, new and old, in existence, that pigeon shooting is a difficult business, that results may be inconsistent, that statistics should be considered over several years and that there is a requirement to drop the bird within 'a certain space'—as noted in *The Sporting Magazine* with more detail. It all implies an activity that had been in existence for some considerable time and which had attained significant popularity circa 1800.

William Taplin also mentions pigeon shooting and provides rules for it in his *Sporting Dictionary* of 1803:

> Pigeon shooting is a sport principally resorted to at that season of the year when guns are lying dormant and game of every other kind is, by privilege of Parliament, permitted to enjoy its rest. Pigeon shooting is a match between two individuals or any fixed number on each side and is decided by one or the other killing the greatest number of pigeons within an equal number of shots.
>
> The match made and the place agreed on where it is to be decided, the dovehouse pigeons are provided in proportion to the parties who stand engaged to shoot, of which there are generally four, five or six on each side; and, as every individual feels disposed to shoot at least five or six times, less than eight or ten dozen are hardly ever procured for the occasion.

Taplin's reference to 'dovehouse pigeons' is interesting as, later, as the sport became more sophisticated, blue rocks became the favoured target. Taplin confirms the organisation of a match much as it is described in *The Sporting Magazine*—a 20/21 rise, a 100-yard boundary and a gun down stipulation—but adds some important extra detail:

Previous to the commencement of the match, an open spot is fixed on, agreeable to the arbitrators, one appointed by each side. Here, 20 yards are measured with accuracy and both extremities correctly marked. At one end, a hole is made in the earth, in which is deposited a small box, about 8in deep, 6in wide and 1ft long, its surface 2in above the level of the ground, with a sliding lid running in a groove. To the front of this lid is affixed a string or small cord of 21 yards in length which, extended, will reach a little beyond the precise distance of 20 yards, where each of the parties concerned will afterwards stand and shoot.

The preliminaries adjusted of having taken the toss—to determine which side is to take the lead—and all parties ready, a pigeon is lodged in the box and the runner (as he is called) resuming his post by the side of the person whose turn it is to shoot, he is there ready to pull the string annexed to the slider and give liberty to the bird the moment he is ordered by the shooter so to do.

It is a fixed rule that the gun is never to be advanced to the shoulder till the bird is upon wing. This is to be decided (as well as every other cause of dispute) by the persons appointed; and every pigeon so shot at must fall to the ground within 100 yards of the box or it is not admitted a bird killed but a shot missed.

The first person having shot (hit or miss) he is succeeded by the opposite side and they continue to shoot in alternate rotation till the match is decided according to the original terms upon which it was made, in respect to the number of pigeons to be shot at by each distinct party, when those who kill the most are declared the winners and entitled to the stakes made.[12]

Colonel Peter Hawker expressed strong opinions on pigeon shooting. He is as rude about it as Daniel and *The Sporting Magazine,* but rather more amusing.

In the 1816 (second) edition of his famous work *Instructions to Young Sportsmen,* Colonel Hawker writes (and repeats the assertions in later editions):

> The shooting of tame pigeons I have always had want of taste enough to consider an amusement to be classed with baiting a badger... But as it becomes a glorious opportunity for assembling parties to gamble and get drunk, I must not be so unfashionable as to moralise about cruelty; particularly as the human professors of this elegant accomplishment might ask me, 'Why is it worse than hunting a bag fox?' or 'May not every sport be more or less condemned for cruelty.'

Hawker deigns to give some brief technical advice. Its depth of understanding, however, leads one to wonder whether or not the gallant hero of Douro and Talavera had rather more experience of pigeon shooting than he might like to admit:

> As pigeons are commonly turned out at 21 yards, it may easily be observed, that the knack of killing them consists merely in firing the instant they are up and being careful not to shoot under them, as they take so hard a blow, particularly on the rump, that, if suffered to fly any distance, they are apt to get out of bounds before they fall.

By the 1833 edition, Hawker has added some extra practical material to the passage quoted above. It could indicate his perception of increasing public interest:

> The larger the gun and the charge, the wider the circle of shot; and therefore the better to assist that shaking hand, which among the most expert marksmen, may be occasioned by anxiety. Plenty of powder and a light charge (in proportion) of no 6 shot will do better for a man while nervous than very close shooting; or, at all events, till he has become cool and confident, which he generally will find himself after he has killed a few birds in succession.

The Colonel then concludes in splendidly biting style:

> So little is the art of pigeon shooting the criterion of a good shot, that many of the very best performers at this are scarcely third-rate shots at other birds and some of them perfect cockneys in every other kind of shooting. In short, pigeon shooting is simply this—if you miss, you are disgraced—and if you kill, you get no credit. *It must, however, be admitted that*

Live bird shooting in 1828

FAMOUS EARLY pigeon shot Captain Ross's description of how he won the annual prize at the Red House in 1828 (he also won the event in 1829):

A pigeon shooting match in London during the 1820s

> The members shot for four days, firing twenty shots each day: the traps five in number were place at a distance of thirty yards from the shooter; we were allowed to use both barrels, if required and the charge was unlimited. I shot with guns made by William Moore, 12-gauge; I killed seventy-nine birds out of eighty I fired at, but I only scored seventy-six, as three of the birds settled on the top of a fence which enclosed the shooting ground and then fell back dead. According to the rules of the club, a bird settling on the fence was reckoned a missed bird, although it subsequently dropped dead. I have little doubt I should have killed all the birds if I had not had a mis-fire with my right barrel.[13]

there is more difficulty in shooting pigeons at a regular match than bystanders are aware of.

The last sentence—my italics—is not included in the 1816 edition, which is otherwise very similar as far as this passage is concerned. The addition could be another indication of Hawker's perception of growing interest in the subject in the second quarter of the nineteenth century.

Not so much fun as Hawker, or, ultimately, as informative or damning, is a report in Blaine's *Encyclopaedia of Rural Sports of 1840*. It disguises ill-feeling towards trapshooting with rather less wit: 'The zealots in pigeon shooting, of which there are many among the wealthy and influential, are loud in praise of this sport and consider it the perfection of the art of shooting flying'. Blaine's also appears to confirm that the activity was practised in the mid-nineteenth century much as it had been in the 1790s.

> A match thus made, several dozens of pigeons having been provided for the purpose are disposed in baskets behind the company, there to await the destructive crisis.
> A shallow box about 1ft long and 8 to 10in wide, is sunk in the ground parallel with the surface and just 21 yards from the foot-mark where the gunner takes aim.
> The box has a sliding lid to which is affixed a string held by one appointed to that office and who on command of the gunner will release the pigeon. The gunner is not permitted to raise his gun until the bird is on the wing. The bird must fall within 100 yards of the box or be deemed a lost shot.

The work, however, merely plagiarises *The Sporting Magazine* article of fifty years before. Sadly, this is a common practice in British sporting literature and one for which researchers must be alert if mistakes of attribution and chronology are not to be made.

Bell's Life, a weekly London magazine begun in 1822 and that would play a significant role in the evolution of pigeon shooting, includes some coverage in its early issues in the 1820s. The earliest that the present writer could find is for 24 March 1822 headed 'Uncertainty of pigeon shooting':

> Two crack shots, who were backed to kill seventeen birds, from twenty guns, had a match for twenty guineas, on Thursday morning, in a meadow adjoining Hampton Common; when, at each shot, their guns were backed at four to one to kill. The performers were Messrs Anderson and Thwaites; and, strange as it appeared, Mr Anderson, who was considered an eighteen [out of twenty] man, bagged twelve only; he, however, won the match, his adversary hitting only nine.[14]

The next *Bell's Life* report appears on 14 April 1822 concerning a 'great pigeon match' which took place 'on the Forest at Farnham Heath, when the 'Migham Crack Club', which we are later told had eighteen members, was defeated by 'the picked men of three Counties'. Several matches actually took place on the day in question, at least two of them involved thirteen birds presented at 21 yards rise. Competition was close; the high gun in the first match was Mr Grosvenor of Berkshire who shot all thirteen of his birds.[15]

Coverage becomes much more extensive by the 1840s. An issue of *Bell's Life* for 11 February 1849 (brought to my attention by Donald Dallas) reports that out of no less than twenty venues, sixteen were public houses. Three of the more colourfully named were the Beehive Inn at Belton, the Blue Dumpling at Oughtibridge and the Six Bells at Bexley. Two metropolitan hostelries feature particularly in the reports of this era: the Red House at Battersea and the Hornsey Wood Tavern.

The Red House, as noted, had been in existence as a pigeon shooting pub in the early 1820s. It was still popular a generation later and closed about 1850. The less central Hornsey Wood Tavern came into existence sometime around 1800, was frequented in early decades of the nineteenth century, but became prominent in the 1850s when it metamorphosed into 'Hornsey Wood House' or 'Hornsey Wood Rise.'

Greener notes, contentiously, in later editions of *The Gun and Its Development* [see, for example, p457 of the seventh edition] that the first bona-fide club was formed at Hornsey Wood. The venue is certainly known to have been associated with the standardisation of rules and developments in trap technology. *Bell's Life* also makes interesting reference to Hornsey concerning the shooting at starlings and sparrows—the cheaper and frequently forgotten, alternatives to dovecote pigeons and the blue rocks later favoured bird for high-wager competition. The issue for 2 July 1848 notes:

> At the Hornsey Wood Tavern, on Monday, Messrs Wooley, Godwin and Harvey shot a match with Messrs Herbert, Ashley and Charlton for £10 a side, twelve pigeons each, 24 yards, five traps, to use both barrels. The former side won, killing 28 to 23. They shot three sweepstakes of £1 each at twelve starlings each, 21 yards, two traps; Mr Ashley, after two ties, won two and Mr Godwin one. The Swiss rifle society mustered very strong and shot at the 200 yards distance. Their next meeting, to shoot for prizes, will take place on Monday, the 31st instan'. On Tuesday and Wednesday several matches at pigeons and starlings were shot. The Hornsey Wood Rifle Society had an excellent day's practice and several matches at 100 yards took place. Messrs Davies, Marshall, Lucas and Robinson, shot for £1 each, twelve starlings each, 21 yards, two traps; Mr Marshall won, killing nine. Mr Marshall and Mr Robinson shot three matches for 10s each at twelve starlings each; Mr Robinson won two. Messrs Holland and Newton shot at twenty-four starlings £2 each; the former won, killing seventeen. On Thursday the Acrotormeatarian Rifle Society met to shoot for their gold and silver medals, but the day was extremely boisterous and the silver medal only was shot for, which was won by Mr Lancaster. The Hornsey Wood Pigeon & Sparrow Club met and a vast number of sweepstakes and matches were shot. On Friday Messrs Dickinson, Bailey and Reynolds shot a match for £2 a side, at twenty-one starlings, 21 yards rise and twenty-four sparrows, 19 yards rise. Mr Bailey won, killing sixteen starlings and eighteen sparrows.[16]

And, as well as the references to starlings and sparrows, the *Bell's Life* article is interesting because it confirms the growing popularity of Hornsey Wood circa 1848 and shows that a number of clubs and societies were operating there through the week. The mention of rifle shooting suggests a sport that was growing as quickly as trapshooting and which, like it, offered a means for the test and development of guns. Successes by Messrs Holland and Lancaster are witness to the personal marksmanship skills of soon-to-be-famous makers.

Robert Blakey, in the first, 1854, edition of his useful, but part-copied little work *Shooting: A Manual of Practical Information* comments on trapshooting:

Pigeon shooting is still practised in many parts of England and in the metropolis and suburban localities. The terms of these matches vary, according to the fancy of the concocters of them. Sometimes they are arranged for single, sometimes for double guns, sometimes for this weight of shot, sometimes for that. We think, however, *within these few years these matches have been decidedly on the decline and are not now considered so fashionable as they were wont to be some years ago.* [my italics][17]

This is interesting intelligence, not least his comments on double guns, which had been made in England since about 1750, but which did not become commonplace until the percussion era.

Blakey repeats the passage in the editions of 1859 and 1865. We must be cautious, though. He is a plagiarist and to complicate the issue, he plagiarises Blaine, another plagiarist. He does, however, seem to make an effort to achieve some balance on the subject of pigeon shooting. Republishing the key 1793 *The Sporting Magazine* article with proper attribution (which is why I risked using him earlier as a source). He also quotes 'Mr Daniel', (in fact, the Rev WB) and, anonymously, a 'decided favourer of this sport' who memorably opines:

…whatever degree of utility may otherwise attach to it, pigeon shooting has the further merit of annually delivering some hundreds of birds from the miserable clutches of metropolitan blackguard fanciers, by whom they are often kept in an unnatural and torturing state of confinement. Indeed their carriage in sacks to the place of execution is no mitigation of their tortures, yet happy are those which there find their quietus. Further, it is an Englishman's sport, since it is a free one, in which a man may exercise his gun, although of the unprivileged class.

The Field was founded in 1853 and was soon adopted as an arbiter of fashion by the landed classes. In its issue for 14 June 1856, an account of a pigeon shooting match 'highly interesting to lovers of the trigger' is reported. The contest was between Robert Southby of Berkshire and William Hall of Oxfordshire and was evidently the subject of considerable interest. The event was at 21 yards rise, 100 yards boundary and made use of a 'Red House Trap'. It did not turn out to be a good day for Hall. The sporting periodical recorded: 'The Oxonions were quite disappointed their pet could not shoot a bit.'

1856 is a significant date for pigeon shooting. During it, Frank Heathcote, who would later become famous as the founder of the Hurlingham Club, is credited with introducing a handicapping system[18]. This was a major development and changed the character of competition substantially; it opened it to participants of widely different abilities and encouraged a more sociable activity. Formal handicapping appears to have been first adopted in some contests at Purdey's ground at Willesden, with handicaps ranging from 24 to 30 yards, and subsequently at Hornsey Wood[19].

Greener writes in the third edition of *The Gun and Its Development*:

Many years before it became fashionable, pigeon shooting was practised by the frequenters of low public-houses in most large towns... But about 1856…it was patronised by Lord Huntingfield, the Earl of Stamford and other noblemen and *suddenly became fashionable* [my italics]. Since that time clubs have been formed and grounds reserved for this sport, wherever the Anglo-Saxon race are found.'[p.543, third edition, Cassell & Company, London, Paris and Melbourne, 1892.] Pigeon shooting 'as a sport,' Greener claimed in the ninth edition, 'may be said to date from about the middle of this [the nineteenth] century, although there were occasional matches and contests earlier.[20]

In *Modern Shot Guns*, WW gives us a bit more information whilst reinforcing the idea that early trapshooting and/or un-regulated trapshooting were distinctly suspect:

Pigeon shooting has long been a holiday pastime with the frequenters of low-public houses and has been and still is used a means by sharpers [conmen] to fleece the unwary young sportsman. It is wise to shoot pigeons at recognised clubs only whether in England or elsewhere; and before accepting an invitation to shoot a friendly match, to make sure of the character of the person who invites the contest, or experience at the trap may be very dearly bought.[21]

He states that the first handicap 'is said to have been shot upon Mr Purdey's grounds at Willesden in 1856 and notes that the first 'bona-fide' pigeon club was formed at Hornsey Wood House. He also suggests that 'traps' were introduced at this venue—does he mean iron traps?—and that the 'small cannon' formerly favoured gave way to 'the ordinary double-barrelled fowling piece.'[22]

Greener underplays, indeed denies, the whole era of Osbaldeston and Ross in his writings. It is clear, nevertheless, that a significant number of well-born Regency bucks as well as some more Hogarthian characters sported at the traps and lost or won a guinea or two. These early sportsmen played an important part in the evolution of pigeon shooting before the advent of what might be called the aristocratic movement of the 1850s and 1860s. Greener may want to distance himself and his products—his pigeon guns would become especially famous in the 1880s—from the disreputable associations of the early game. It is notable, for example, that in the definitive 1910 edition of *The Gun and Its Development*, the reference to 'low-public houses' is removed as is the reference to Huntingfield and friends. Whatever Greener's reasons, he appears to have sanitised history. Happily, *The Field* of 26 June 1858 contains an editorial that casts much light on the chronology and development of mid-nineteenth century pigeon shooting:

> Fashion reigns omnipotent in sport as well as in other matters and each kind seems to have a rise and fall in succession, the only predictable point being that sport-in-general is always in vogue among the inhabitants of the British Isles. During five or six years past, for instance, pigeon shooting has been voted low and the matches have been confined to the denizens of sporting public-houses, who in the country shot for a fat pig, or in the suburbs of London for a small sweepstakes, or at the outside for a gun. This year it is ruled, however, by the members of the 'Upper Ten' that it shall be the sport of the summer and, as a consequence, Hornsey Wood House is patronised by the Four-in-hand Club and other fashionables at least once a week, with great advantage to Barber [a famous supplier of pigeons] and a most direful effect upon the blue rocks, who, moreover, vote the double-barrelled no 12 'a greater bore' than the old-fashioned single-barrelled no 6.

The article goes on to describe the use of both Lang and Lancaster breechloaders and notes that ordinary game guns were in use amongst upper class pigeon shooters previously, big bore guns—single and double-barrelled—throwing as much as 2oz of shot had been popular. It appears from all this—and the magazine is usually a reliable source—that pigeon shooting, rather suddenly, came back into high fashion during the late 1850s. To those who were not familiar with its origins, it might have seemed as if it had just arrived. The past is so easily ignored when the present feels pleased with itself.

In 1858, Deane's *Manual on the History and Science of Firearms*, a book that appears to have been written with the benefit of some direct knowledge unlike many, offered some disparagement of pigeon shooting, common to shooting literature but not, generally, to periodicals pre-1860. As in *The Field*, there is corroboration that pigeon shooting had recently come into vogue and, as interestingly, that it had spread abroad:

> In pigeon shooting matches, self-love and money-love being mostly at stake together, to ensure the safety of those two imperilled sentiments resort is had to guns of great bore, 8, 10 and 12, very artillery, throwing from 1½ to 2oz of shot, circa 138 grains of powder; so that in this kind of shooting, the skill of the shooter may rather be measured by the calibre of his gun than attributed really to himself. This modern fashion... has extended from this country both to the north of France and to Belgium; and the birds for the indulgence of this amusement have become a staple export to a very considerable amount from the latter country to London.[23]

Pigeons

ALTHOUGH THE small-bodied, tough and fast flying blue rocks (*Columba livia*) were the favoured birds for high level competition in England from the mid nineteenth century onwards, feral pigeon and domestic doves were also employed. When pigeons were unavailable or considered too expensive, sparrows, starlings and larks might be used. In the United States the replacements were purple martins and blackbirds as well as sparrows. Some American matches were even settled with bats.

The best of the blue rock pigeons were from Lincolnshire. These were sometimes called 'tin rocks' because of their distinctive colour. Slightly inferior birds came from Oxfordshire and Yorkshire. The 'English skimmer' is also mentioned as being a popular alternative though precisely what this was seem to have been lost in the mists of time. Birds were imported from the Continent (notably Antwerp) in vast numbers and breeding stocks were also exported to Belgium and France.

One of the most famous purveyor of pigeons in London was a man named Barber. He provided a complete service to ensure fair play. As well as nurturing and preparing the birds in all respects, he supplied a handler whose responsibility extended to placing the birds in the traps. A club servant acted as puller, however. This handler was also responsible for gathering shot and wounded birds and typically included the services of a dog in his package to the club.

Escapees from the traps have influenced the gene pool of feral pigeon flocks in London's Trafalgar Square and similar metropolitan locations. It is interesting when watching city birds today to consider how many of their ancestors—the purer scions of whom may still be found in North West Scotland and West coast of Ireland—might have run the gauntlet at the Red House or Hornsey. You may also ponder on the biological imperative to nest on cliff-like buildings.

A sophisticated 'sport' develops

FROM THE 1860s, positive references to pigeon shooting become much more common than negative ones in sporting literature. Coverage in the sporting press becomes more extensive and methodical, reflecting the growing sophistication of pigeon shooting itself. The fourth, 1866, edition of *The Dead Shot*, a work first published in London in 1860[24] is full of praise and filled with practical tips.

Iron traps, it reports, were in use at the Red House Battersea—a bit perplexing, however, as this venue closed a decade or so before the first publication of the work—'and other distinguished match shooting localities' and also informs that the earlier pattern wooden traps 'are seldom used now at public shooting grounds, except for sparrow and starling shooting'. In a plug for its own 'Marksman's Rules' it declared that:

> Strange to say, until the first publication of this work, there was no other printed or authorised rules in regard to pigeon-shooting save those of the old Battersea school; and though some are quite useful, they are quite inadequate to the requirements of the present day.[25]

The pages of *The Field* reveal on 4 May 1867 an important letter from Frank Heathcote written from Paris (in the year of its International Exhibition) concerning a cup that had been put up by the Emperor of France for a grand prix. It was 'to be shot for by the elite of the two nations, all at 28m (quite 30 yards)'. Noting other contests to be held as part of the same festival Heathcote, declared:

> I hope all my friends will respond to the handsome and generous way the Emperor has behaved, by flocking over in their quantities and quality. My anxiety is to see the cup come to England and it will not unless the very best men are sent, as some half dozen here are quite a match for the best in England. So, British gunners mind and have straight powder and good tempers: I have done my duty to you, now do yours to me.

Immediately below the letter (but not apparently a postscript to it) are two small news items:

> Aristocratic pigeon shooting handicap—The first great handicap of 5 sov[ereign]s each will take place at Hendon, Welsh Harp [another venue on the rise], as last year, on the Saturday before the Derby, under the usual conditions.

> The new Red House Club—This new aristocratic pigeon club, we understand, will very shortly have filled up its number of 100 members, after which admissions will only be made by ballot.

Though he was temporarily abroad, the first story may, nevertheless, be linked to Heathcote. After the closure of Hornsey Wood some years previously, he was in 1867 using the Welsh Harp Inn as a venue for his pigeon contests that were both upmarket and handicapped. The second report is also connected to Heathcote and probably relates to the beginnings of his Hurlingham Club. Both pieces are evidence of a trend amongst the elite to corral themselves away from a growing hoi polloi who, more than ever before, could afford to buy and use guns themselves.

On 20 July 1867 Heathcote's name is mentioned again in *The Field* in relation to 'The Second Lake Match at Hendon'. The aquatic reference almost certainly referring to a pontoon built in the middle of a lake at the Welsh Harp shooting ground in imitation of one used in Paris at the *Patineurs Club* in the Bois de Boulogne. An Englishman, Peters, had won the Emperor's Cup and the pontoon from which the contestants shot had drawn much positive comment. Evidently, this was not lost on Heathcote who resolved to copy the idea, or cause it to be copied, as a means to bring in the carriage trade.

On 30 May 1868, we find Heathcote's name mentioned as organiser at what is by then called the new Red House and Riverside Club. While he had been organising contests at the Welsh Harp and elsewhere, Heathcote had been searching for a major site for development as a pigeon shooting ground. He found the splendidly situated riverside estate Hurlingham in Fulham and, good businessman that he was, he appears to have canvassed for the first 100 members in 1867 at the same time or before he had acquired the rights to it. We know that in the same year, he 'obtained the leave of Mr Naylor', the last private owner of Hurlingham, to promote pigeon shooting matches there. A lease was taken out in 1869 and the freehold purchased in 1874.[26]

By 1882 the Hurlingham had 1,500 members—500 of them involved with polo or shooting—and the Prince of Wales, a keen pigeon shooter as well as driven game shot, was club president.

More information concerning the background to Hurlingham may be found in the 1911 work *The Victoria History of the County of Middlesex*, edited by William Page FSA. It records in volume II:

> A few years after the establishment of the Gun Club, the spread of London northward obliged Mr Frank Heathcote to abandon the Old Hornsey Wood House and, in 1867, he rented the Hurlingham Estate at Fulham for £700 a year. This action was followed shortly afterwards by the formation of the Hurlingham Club, which purchased the property for £20,000. It achieved such success under the management of the Hon DJ Monson that for several years prior to 1891 it had the full complement of 1,500 member under the presidency of his late Majesty, King Edward, then Prince of Wales.[27]

Like the dynamic Mr Heathcote, *The Field* itself seems to have played a significant role in developing pigeon shooting. During the 1860s, the magazine published the odds on the top shots and recorded the make of gun with which they won, creating a league table that takes on enormous significance to British gunmakers for the remaining years of Victoria's reign.

By this era, pigeon shooting had become much more regulated. The big new clubs take on a special significance. They were not just meeting places for the haute monde, they were also centres of excellence for shooting and gun development. And they were rule-making and handicapping institutions operating much like the Jockey Club does today in the case of racing.

The Hurlingham—also known as the Hurlingham Gun & Polo Club—had begun in the late 1860s as noted. The Gun Club at Shepherds Bush—also known as the Gun Club, the London Gun Club and the Gun Club Notting Hill—was the other pre-eminent institution. It had started a little earlier, probably in or around 1861, soon after the closure of Hornsey Wood. The rules introduced for pigeon shooting by Hurlingham and the Gun Club were used at many lesser clubs. Those rules became international too, being extensively employed in the United States as well as Empire and beyond.

Greener qualified Hurlingham as the 'most select', but the Gun Club he called 'the first shooting club in the world' noting its forty fixtures a year. WW's readers are told that the club was started by 'Sir Gilbert East, Colonel Vansittart and Mr G Batcock hiring a field at Wormwood Scrubs'. It was initially rented for friendly matches and practice once a week, but the numbers attending rose so rapidly 'that it was proposed by Mr Batcock to establish it as the Gun Club and a lease of the ground was taken, the club subsequently growing to 'vast proportions'.[28]

Greener published a line illustration of Hornsey Wood (see page 23), taken from the earlier work *Manual of Rural Sports* by JH Walsh aka 'Stonehenge' and repeated it in several of his books. It shows a pleasant rural idyll with the corner of a marquee just visible and has a boundary fence in keeping with a serious venue for match shooting. He also offers a line drawing of the Gun Club in several of his works. It shows, by contrast, a much more sophisticated establishment buzzing with activity, with a large circular pavilion and other buildings, numerous gun racks and plenty of spectators.

I have not seen any images of Hurlingham operating as a shooting venue, but I can note from personal acquaintance—I spent a significant amount of my youth playing tennis there—that its site is dominated by the neo-classical mansion, Hurlingham House built for John Ellis by the architect George Byfield.

London clubs

IN THE second edition of *Modern Shot Guns* (1891), one of Greener's most succinct works, WW notes the most celebrated clubs in England as:

- The Gun Club, Notting Hill
- The Hurlingham Gun & Polo Club
- The International Gun & Polo Club Brighton
- The Union Gun Club at the Welsh Harp, Hendon
- The Manchester Gun Club
- The Wolverhampton Gun Club
- The Oldham Gentleman's Club
- The Witton Gun Club at Birmingham

The Hurlingham Club today

Moreover, he tells us that 'winter shooting' at the Gun Club commenced in the first week of November and continued 'every Saturday' until March. Summer shooting began in April and went on 'twice or thrice weekly' until July. At Hurlingham, where the Secretary was the Hon D Monson (later Lord Monson) shooting started in April and continued twice or thrice weekly 'through the summer'[29]. We also discover that the 'International Week' of the Hurlingham and the Gun Club—a major social fixture that might be compared to Henley or Ascot today—was 'generally fixed for the 15 July'.

We learn that the combined prize fund circa 1891 was about £3,700 —a fortune in that era. The event might be compared in importance to modern Wimbledon.

Greener states that 'in or near London' there are a number of other clubs: the Commercial Gun Club (which met at Hendon); the Licensed Victuallers Gun Club; the Wimbledon Gun Club (which met at New Malden); and the Mid Kent Gun Club. And, he notes that pigeon shooting was available 'by arrangement' at the exclusive Ranelagh (the birthplace of British clayshooting) and Orleans clubs. He might also have included: the Invicta, which met at Plumstead; the Shire club at Hendon; the Reform; the South London Grounds at Nunhead (near Peckham); and the Beaufort Gun Club at Chelsea.

Public houses, though excised from Greener (with the exception of the Welsh Harp, Hendon) were still frequent rendezvous for pigeon shooters and their gambling entourage. Among the better known pigeon shooting pubs were: the King William the Fourth, Kensal Green; the White House, Hackney Marsh; the Prince of Wales, Hampton Court; the Hare & Hounds, Lea Bridge Road; the Lord Raglan, Windsor; the Chequers Inn, Dagenham; the Hook & Hatchet, Chatham, Kent; the Cricklewood Arms, Cricklewood; the Cauliflower Inn, Ilford; the Two Brewers, Maidenhead; the Swan Inn, Ashington, Sussex; and the Norbiton Park Hotel, New Malden.

'In the provinces,' Greener draws attention to 'good clubs' at Cheltenham, Maidenhead, Redcar, Barrow, Taunton, Exeter, Chester, Newton-le-Willows and Stockton-on-Tees.[30]

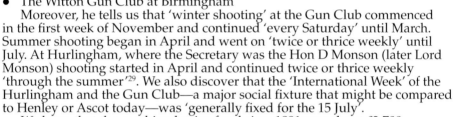

Other well-known clubs of the 1880s included: the Taplow; the Worcester Gun Club; the Wye Gun Club in Kent; LV Sturry (Licensed Victuallers at Canterbury?); the Clifton Gun Club near Bristol; the Redcar Gun Club; and the Bradford Gun Club. In the 1880s shooting was also taking place at: the Racecourse, Hampton; Rye House in Kent; Brentwood in Essex; the Victoria Hotel, Banstead, Surrey; Egham, also in Surrey; Hooton, Cheshire; the Greyhound Hotel, Wadhurst, East Sussex; the Angel Hotel, Tunbridge, Kent; the Star Hotel, Edenbridge, Kent; High Gosforth Park, Newcastle; the Queen's Grounds, Barnsley; Trent Bridge Grounds, Nottingham; the Salway Arms, Hotel, Wooferton, Shropshire; and at Dalbeattie in Scotland.

Holt's Shooting Calendar—the source of much of the above not otherwise provided by Greener—is an almanac of sports focused on pigeon shooting. It is a work so scarce today that is rarely encountered even among specialist book dealers. The 1882 volume was the first published, which itself may be some indication of the date of pigeon shooting's zenith. Both 1882 and 1883 editions are mines of information. You discover, for example, in the 1882 edition that 'at least 500' dozen pigeons are sold for shooting in London every week[31]. There is considerable reference to Continental shooting and there is section on 'Our Fashionable Resorts'. It confirms the pre-eminence of Hurlingham:

> Unquestionably foremost among fashionable resorts of the aristocracy in this country is the Hurlingham Club, which sprang into existence some fourteen years since [1882]. From that time down to the present it has never ceased to be the most popular rendezvous of the haute monde.[32]

Holt's also notes that before the opening of Hurlingham, it was the custom of 'noblemen and gentlemen' to hold pigeon shooting meetings at Hornsey Wood 'a well known hostelry on the north side of London' where competitions were conducted 'under the supervision of Mr Heathcote' and patronised by many of 'the most influential sportsmen of the day.' Many of the Hornsey Wood regulars it states had previously attended shoots at the Old Red House, Battersea and had 'found it necessary to migrate northward with Mr Frank' when that establishment was closed (also confirming the peripatetic nature of Heathcote's activities in the 1860s). *Holt's* is also an excellent source on the Gun Club:

> Of the many clubs which have been organised in this country since pigeon shooting became a popular sport, the Gun Club has attained a position that it has every reason to be proud of, for it now ranks with the first of the sporting institutions of the United Kingdom. From small beginnings it has gradually grown in influence and prosperity...
>
> In the year 1860, Sir Gilbert East, Colonel Ibbetson, Mr Broadwood, Mr Battcock, Mr G Powell, Mr James Bird and some friends held a few meetings for the practice of pigeon shooting in a field adjoining Wormwood Scrubs and upon this site the present Pavilion now stands. Mr Battcock proposed to establish a club and at his suggestion it was called the Gun Club. Noblemen and gentlemen from all parts of the country joined and many well-known sporting celebrities became identified with the undertaking. The club quickly grew in popularity and new members joined in such numbers that it was decided, in 1862, to appoint a secretary and Mr Arthur Battcock was unanimously elected to that office...
>
> For the convenience of members a pavilion was built in the years 1877-1878... but in course of time, the club having grown to such dimensions, it was decided at a general meeting to spend a large sum of money upon the further improvement of the ground... The energetic committee of the club determined to carry out the necessary reforms in the most liberal spirit and at the conclusion of the season of 1881 a start was made and, early in the present year, a perfect transformation was effected. The grounds occupied by the club at present comprise, with the road, garden, carriage-drive, &c, about seven acres and the general arrangements are all that can be desired.
>
> ... the clubhouse, as it now stands, is unique of its kind for convenience and general completeness and contains clerks' office, luncheon room, members' writing and reading room, committee room, refreshment department with kitchen, grill room, cellars, &c, dressing rooms fitted with lockers, for the convenience of members and ample lavatory accommodation. The

The gilt trigger guard bow on this James Purdey 12-bore percussion pigeon gun, serial no 7628, was made for renowned pigeon shot Lord Hill in 1867. Lord Hill was among the best pigeon shooters of his day and this wonderful old gun has engraved on the guard bow a record of the owner's wins fro the year 1867-1871 at the Notting Hill Gun Club, Hurlingham, Paris and Baden-Baden.
Picture courtesy: Roosevelt & Drake www.drake.net

main entrance to the pavilion on the shooting ground side is screened by double glass doors… the general public [is] admitted to view the shooting on payment. There is also a good gallery running round the structure which will accommodate about 200 persons and this is largely patronised on the occasion of important contests, as it affords a capital view of the whole surroundings.

The description of the facilities at the Gun Club makes clear just how significant a sport pigeon shooting had become by the early 1880s. Of the major London venues of this era, we have considered the two most famous in some detail, but there is another that definitely deserves more attention—Hendon, in particular the Welsh (or Welch) Harp there. This establishment was used by Frank Heathcote after Hornsey Wood and before be acquired the lease of Hurlingham. It advertised itself in Holt's as 'Warner's Welsh Harp'—'The great London holiday resort', 'Pleasure grounds' with 'Public shooting ground'. 'Only five miles from London' and readily accessible by means of the Midland Line railway. The dining saloons were capable of catering for up to 1,000 visitors according to the advertising. There were facilities for angling that included a stocked 400-acre lake. Cricket, lawn tennis, boating and archery were also catered for with shooting. It was the proud boast of owner WP Warner in 1883 that his establishment had been used as the 'favourite headquarters' by both 'Dr Carver and Captain Bogardus, the champion American shots'.

Bogardus and Carver

THE AMERICAN professionals, 'Captain' Bogardus and 'Doc' Carver had a deep impact on both British and American trapshooting in the 1870s and 1880s. The handles to their names were suspect: Bogardus was not a regular military man and Carver was certainly no doctor, nor dentist as suggested in some accounts. Nevertheless, both did a great deal to promote pigeon, glass ball and, later, clayshooting.

Bogardus was in England in 1875 and came again in 1878, Carver arrived in 1879 and also returned after touring the Continent. Their itineraries included challenge matches for high stakes at pigeons and theatrical displays of shooting skill at inanimate targets. Both would later perform in Buffalo Bill's Wild West Show too (but before it reached London and played at Earl's Court). And, both would enter into partnership with William Cody—the man who 'played' Buffalo Bill—and later regret it.

Carver went into litigation with the now iconic figure over various matters and claims to have lent him the money to develop the original western show (allegedly US$29,000). He also claimed that Cody was a violent drunk whom he had periodically to disarm. The legend was apparently in the habit of arriving in the arena between performances completely plastered with revolvers blazing. The fact that Cody was a heavy drinker is a matter of historical record. Carver even states that their mutual acquaintance Wild Bill Hickok—a serious hombre by all accounts—had once forced Cody to his knees and threatened to shoot him for being a cowardly wretch. Mind you, it might be remembered that Carver and Cody's shows became direct rivals.

Bogardus seems to have developed less personal animosity towards Buffalo Bill but experienced a run of extraordinary bad luck when associated with him. He was almost ruined when his guns and all the props and animals for a new Bogardus-funded Buffalo Bill / Bogardus show went down in a riverboat disaster. A little known female trick-shooter, Annie Oakley, took his place having developed her act on the Vaudeville circuit.

Financial disasters and personal peccadilloes not withstanding, Bogardus and Carver were headliners among a new breed of performer—the professional exhibition shooters. Their exploits became legend and parallel the final developments of the modern breechloader. Although over-hyped or misrepresented on occasion, their much-practised abilities were genuinely extraordinary. WW Greener wrote that 'for speed and accuracy, the professional pigeon shots of America must have the palm'. Stage performers and hustlers with a gun, they rose to the top by natural selection. The names of dozens less talented are now long forgotten.

'Champion Wingshot of the World' Adam H Bogardus had beaten fellow American, Ira Paine, in the USA for 'the Championship of the World' in 1871

A fancy Model 73 rifle featuring (l-r) Bogardus, Buffalo Bill and Carver. Picture courtesy: America Remembers

Choke bores and concentrators

IN THE 1870s, there were a number of famous gun trials in both the United States and England (New York 1873, Chicago 1874, London 1875, 1876 and 1877). Trials in the 1860s had, essentially, been contests between muzzle loaders and breechloaders. The trials of the 1870s, by contrast, pitted choke bores against cylinder guns. The 'Great London Trial of 1875' at the All England Croquet Club at Wimbledon was sponsored by *The Field* and supervised by Dr JH Walsh, its editor. It had shown WW Greener's choked guns (actually bored by William Ford, then an artisan working for Greener) clearly superior. But the issue was still contentious and a trial at pigeons was scheduled for 1876—the 1875 trial at the All England Club having considered pattern and penetration at static targets only.

The new event took place at the Gun Club Notting Hill on 21 July 1876. There appears to have been some gamesmanship. Those using cylinder guns also employed shot 'concentrators' (cylinders of card in their cartridges that contained the pellets as they left the muzzles and fulfilled a similar function to a modern plastic wad). The cylinder bores using these devices won, but it was not really a fair contest. Greener was obviously irked by this subterfuge and wrote in the fifth (1892) edition of *The Gun and Its Development*:

> The smooth-bores scored 59 at 27 yards rise and 47 at 33 yards rise; the choke-bores scored 57 at 27 yards and 40 at 33 yards. In this match concentrators were used in the cylindrical barrels; this made them about equal to modified choke. Besides this, the majority of the best shots were on the smooth-bore side… had the sides been equal it is probable that the choke-bores would have been victorious.

To settle the issue finally, Dr Walsh, the honest broker of the Victorian shooting scene, set up yet another trial for 1877. Concentrators were banned. There would be nine guns on each side. Mr Purdey put up a fifty-guinea cup for the first day, the same sides would compete for a sweepstake the next. Greener's guns won both. The high gun of the fist day - scoring 5 birds straight at 30 yards rise and 3 ex 5 at 40, was Mr HC Pennell (who also appears in shooting literature as H Cholmondeley-Pennell). He would go on to become an early clay pigeon enthusiast. Greener's reputation as the first master of choke boring was established, meantime. He concluded happily a decade and a half later: 'The choke bores were first by fourteen birds [on the second day]. This trial fully proved that choke-bores were the best weapons for this shooting and they have since come to be generally used at all the gun clubs.'[33]

and, on 8 August 1875, he beat an Englishman, George Rimell for the same title at the Welsh Harp, Hendon, England. The auspices under which either match were shot are not altogether clear. There is also a record of Bogardus beating Rimell on 2 July 1880, in a match for US$250 a side, presumably in the United States, with the remarkable score of 99 ex 100[34]. This would have been almost impossible with British Blue Rocks, where scores over 80 were rarely recorded.

Bogardus's most famous tour of the British Isles was in 1878. At the start, he had used the British sporting press to issue an open challenge to those who fancied their chances against him. This was a common practice at the time.

On 21 June 1878, Bogardus gave an exhibition of his remarkable skills at the Welsh Harp—no doubt to stimulate interest. Offers soon came flooding in.

In a match in July 1878 with a Mr Wallace for £200 (£100 a side), he tied on 69. This sounds low ex 100 save for the fact that the shooting was at the experts' rise of 30 yards and the birds were best blue rocks—much tougher than the passenger pigeons used in the States or the inferior varieties used in some lesser matches in England. A decider was arranged with stakes doubled. Bogardus lost to Wallace 62 to 71 ex 100. The wily pro had better luck with H Cholmondeley-Pennell, the much-fancied winner of the Grand Prix of Monte Carlo earlier in 1878 and who would later become a clayshooting pioneer. The marvellously over-monikered Brit was defeated twice by Bogardus in 1878, once at the Gun Club and once at Hurlingham for £300 a side.

The Field of 27 July reported: 'As little was known of the event coming off, attendance was very small and there were never more than one hundred persons present in the inclosure during the afternoon'—which makes you wonder just how many attended the well-publicised matches—The same issue of magazine concluded: 'Captain Bogardus—who we may remark, is forty-four years of age and stands 5ft 11in—shot throughout the contest with the greatest fairness, holding his gun below the elbow until the bird was on the wing.'

Bogardus also had good fortune with a Mr Boulton and with Captain Shelly, another well-known 'crack'. He beat the latter at 30 yards rise for £400 by the wide margin of twenty birds (84-64) at the Gun Club on 29 July 1878. In this much-reported contest he used a choked 12-bore Scott gun weighing 10lb and his usual heavy charges of powder.

The Captain was, however, beaten by Dudley Ward. They both made the high score of 84 ex 100, but Ward won the shooting off. I have not yet found record of the stakes involved, but doubt if they were less than £100 a side. Bogardus's greatest victory as far as financial reward was concerned was with one Aubrey Coventry for a mighty £500 a side. This contest took place at a fashionable venue outside of London—the International Gun and Polo Club, Preston Park, Brighton on 6 August 1878.

The American had some bad luck, but still managed to win by a bird, shooting 79 to his opponent's 78 (again, at the expert's rise of 30 yards). Bogardus's scores during his English tour of 1878 were typically in the high seventies. This may sound low, but Greener confirms that Bogardus's scores were, nevertheless 'amongst the best ever made in England'. They were certainly enough to impress *The Field*, which noted favourably of Bogardus on his departure:

*Colonel William F
'Buffalo Bill' Cody*

Capt Bogardus has shown us that he can hold his own with the best men we have in this country; and when it is taken into consideration that he always has to shoot in fresh grounds, his performance is all the more meritorious. That Capt Bogardus will return well satisfied with his reception here there is no doubt, for every courtesy has been shown him at Hurlingham and the Gun Club and the members have been nothing loth to accept the challenges offered by the American champion. Capt Bogardus leaves on Saturday [10 August 1878] on the SS Bothnia.

Bogardus's own account of his 1878 visit to the UK is fulsome in its praise of all things English but with one rider:

…during all my stay in England, I met with kindness and courtesy on every hand, especially from the press and I am convinced that any straightforward man who may go there will never have to complain of his reception by English sportsmen. The truth is, it is rather the other way and some mercenary charlatans have been tolerated [to whom does he refer?] and applauded in London when they ought to have been discouraged and denounced.[35]

He gives an account of various matches in his book, quotes stories in his favour from *The Field* and *Bell's Life* and records that he made a tour that began and ended in Liverpool with Oldham, Sheffield, London, Ireland and Wales on the itinerary. He might also have mentioned that his total winning exceeded £2,000—perhaps as much as £500,000 in modern money.

Carver arrived in England early in 1879 hot on the Captain's heels. In *Bell's Life* of 22 February 1879, following his great rival's example, he issued a challenge to the sportsmen of 'England or the world'. It must have seemed quite exotic to the club-men of London, as its terms encompassed horseback shooting and rifle shooting as well as trapshooting at pigeons.

This is the less colourful challenge Carver issued in October of the same year once he ad got the measure of the Brits:

Doc Carver and his ball-throwing assistant Jim Williams, in front of the Crystal Palace in London, in 1879

> To the Editor of *Bell's Life* in London
> Dear Sir, I will shoot any man in England a match at pigeons for £1,000 a side, 100 birds each. Or I will shoot the two best men that England can produce for £1,000 a side at 400 pigeons, I to shoot at 200 and my opponents to shoot at 100 each. The match is to commence and finish the same day, 30 yards rise and English rules. The Editor of *Bell's Life* to be the stakeholder and appoint a referee. Yours most respectfully, Dr William F Carver, Champion Rifle Shot of the World, 25 Oct 1879.

Carver's tour was a considerable success, too. Frequently commended for his modest manner, he nevertheless attracted considerable attention on Rotten Row in London's Hyde Park riding out in full western rig, *The Whitehall Review* of 3 April noted 'The man an athlete, the horse a picture'. PR, clearly, is not a modern science.

Carver shot a variety of matches in 1879—though some accounts suggest he did not especially like pigeon shooting. He also gave exhibitions with his Winchester lever-action 73s before being invited to the ultimate shooting gig—the royal estate at Sandringham. There he performed one of his greatest recorded feats—breaking a hundred glass balls straight with a rifle—in front of the Prince of Wales (who acted as scorer) and guests. It was reported in the 19 April issue of *The Field*.

In the same month his name appeared in the press for quite different and less happy reasons. A London policeman accidentally shot Carver's black assistant, Jim Williams, during a Crystal Palace performance. The officer of the law had picked up one of Carver's guns and foolishly pulled the trigger assuming it unloaded. Happily, Jim recovered.

WW Greener and others supply detail on Carver's conventional matches. He beat W Scott 66 to 62 on 7 February 1881 at the Union Gun Club, Hendon (referred to as the Welsh Harp in some accounts), in a contest under the auspices of the International Polo & Gun Club. The stakes were £400. The weather conditions were most unpleasant—WW Greener noting that 'the greater part of the match' was 'shot in a blinding snowstorm' and the birds 'the finest and quickest seen during the winter'. *The Sportsman* of 8 February 1881 reported pithily:

Both Dr Carver and Mr Scott, it must be admitted, are champions in the use of their 'weapons', but though the former has styled himself champion shot of America and Mr Scott that of England, the appellation in either case is somewhat ambiguous. Since his sojourn in this country, the doctor has devoted great attention to pigeon shooting and with such success that at the suburban meetings which he attended he was nearly always found in the front ranks and soon came to be regarded as one of the 'warm ones' to fight out a tie with. Dr Carver's free, manly, courteous manner soon won him a host of admirers and those who know him and in sweepstakes have competed with him, will readily admit that his best form has been invariably shown without the slightest ostentation.

The following month, Carver beat Scott again at Hendon, 79-74—the match being a hundred birds at 30 yards rise. This contest was the final of a three-day event—14-16 March 1881. Between his arrival in 1879 and this date, Carver had travelled with his show on the Continent, developing a formula later adopted and improved upon by William Cody. Greener was happy to report that Carver used a Greener choke-bore and WW continued to report on Carver's victories with a Greener in his advertising throughout the 1880s.

Archibald Stuart-Wortley in *Shooting: Field and Covert* praises Carver's shooting but is more circumspect concerning Bogardus, by whom he was beaten twice. Reading between the lines of contemporary accounts, the Captain clearly impressed the Brits as a pigeon-killing machine but bruised a few delicate egos with his consistent if not inevitable victories. His general success seems to have been explained by his detractors by his unsportingly heavy gun and special loads. The English would use a similar excuse to explain the victory of the first visiting American clay team in 1901. It seems likely, nevertheless, that the publicity attending him and his matches was a significant factor in stimulating interest in pigeon shooting at a key point in its development.

Bogardus preferred a 10lb W&C Scott 12-bore and was an exponent of relatively light pellet payloads and small shot as well as heavy powder charges. His preference for match pigeons was no 8 shot. Stuart-Wortley notes the American beating a Captain Shelley (the final score was 84-64) easily at the

Gun Club, Notting Hill, and comments that soon after many British pigeon shots adopted heavy guns (which he disliked) and 'smashing charges of powder'. The effectiveness of the latter—and Bogardus sometimes used nearly 5 drachms—were evidently a revelation to British sportsmen. They led the Gun Club to change its rules limiting the charge to 4 drachms and gun weight to 8lb.

Stuart-Wortley, an egotistical snob, suffers some amnesia concerning Bogardus's victories. He had kinder words for Carver 'whose marvellous skill with the rifle had fairly astonished the world' and whom he noted shot 'many matches' in England 'never being beaten or approached', save in one twenty-five bird contest at the Gun Club which ended in a draw and in another match with old Archibald himself. This took place in December 1882 at Hendon, the stakes being a massive £500 a side. It ended in a tie—which may explain Wortley's different attitude—each shooting 83 ex 100. The Englishman writes:

Doc Carver, as he appeared at shooting performances in Britain

There was much betting on the contest and it was rendered peculiarly exciting by the fact that it was a tie at the fiftieth bird and again eight or nine times during the last half of the match. The writer was unlucky, for his fiftieth bird fell dead upon a small building within the enclosure, but by the custom of the ground was given a lost bird.[36]

This expensive 'miss' evidently rankled Wortley and he could not help concluding: 'Carver did some wonderful things, but though he and Bogardus—who were, it should be remembered, professionals—claimed to be better than our best men, they certainly failed to prove it by their public performances.'

There seems spin if not even spite here. Both Bogardus and Carver showed themselves to be first-class shots on British soil. They won a lot of money. And they certainly made a lasting impression as is confirmed by the many reports about them in British periodicals and books.

What's it worth?

THE YEARBOOK *Holt's* presents an interesting but shamelessly partisan view of pigeon shooting in 1882. Having set out a case for the sport and dismissed its detractors, the almanac notes some of the extraordinary prizes on offer. They were of an order seen in major golf and tennis tournaments today. The 'circus' surrounding the major shoots, however, is reminiscent of nothing so much as modern Formula 1.

It is not to our purpose to exhaustively discuss the merits of pigeon shooting; but it may not be out of place to make a few remarks in connection with the sport. Its enemies contend that it is a wantonly cruel pastime and that the unfortunate birds are slaughtered without a chance of escape. Those who indulge in this notion would, in all probability, have reason to modify their ideas were they actually engaged in a properly conducted pigeon shooting contest; and the distinguished and thoroughly representative body of noblemen and gentlemen who patronise the sport is a sufficient guarantee that it is in every way a legitimate and sportsmanlike recreation and it is inconsistent to contend that there is any cruelty involved in the matter.

The birds used for the purpose of trap-shooting are bred in enormous quantities in England and elsewhere and are a source of considerable profit to the farmers who rear them. Practically, there is little difference whether they meet their death by a charge of shot or are killed as ordinary poultry; but there is this to be said in favour of encouraging pigeon shooting, that whereas it would not pay a farmer to breed pigeons for the market as an article of food, it is a remunerative branch of his occupation to rear them for shooting purposes; and the dead birds can then be sold at such a low price, that they become a most nutritious and economical article of food. In the London district alone, at a very low calculation, at least 500 dozen are sold every week, at an average cost of 2s a dozen.

Taking a general review of the events of the past year, there is every reason for congratulation that the sport has taken a further step towards healthy development and increased popularity. The meetings held at our principal clubs have been on the whole numerously attended and the interest taken in the sport well sustained.

The first series of contests involving more than usual importance were those decided at Monaco. The Grand International Series commenced on 18 January and it will be remembered that the *Grand Prix du Casino*, which consists of a valuable *objet d'art* and 18,600L, was won by Count de Quentin, who stood at the head of the poll out of a field of eighty competitors, with a total of twelve consecutive kills to his credit. Signor Guidicini ran second and Mr Wingfield Stratford third. The other principal prizes were won by Lord de Clifford, Comte F du Chastel, Mr HJ Roberts and Mr EC Ellis.

The International Shooting Meetings, held in London, were a great success and the series commenced on 12 June. Continental sportsmen were fairly represented and some of the most skilful marksmen from abroad tried conclusions with the members of Hurlingham and the Gun Club; and although the events were carried off by Englishmen, they had to show their best form to hold their own against their foreign rivals.

The Hurlingham Cup, value £200, together with £300 in specie [gold coin], won by Sir Harry Paul Burrard (25½ yards rise), who killed seventeen birds without a miss; and Vicomte de Quelen (29½) and Mr Wykeham Martin (25½) divided the second and third prizes, amounting to £132. On this occasion, the largest field of shooters has taken part in an international pigeon shooting meeting competed.

The International Cup, value £300, was shot for at the Gun Club and eighty-seven shooters tried conclusions. This trophy, together with £250 was won by Mr A Grimble (30 yards rise), who was fortunate in scoring eighteen birds without a miss; Vicomte Olbert (28) and Captain F Gist shot well up and took respectively the second and third awards.

The winners of the other principal prizes during the meeting were Mr Gould, Mr Turner-Turner, Mr Elsen, Mr Ford, Mr Craig, Mr Berkeley Lucy, Mr F Leighton, Lord Grenville Gordon, Mr HC Bentley and Mr ERG Hopwood. Besides these gentlemen, numerous others have won valuable prizes, which will be seen by reference to the statistical tables contained in this volume.

During the year just passed, a large number of matches have been decided but it would be

HONOURS TO THE GREENER GUN.

The Purdey Cup. Choke-Bores v. Cylinders, 1877.

Grand Prix du Casino, 1891.

The "American Field" Champion Wing Shot Cup.

tedious to review them in detail. The most noticeable contest was that on 22 June, at the Gun Club, between Mr Turner-Turner and Mr Montague, when the stake at issue was £1,200. Both marksmen showed fine form and Mr Turner-Turner won by killing 84 out of 100, at 30 yards rise, against his opponent's 80 out of 100.

Besides the ordinary meetings at Hurlingham and the Gun Club, the International Gun & Polo Club and other prominent organisations in the pigeon shooting world have held very successful meetings during the last twelve months and most of our provincial clubs are in a flourishing state; there is therefore every prospect that this popular sport will continue to grow in favour and that it has now become so firmly established as an institution amongst sportsmen both at home and abroad, that it will long survive the puritanical attempts of that over-zealous and uncharitable section of the community who would do their utmost to put a stop to all sport, because they find no pleasure in participating in it themselves.[37]

In the year to which this refers, 1882, *Holt's* informs that the winning guns at Hurlingham and the Gun Club were predominantly those of EM Reilly and Co with ninety recorded wins and cash prizes of £6,148. Next came Purdey with seventy-six wins and £3,382 10s. Lang was third with forty-three wins and £2,128 10s and Stephen Grant fourth with thirty-seven wins and £1,200. These were vast amounts of money for the day—cottages could be bought for £50 and many earnt far less in a year. The totals, moreover, ignore the value of cups and other non-cash prizes.

In the season 1900/1901—these figures now taken from *Sporting Goods Review*—the guns of EJ Churchill topped the list with total winnings of £4,283 3s 4d, Powell was second with £3,237 6s 8d, Boss third with £2,518 6s 8d and Purdey fourth on £2,413 10s. Purdey regained its pre-eminence the following year, taking £4,606 10s and pushing the then relatively young but clearly successful firm of EJ Churchill into second place with £3,774 6s 8d. Several members of the Churchill family were skilled pigeon shots and this was a significant factor in the gunmaker's rapid growth. When pigeon shooting lost its appeal in the years that followed, EJ's nephew Robert Churchill—the man who would take over the business—came up with the clever notion of a special short-barrelled gun and a new shooting method to revive the firm's fortunes.

Shooting abroad

PIGEON SHOOTING not only prospered in England, the Empire (notably Australia, New Zealand, India and Canada) and the Continent but, most notably, in the United States, where the first reference to the activity is at the Sportsman's Club of Cincinnati in 1831. A cup of 1836—probably the earliest for trapshooting—is still in existence and was awarded to P Shelk by members of the Cincinnati club.

A club was formed on Long Island in about 1840 and, soon after, the New York Sportsman's Club was founded. DH Eaton notes that the members of the Long Island Club were game shots who saw pigeon shooting as a means of practising for the field. He also tells readers that the club imported a mysteriously large trap from England. Some thirty years later, it was described by one of the members 'as made of sheet iron, and… almost large enough for the body of a coach such as we run today. The weight of it was a decent load and it would easily hold a dozen or fifteen pigeons.'[38]

The *Cercle des Patineurs* was the leading club of France with grounds in the Bois de Boulogne next to an ornamental lake. Shooting—Skeet and Hélice—still takes place there. It is now one of the most exclusive social clubs in the vicinity of Paris and is populated predominantly by elderly folk playing cards (or so it appeared when I made my pilgrimage there a couple of years ago).

There were two other well known Parisian clubs: the *Tir d'Archeres, Foret de Saint Germain* and the *Tir du Parc de Saint Ouen*.

The pigeon shooting at Monte Carlo was also especially famous, offered the richest prizes and consequently attracted shooters from all over the world. In the 1890s, the season started in early December, with shooting three days a week until mid January when the international contests began. These attracted some of the finest shots in Europe. The *Grand Prix du Casino* offered £1,000 or more of booty. Every three years there was a championnat universal which, as well as honour, offered £400 in cash.

The English performance became progressively poorer leading Teasdale-Buckell to write rather mournfully in 1906 (published 1907): 'Our country now loses the *Grand Prix de Monte Carlo* with nearly as great certainty as formerly they won it.'[39]

Happily, though, there was a late rally in 1907 with Englishmen winning first and second place. A Mr Hall took top honours having shot 12 ex 12 (and pocketed 24,848 francs—about £1,000—as well as an 'objet d'art') and a Mr Roberts managed 14 ex 15 and took home 19,329 francs.

Circa 1890, there was also shooting at Abbeville, Amiens, Boulogne, Bordeaux (Saumur), Cambrai, Havre, Lille, Le Treport, Lyons, Macon, Nantes, Reims, Rouen, Saumier, Tours and Valenciennes during the summer. And, in the winter, at Arcachon, Cannes, Marseilles, Pau and other resorts. In Belgium, you could shoot at Brussels, Namur, Ganshoren, Ghent, Enghenhoven, Corbeek-Loo, Mons, Liège, Antwerp, Spa or Ostend *.

Within the Austro-Hungarian empire there were clubs at Vienna and Trieste and no doubt elsewhere (Prince Louis Esterhazy was a keen pigeon shot). In Germany, the Union Club of Berlin shot pigeons near the racecourse at Hoppergarten. Teutonic marksman and visitors might also face the traps at Ems, Baden-Baden and Wiesbaden. Spain had clubs in this era at Madrid,

---

* In 1900 one of the richest contests ever would take place at Ostend. 50,000 francs—about £2,000—went to the eventual winner, Hodgson J Roberts using a Churchill gun. The following year, he also won the Grand Prix du Namur in Belgium and collected another 25,000 francs shooting from 30.5 metres.

Monte Carlo winners

WINNERS OF the *Grand Prix du Casino: Monte Carlo* are:

1872	Mr George L Lorillard (USA)
1873	Mr J Jess VC, CB (England)
1874	Sir William Call, Bart (England)
1875	Captain Aubrey Patton (England)
1876	Captain Aubrey Patton
1877	Mr W Arundel Yeo (England)
1878	Mr H Cholmondeley-Pennell
1879	Mr ERG Hopwood (England)
1880	Comte Michel Esterhazy (Hungary)
1881	Mr MG Camaueur (Belgium)
1882	Compte de St Quentin (France)
1883	Mr HT Roberts (England)
1884	Le Compte de Caspela (Italy)
1885	M Leon de Dorlodot (Belgium)
1886	Signor Guidicini (Italy)
1887	Count Salina (Italy)
1888	Mr C Seaton (England)
1889	Mr V Dicks (England)
1890	Signor Guidicini
1891	Count Cajoli (Italy)
1892	Count Trautmannsdorf (Austria)
1893	Signor Guidicini
1894	Count Zichy (Austria)
1895	Signor Benevenuti (Italy)
1896	Monsieur Journu (France)
1897	Signor G Graselli (Italy)
1898	Mr Curling (English)
1899	Monsieur Moncorgé (France)
1900	Signor O'Brien (Spain)
1901	Monsieur Guyot (France)
1902	Signor J Grasselli (Italy)
1903	Mr Pellier Johnson
1904	Signor Schiannini (Italy)
1905	Signor Hippolyte Grasselli (Italy)
1906	Signor Hippolyte Grasselli (Italy)

Seville, Cordoba, Cadiz, Granada and Valencia. In Portugal you could shoot at Lisbon or Oporto. In Italy, there were clubs at Rome, Milan, Florence, Genoa, Venice, Bologna, Padua and Turin. You could shoot in Russia at St Petersburg where there were two clubs and Moscow. Constantinople, Budapest, Buenos Aires and Montevideo offered pigeon shooting too. And clubs were to be found in every major town in Australia and New Zealand.

WW Greener tells his readers in the third edition of *The Gun and Its Development* that the International Concours—a social calendar event in the UK which took place during January and February—surpassed 'any tournaments of a like kind held on the Continent and attracts the best shots of all nations, many English and American professional shooters attending year after year'. He also notes that prizes were remarkable and included 'rare works of art and vertu'.

Characteristically, he gives an unabashed plug for his guns, noting Cholmondeley-Pennell—the man who was beaten by Bogardus and who would go on to write the first set of clay pigeon shooting rules in England—won in 1878 with his WW Greener patent wedge-fast 12-bore; the prize was worth £160 and another £1,328 in other stakes. This was the most valuable prize ever shot for at Monaco up to that time according to Greener.

All things considered, the great gunmaker paints a most appealing canvas of shooting on the Continent, assuming you had the funds to enjoy it. His analysis is valuable too because it puts this lost world into perspective:

> The shooting at Monaco usually commences in the middle of December and closes the last fortnight in March. At Cannes… there is also fair pigeon shooting during the winter months but the prizes are not so valuable as those offered at Monaco, nor is the shooting ground so good or the conditions so rigorous. In the winter there is also shooting at Pau [Basses Pyrenées].
>
> In summer months at Paris, Dieppe, Bordeaux, Reims, Boulogne and Pau are the most important; the rules of *Cercle des Patineurs* being observed at all.
>
> In Belgium good pigeon shooting is to be had during the season, both at Brussels and Ostend. The meetings at Brussels, under the auspices of the *Tir du Bois de la Cambre*, are well worth attending.
>
> In Germany the best meetings are at Baden-Baden and Ems; in Italy, at Milan and Florence.[40]

Practical Hints on Shooting by '20-bore' (Basil Tozer), published in 1887, is another outstanding, but now scarce Victorian work and one of my favourite technical volumes of this era. Tozer corroborates much of what Greener has written about shooting abroad and also adds useful information. His list of continental clubs is virtually identical to Greener, save for the mention of Reims. He also tells us that the boundary distance and fence at the various clubs varied widely (this may seem a trivial point but it had a profound effect on the style of shooting required to succeed):

> The boundaries of the Hurlingham and the Gun Club enclosures, for instance, are much higher than the fence at the Hendon ground [the Welsh Harp], which have the effect of scoring many birds 'dead' which at Hendon would be scored 'lost'. Perhaps nowhere is prettier shooting ever witnessed than at Monaco. Here also the fence is very low indeed and being but 20 yards or so distant from the traps, it needs the utmost skill to drop fast-flying English blue rocks inside the boundary. This accounts for the fact that many of our English competitors, accustomed to shoot at Hurlingham or The Gun Club, are frequently defeated at Monaco by foreign sportsmen who, from constantly practising on the same ground, get into the habit of killing their birds with the first barrel and who, when they come to England, naturally find our shooting grounds much easier to score upon.

The zenith of pigeon shooting

BY THE 1880s, it is clear that pigeon shooting had evolved into a much more sophisticated activity than it had been a generation before and one which might more properly claim the title 'sport'. The activity was also growing. 'The Marksman' writing in 1866 edition of *The Dead Shot* had propagandised:

> Pigeon shooting is, unquestionably, the finest practice for the aspirant to excellence, in the use of the gun at flying objects… At the same time it is a sport which requires considerable skill and there is none in which so much depends on the perfect coolness and steady deliberation of the shooter.[41]

The 1896 edition seems even more assured (though by this date pigeon shooting was already entering its decline in England):

> Pigeon shooting, as practised at the Hurlingham enclosure and at some other shooting clubs in town and country, is a very attractive recreation, particularly to those who desire to excel in the art of killing birds on the wing. Its patrons may therefore be found amongst sportsmen of every class… Pigeon shooting matches at the present day are attended by sportsmen of the highest repute and by prize-shooters and champion prize-shooters from various parts of the world.

We must go back a few years for the most memorable bit of propaganda— and one that again intimates that pigeon shooting, even at its height, was defending itself from detractors. It was created by Archibald John Stuart-Wortley, the pompous and vainglorious fellow who had not been too kind in his comments regarding Bogardus. He expostulated in the *Badminton Library Shooting: Field and Covert* in 1887:

> We may fairly point to the names of those who have followed with zest the pastime of pigeon shooting, a list spread over four or five generations [which suggests that he is aware of an early beginning] and comprising most of the best known sportsmen of this century, as an answer to the diatribes of ignorant sentimentalists. The leading pigeon shooters, since the days when the 'Old Hats' at Ealing was the principal rendezvous, have been men noted for their devotion to sport of every kind and to write down their names in order should be sufficient to convince an unprejudiced person that a pastime to which they were addicted cannot be dismissed as contemptible, brutal or un-English. Surely Mytton, Osbaldeston, Ross and Anson may appeal to us as the bearers of good English names, giants of sport, men trained to feats of endurance and nerve on foot and on horseback. Later, we find the late General Hall and Mr Stirling Crawfurd (one of the best), Mr Walter de Winton, Lord Leconfield, Lord Huntingfield, Mr Corrance, Mr WG Craven, the late Mr Dudley Ward and a host of others well known at the covert-side, on the turf, or on the moor and stubble; while to pass to our more immediate contemporaries, the names of Bateson, Hill, Cayley, de Grey, Rimington-Wilson, Shelley, Hargreaves and many others need no recommendation to modern sportsmen. The jungles of Africa, the precipices of the Himalayas or 'Rockies', the corries of Inverness-shire, or the Wolds of Yorkshire have known them alike in their generation and we might be safe in assuming that a pastime with which they have not been ashamed to identify their names needs no further defence.

Captain Albert W Money ('Blue Rock'), an Englishman who became manager of the EC powder company in the United States yet retained membership of the Gun Club, devoted a whole book to pigeon shooting in 1896. Entitled simply, *Pigeon Shooting*, it turned out to be something of a last hurrah. It is a most interesting and informative little volume, nevertheless, and one worth reading by anyone with an interest in shotguns, whether or not they have a special interest in the history or practice of captive bird shooting. It contains, for example, interesting material on early clayshooting. Money was an enthusiast for the newer sport as well and a member of West Kent Gun Club, an early venue. On the subject of pigeon shooting he declares:

> For many years past, pigeon shooting has been such a fashionable amusement that for a man to say he has never shot pigeons at the trap is almost equivalent to saying he is not a shooter. There are, of course, exceptions to this rule and one, I think, of the chief causes of these exceptions is that live pigeon shooting is and always must be, an expensive luxury; but it is made more so from the fact that a beginner has little or no chance of winning when competing with those who have practised this particular form of sport for any length of time an so become expert at it.

Money compares field and pigeon shooting, noting tactfully:

> It is really far easier to become a good pigeon shot than a good game shot... But there is a wide difference between the two sports. In field shooting, a man cannot study his position; he is probably moving along at the moment the game rises; his right foot may be in front of his left... he may have one foot on a rock... Pigeon shooting and gameshooting are so different that you cannot make them alike.

Like the Marksman, he draws attention to the constitutional qualities required:

> To be a first-class pigeon shot, a man must have nerves like iron; no weak point about him. He must be able to concentrate all his thoughts and energies on the work he is doing. Good luck nor bad luck must make no difference with him; he must not be easily cast down or easily elated. Nothing brings out the points of man's character more than pigeon shooting. If he has a weak spot, it is sure, sooner or later, to come to the front. The niggardly man, the selfish man, the bad tempered kicker and above all the crooked man will surely come to grief.

It is almost a statement of Victorian virtue, *mens sana in corpore sano*, but every word of it would or should apply to a competitive clay shot today. For a rather different point of view to Money or the Marksman, we may turn to the thundering Teasdale Buckell, editor of *Land and Water* from 1885-1899 and author of a monumental tome *Experts on Guns and Shooting* published in 1900. In the latter work he writes:

> Pigeon shooting is a growing amusement in the States of America [in fact, it was in decline at the time, proving that one should never trust 'experts'], whereas in England it is a survival... Pigeon shooting is not a subject which appeals to us very much, nor can we, like Captain Money, call it sport. It ranks as an amusement... you shoot pigeons with a gun and a load that you would never dream of shooting game with, for your object is to plaster your pigeon and render it thereby totally unfit for food... not only are the gun and the load different but the very position of the shooter and the way he holds his gun are at variance with those prescribed by necessity for gameshooting.[42]

What caused this hostility? Well, it is perhaps first necessary to point out that Teasdale-Buckell was not especially consistent. We may, nevertheless, be able to take some of what he writes at face value. He appears to have genuinely disliked the idea of specialist guns for either pigeon or clayshooting. He notes, interestingly, that Money advised different comb heights for both (higher for pigeons than clays): 'shooting that necessitates a special gun, one that will not do for game, will never become popular amongst game shots'. There is something else, however—contemporary social values. The late Victorians were famously prudishness and hypocritical.

There is an oft-repeated story—but one that fails to be pinned down precisely—concerning Princess Alexandra, wife of Prince Albert 'Bertie' Edward. Apparently, she was gravely offended when a dead or wounded pigeon landed in her lap while watching tennis at Hurlingham in the early

1890s. It is suggested that she openly campaigned against pigeon shooting afterwards. It is remarkably similar to a story concerning Princess Grace and the cessation of pigeon shooting at Monaco more than half a century later.

Teasdale Buckell is negative about pigeon shooting in *Experts on Guns and Shooting* but discusses it at great length in the same work nevertheless. He also devotes half a short chapter to it in his later work *The Complete Shot*. Confusingly, however, he changes to a much more positive tone. This might be explained by the change of fashion, feeling and monarch circa 1901.

A stuffed blue rock pigeon given as a prize for shooting

The late Victorian era was an age when legs of grand pianos were sometimes covered up for decency and when young ladies might be barred from sniffing certain orchids lest their passions overcame them. The idea of sport changed significantly in the second half of the nineteenth century. It was vastly different to the rumbustious and ribald Georgian epoch—a time of cockfights, badger bating and bare knuckle contests.

You can time the change in national character almost to the year. Harry Flashman might take his turn at the traps, but not Tom Brown, his victim at Rugby School. With the dawn of the new century things began to loosen up in some respects but the nature of sport was forever changed—doomed to even more regimentation and regulation. Pigeon shooting had simply had too much bad press to survive, and, critically, lost its royal approval.

In the United States, the last Grand American shoot at live pigeons was in 1902 in Kansas City. Annie Oakley competed. Meantime, the Humane Society—the US equivalent of the RSPCA—was lobbying for legislation to ban pigeon shooting. Keith Buchert, who has researched this, notes: 'Pigeon shooters like JAR Elliot and Crosby were taken to court… as early as 1901 in Missouri for shooting pigeons. They were acquitted at that time because no laws were on the books.'[43]

Another major issue was professionalism and cash prizes. There was much potential for gamesmanship and dishonesty, hence the elaborate rules that evolved to control serious competition. The issue of professionalism would continue to cause considerable difficulties for inanimate target Trap shooting well into the twentieth century—and led to it being eliminated from the Olympic Games of 1928, 1932 and 1936.

There may be another component to criticism of live bird trapshooting. Pigeons are extremely hard to shoot out of traps consistently—something which in more recent years has sometimes caused some game shots to criticise clayshooting for the wrong reasons. Simple snobbishness is another factor. Although Hurlingham and the Gun Club attracted the carriage trade, more than a few matches took place behind pubs or other 'low resorts' even in the later years.

Finally, there is the issue of cheating. Methods became quite creative. The Marksman noted that the foul practices prevalent circa 1866, included spring traps designed to send the bird out in a particular direction, the use of massive guns as noted and, intriguingly, 'loaded waddings'—wads created with a hollow to conceal extra quantities of shot above the stipulated limit:

> There are many other equally disgraceful tricks which are sometimes resorted to by 'professionals'; and I need scarcely say, that such are the practices which bring pigeon-shooting into disrepute.[44]

Even Money, who—Teasdale-Buckell's comments notwithstanding—seems a wise and knowledgeable old cove, felt the need to include a chapter in *Pigeon Shooting* entitled: 'Responsibility of Handlers—The Tricks of Unprincipled Men' in which six methods of cheating are precisely noted. These include, slow or fast pulling, deliberately deceptive pulls (causing a trap to rattle as if it were about to be released), varying the the timing of the pull, tampering with birds, secret signals and altering the release sequence of traps.

Because there was scope for profit by foul play and potential for accident, the *Rules of Pigeon Shooting* became precise and quite complex. New shooters began at 27 yards (Gun Club rules circa 1892), with the maximum handicap distance being 31 yards, later extended to 35. Pigeons were rarely shot at less than 18 yards rise, a distance later adopted for early clayshooting matches in England (but not in the US where 16 yards was the norm in 1890s as it would eventually become in England for inanimate shooting).

A gun-down rule was universally enforced but, like most such rules, was subject to change and argument. Guns had to be loaded and unloaded on the firing point or 'mark'. There were significant differences from club to club, although the Hurlingham and Gun Club Rules were widely adopted by others. *The Field* also offered its own regulations.

Pigeon shooting introduced many, now familiar shooting terms—'trap', 'pull!', 'dead bird', 'lost bird' and 'no bird' and a variety of prohibitions concerning equipment. Limits were placed on gun weight (8lb at the Gun Club as noted, 7lb 8oz at Hurlingham circa 1890), pellet payload (typically set at 1¼oz in the later era), pellet size (5, 6, 7 or 8) and powder charge (4 drachms at the Gun Club circa 1890, 3½ at Hurlingham, raised, sometime between 1892 and 1896, to 4 drachms).

In later years at British clubs, wire mesh cartridge cups used to increase range with muzzle-loaders were forbidden, as were shot 'concentrators' —as previously mentioned, card tubes that held the pattern together in a similar manner to a modern plastic cup wad and helped cylinder bored guns to throw tighter patterns.

The use of bone meal as a buffering agent to improve patterns was also banned by the increasingly comprehensive regulations.

In the flint era, small bores were popular for field use—18s, 20s and 22s. With the advent of percussion ignition, 14 and 16-bores were still favoured for gameshooting. Large bore guns were, however, seen as a significant advantage at the traps. Consequently, massive artillery had become commonplace in the 1840s and 1850s. Donald Dallas notes that Harris Holland, tobacconist turned gun seller, produced nearly twenty large bore guns in 6 and 8-bore for pigeon shooting 1855-1865. He also appears to have had a double 4-bore (no 575) made for his own competitive use in 1856.[45]

Again, in later years, limits on bore size were near universal. Even in 1866, the Dead Shot's *Marksman's Rules* stipulated no gun greater than 10-bore. The sophisticated English clubs of the last quarter of the nineteenth century usually allowed the use of 11-bores but with a half-yard handicap. Guns smaller than 12 were given a range advantage of 18in per bore size down to 16. It is interesting that this did little to increase their popularity. The popularity of the 12-bore pigeon gun we might therefore speculate may be an important factor in the near universal adoption of the 12-bore sporting gun in Britain.

The Parisian *Patineurs*, accepted 10-bores but at a cost of 1m on the handicap distance. 11-bores were given a handicap of 0.5m, but 14-bores were allowed to advance 0.5m and 16-bores 1m. The *Patineurs* also allowed the use of shot concentrators without penalty.

Double guns had come into general use at pigeon shooting matches from about 1850—about the same time that they had become common amongst game shots and as the battue was beginning to become fashionable. There was a significant variation in club rules here, however. Some allowed the used of both barrels, some only one. Breechloaders were also coming into vogue in the 1860s in Britain. Competitors using muzzle-loaders, meantime—and significant numbers still did well in the 1870s—were required to take their shot from a communal bowl. They also had to use a communal shot measure and a common ram-rod, one with an enlarged head than ensured good seating of the wad. Gun collectors might note that muzzle-loaders which have no means of carrying a ramrod beneath the barrel or barrels, may well have been built as pigeon guns.

Pigeon traps

I HAVE noted that early traps might be improvised. The first dedicated traps appear to have been wooden boxes with sliding lids. The boxes were set in the ground, their tops just visible.

The idea may have originated from the use of simple slates over holes. Basic wooden traps might also have been made with simple hinged lids, though this is speculation. Wood was subject to damp, of course, and was easily broken— or shot.

Metal traps were an obvious improvement. The most common pattern involved a floor with four sides that fell away when a string was pulled. These traps—which appear to have come into use from the 1840s—did not need to be sunk below the surface and are consequently sometimes referred to as 'ground traps'.

They developed some interesting features. Holes were put in one side to encourage the bird to look and hence fly forward. An opening of about 4in in diameter and an escutcheon-like cover were provided to load the pigeon once the mechanism was set. Mechanical arrangements were made so that the roof and side walls fell first, leaving the back wall till last. This was another attempt to ensure that the bird flew away from the guns and also a means to prevent it being shot prematurely.

Traps were typically designed to rattle and clatter on springing to encourage the bird to fly out immediately. Floors were patterned for grip. Spring, plunge and lever traps with moving floors were also developed to assist the birds in their ascent to an uncertain future. The plunge trap manufactured by Parker Bros in the USA looked like a pyramid and was mounted on a post, down which it partially slid on activation.

Many cautioned against the use of such devices, however. They were pronounced 'cheat's traps' because they made the moment and direction of flight more predictable and might offer an advantage to those who knew them or who brought them to a match.

Bringing your own traps was a common practice when contests took place outside established club grounds. Sometimes, to ensure probity, shooters would bring traps to a well known venue when others were available.

Spring and similar traps were not used at the premier English clubs and writers such as the Marksman specifically cautioned against being drawn into matches with persons who made use of them. Fair play was taken very seriously when vast sums could be at stake. A notable feature of the Gun Club was that the wires for pulling traps were placed beneath the ground, so that no 'twitching string' cues—false or positive—could be given to the guns.

The distance between traps—of which there were usually five—and of boundaries varied. For Single Rise shooting, five traps were usually placed in a semi-circle in front of the shooter with the possibility of shooting at ranges of 21-31 yards depending on handicap—and further on occasion. In the late Victorian era, new (ie unknown) shooters usually began at 27 yards. A foot rail was placed in line with the right edge of the centre trap and on this the various handicap distances were marked. The Marksman wrote in the 1896 edition of *The Dead Shot*:

> In matches at the Hurlingham and other gun clubs, it was usual to have five traps ranged upon the ground in arc-like form, each five yards apart. The object of the traps is to deceive the shooter, or rather to prevent his knowing the precise spot from which the bird will rise and, with that view, a bird is placed in each trap before the competitor comes forward to shoot.

Pigeon shooting with the pistol

THE PHENOMENAL revolver shot, Walter Winans (who also won two gold medals for the United States at the Olympic Running Deer rifle event—London 1908 and Stockholm 1912) is one of the few men to have seriously practised pigeon shooting with a pistol. He had the Parisian gunmaker Gastonne Renette make him a duelling pistol with an interchangeable shot barrel in .32 bore. It was designed to fire 3/8oz of shot propelled by 1¼ drams of black powder. Winans claimed it shot as well at 12 yards as a cylinder 12-bore at 40.

With it, he engaged pigeons at 12 yards rise and managed, by his own report, 44 out of 80 (which sounds honestly unimpressive). 'I should think,' he wrote:

> …that such a pistol would be very good for sparrow or starling shooting out of traps… in this sort of pigeon shooting the arm must be held straight and the pistol pointed just below the middle trap; the eyes must watch the traps, not the sights, and, as you follow the bird with your eyes, the pistol must be brought up as for Bisley rapid-firing or traversing targets, according as the bird is going straight or crossing you. With a shotgun you must have your stock the proper length, bend, cast-off etc; with the pistol, if you keep your arm straight, nature has provided you with a 'stock' of flesh and blood exactly your proper fit.[47]

With regard to the foot rail, which would be in place on any sophisticated installation, the Marksman continued:

> [It] is fixed along the ground on right-hand side of the shooter; and stood a few inches above the ground. When the shooter stands close to it on the left-hand side at whatever range, he is precisely in line with the central trap; and he is, or should be, also equidistant from all five. Along the upper edge of the foot-rail are notches or sockets; one at every ½-yard, for receiving a short wooden cross piece or metal slip, indicating in legible figures the measured range or distance from the traps. Each competitor, as his turn comes round, takes up his position at the foot-rail at the distance indicated, from which he is required to shoot…

We also get much detail from the Marksman on how the release of birds was regulated:

> Behind the foot-rail is the puller's box or station; and behind, or over that, the rostrum of the scorer and referee… In order, therefore, to ensure the most perfect fairness, various expedients were formerly resorted too, such as the use of H and T traps [a system of pigeon shooting which made use of only two traps—one marked H for 'heads' and the other T for 'tails'—to correspond to the coin flicked to decide which would be pulled]… also that of small dies, or counters, marked respectively 1, 2, 3, 4 and 5 which were shaken up in a lottery wheel, or drawn from a ballot box, immediately on the shooter taking his place at the foot rail, when the number drawn indicated the trap to be pulled.
> At the present day, however, a mechanical apparatus, termed a pulling machine (of which there are several different forms), is used at all the principal shooting clubs, both in England and on the Continent, which entirely dispenses with tossing and number-drawing. The machine itself is provided with a revolving apparatus, which puts it beyond the control of the puller, or anyone else, so far as the choice of trap is concerned [Greener describes similar devices as does Money. Two of the most famous patented machines were those of Bear and Fuller]. On the shooter giving the signal 'pull!' the machine is set in motion; and, accordingly, it revolves and then stops by chance at one of five wires, which it instantly acts upon so as to pull the trap and release the bird. The apparatus consists mainly of a drum and ratchet wheel, with the mechanical appliances for manipulating the wires and throwing the traps open. It may be set so as to pull either one or two traps at the same time. The machine is enclosed in a neat mahogany case, about eighteen inches or two feet in width, by three feet in height and no indication is given to which trap will be acted upon, until the trap itself is seen to fly open and sides fall flat upon the grass.

All this makes clear the sophistication of the sport by the 1890s. It is unlikely, however, that all pigeon shooting was regulated within the tight rules of the premier London clubs (though the Victorian passion for games and rules comes across most clearly when one looks back upon pigeon shooting from a modern perspective). In the 1892 edition of *The Gun and Its Development*, Greener notes a simplified but challenging version of the sport as practised in the North of England:

> One trap, 21 yards rise. Gun to be held below the elbow until the bird is on the wing. 1oz shot; boundary 60 yards.

When blue rock pigeons and sophisticated paraphernalia were not to hand, and when even domestic doves were considered too expensive, smaller, cheaper birds might be used. WW quotes a memorable if rather odd little ditty called *Sparrow Shooting* by 'Watts'—probably Mr Watts of the London Sporting Park who was one of the pre-eminent instructors of the time:

> Tomtits and sparrows, pipits, larks
> Are all to me as easy marks.

A bit grim—all the more with Greener's qualification:

> Some sportsmen, when pigeons are not available and many tyros, make use of sparrows and larks for trap-shooting. If no 6 shot is used it is good practice for both game and trapshooting and not despicable sport. Sparrows, starlings and live rabbits were also used in some quantity at the new shooting schools becoming popular in the 1890s.

An intriguing reference to the use of sparrows for shooting contests appears in *Martin Chuzzlewit*, a work by Charles Dickens published in 1865. Chapter 26 tells us about Poll Sweedlepipe:

> He was a little elderly man, with a clammy cold right hand, from which even rabbits and birds could not remove the smell of shaving-soap. Poll had something of the bird in his nature, not of the hawk or eagle, but of the sparrow, that builds in chimney-stacks and inclines to human company. He was not quarrelsome, though, like the sparrow; but peaceful, like the dove. In his walk he strutted; and, in this respect, he bore a faint resemblance to the pigeon…
> … Poll had a very small, shrill treble voice, which might have led the wags of Kingsgate Street to insist the more upon his feminine designation. He had a tender heart, too; for, when he had a good commission to provide three or four score sparrows for a shooting-match, he would observe, in a compassionate tone, how singular it was that sparrows should have been made expressly for such purposes. The question, whether men were made to shoot them, never entered into Poll's philosophy.

The activities of the Limited Gun Club of Illinois might also be noted. Circa 1900, they held regular sparrow shoots using fifteen traps, a rise of 25 yards and boundary of 35. Sparrows were used by a number of other clubs in the mid-West as an alternative to pigeons when the latter became scarce. DH Eaton writes in *Trapshooting: The Patriotic Sport*:

> Each contestant faced three traps, any one of which might be sprung on his command to 'pull!' The traps used were invented by Mr William Hill of Indianapolis, Ind. The traps closed automatically after being sprung, and as there were fifteen of them, it was practically impossible for a contestant, passing from one score [stand] to the next after each shot, to keep trap of which traps had been emptied. When all had been sprung they were refilled and the shooting resumed.

The ideal gun for pigeon shooting

AS DESCRIBED by '20-bore' (Basil Tozer) in 1887:

> For pigeon shooting by all means have a 12-bore with the right barrel cylinder and left full-choked to stand heavy charges… and weighing not less than 6¾lb. The minimum length of barrels should be 29in, but 30in will be found more effective… it must be a very hard-hitting gun and should give a good killing circle up to at least 60 yards with the left barrel… In a gun of this kind, the hammers, fore-end and other minutiae are mere matters of individual taste, but the stock of a pigeon gun should be ¼in straighter and slightly shorter than that of a game gun; the pull of the right trigger not more than 3lb and that of the left about 4lb 6oz.

And, by Greener writing in 1891:

> The gun for pigeon shooting must be so built as to meet the rules of the chief clubs; in England the bore must not be larger than 12, nor the gun heavier than 8lb; the charge to be used must not exceed four drams of powder and 1¼oz of shot. On the Continent and in America 10-bores are allowed, but there is usually some restriction as to charge. The pigeon gun may be made with hammers or hammerless, preferably the latter. It should not have a trigger bolting safety and an automatic trigger safety for this species of gun is the greatest mistake that can be made. The shooting required will in some measure depend on the distance at which the user is generally placed, it being required to have the largest possible killing circle at 1 yard beyond the trap with the first barrels and at 5 yards with the second. In no class of gun is uniformity and regularity of shooting more essential than in the trap gun. The weight may be ½-¾lb greater than in the gun carried for gameshooting, but it is important that the balance be perfect.[48]

And by 'Blagdon' in 1900:

> Such a gun… would scale about 7½lb, being chambered fro the 12-bore cartridge, 2¾in in length and should shoot 1¼oz of shot with a high velocity… For the short distance man, the right barrel should be not quite full choke, but otherwise that barrel as well as the left should be full choke…
>
> An easy alignment of the gun is best obtained with a deadened top rib, broad at the breech and narrowing towards the muzzle, whilst a half-pistol grip stock is generally preferred…
>
> Guns with single trigger…although so recently introduced, are now used by some of the most successful shots of the day, one of the reasons no doubt being the quick and ready discharge of the second barrel without moving the hand to fire the second cartridge and consequently the alignment is not altered and the swing not arrested.[49]

Demise of pigeon shooting

AS IS CLEAR from some of the writers quoted thus far, pigeon shooting had its enemies throughout its history. The first serious attempt to ban it—and it coincides with criticism of other fieldsports—took place in early 1880s. George Anderson, an 'advanced liberal' MP for Glasgow, succeeded in getting a Bill through the Commons with a majority of thirteen votes in 1883. The Lords rejected the Bill, which the *The Field* described as a 'farrago of nonsense'. The editorial of 10 March, however, expounded:

> Except on the score of its attendant gambling, pigeon shooting is quite as unobjectionable as battue shooting; and, indeed, the proportion of wounded pigeons which get away to die a lingering death is very much smaller than that of the tame-bred pheasants with which nearly every battue is largely supplied.

Holt's Shooting Calendar wrote in its pages after the assault had failed:

> Mr Anderson's attempt to suppress pigeon shooting failed, it is true; but only because the House of Lords threw out the Bill. In the Commons, those who might have been expected to strenuously oppose the Bill voted for it. The arguments were all in favour of the opposers; but the numbers were decidedly for suppression. Now that pigeon shooters have roused up a little and have started a Society for the Protection of Sport, we may hope to see any further attempts at suppression met with facts and statistics, which will show that the cruelties at pigeon shooting matches only have existence in the brains of crotchetmongers and hysterical sentimentalists.[50]

The crotchetmongers and sentimentalists continued their efforts, but pigeon shooting continued, more or less unmolested, throughout the 1880s and 1890s. *The Field* reported in 1891 of the successful (and thoroughly deserved) prosecution of the organisers of a contest in Exeter. They had tied 100 yards of string to the feet of their birds to prevent them escaping. Not very British—but it is also an indication of just how expensive pigeon shooting could be in other circumstances. Pigeon shooting survived into the twentieth century. Greener makes clear, however, in the ninth (1910) edition of *The Gun and Its Development*, that live pigeon shooting was by then well past its zenith. He wrote:

> Of recent years the sport has declined in favour, both in this country and in the United States. The Hurlingham ground has recently been closed [this happened in 1905], while in America many of the States have entirely prohibited the trapping and subsequent shooting of pigeons. The nanimate bird, or clay pigeon, has largely taken the place of the live bird and when thrown from suitable traps it affords excellent practice, some of the newer pattern 'birds' being exceptionally difficult to 'kill'.[51]

The Victoria History of the County of Middlesex records in 1911 that even at its height in the late 1880s, the majority of members at Hurlingham were not shooting members:

> [Of its 1,500 members] for several years prior to 1891... only 200 were shooting members, many of whom took no part in pigeon shooting. The sport therefore gradually ceased to be carried on under the favourable conditions it had enjoyed at Hornsey Wood and the Gun Club and owing to the greater popularity of polo, it has now been driven from the scene where it may be said to have attained its zenith.[52]

Live pigeon shooting was finally banned in Britain under the Defence of the Realm Act of 1916, ostensibly due to concern about spies and carrier pigeons. The ban was confirmed after the Great War by the Captive Birds Shooting

George Anderson

(Prohibition) Act of 1921, after a campaign by *The Daily Express* (which shows that not much changes on that front either). The penalty for non-compliance was a fine of up to £25, or not exceeding three month imprisonment. One lawyer expert in this area, Nicholas Everitt, noted in 1927: 'We doubt, however, whether a single individual shooting pigeons released by himself and with no one invited to watch him, could be properly convicted.'

Summary

SO WHAT do we really know of the early history of pigeon shooting? The activity appears to have first become fashionable in the last decades of the eighteenth century. From the start, it attracted less than favourable comment. It appears to have been practised by all social classes, often involved sparrows and starlings as well as pigeons and continued to grow, with peaks and troughs in the years 1800-1850.

In the second half of the nineteenth century, pigeon shooting seems to have come into real vogue, aided by a general Victorian passion for guns and shooting and by the formally organised participation of leaders of fashion. Elaborate rules were developed and large, well-funded, clubs such as Hurlingham and the Gun Club founded. The draft of the Hurlingham rules—probably more copied than any other—were reportedly formulated at a meeting at Stephen Grant's premises in London.

The exhibitions and matches of the touring American professionals in the 1870s and 1880s seemed to have been a significant factor in raising popular consciousness of the activity. There are some other factors worthy of note. This was the same era in which rifle shooting became a widely practised sport through the Volunteer Movement. It was the time that driven gameshooting began to become popular too.

The growth of pigeon shooting runs parallel to the development of the breechloading shotgun. The carefully regulated pigeon shooting clubs of the second half of the century offered an ideal venue for the test and promotion of a new type of scientifically developed double gun. First the breech systems were perfected, then choke-boring and finally the hammerless, self-cocking mechanism (although this advance was not as quickly adopted by pigeon shooters as the others mentioned—they liked the reliability of hammer guns).

It is notable that by 1890 this development work was largely accomplished—the side-by-side gun had taken its modern form—and this coincides with the decline of English pigeon shooting. Gunmakers still took the results of pigeon matches seriously, however. They knew that reputations could be made or lost in the published lists of guns used and money won. These lists ceased to be published in the sporting press early in the 1900s, but makers continued to refer to their pigeon shooting successes in their promotional literature well into the twentieth century. Holland & Holland, for example, was sufficiently proud of the win by Alfred Elby in June 1932 World Championship at Paris to take out a special advertisement in the periodical *Game & Gun* for August of the same year.

Even in its heyday in England—1860-1890—pigeon shooting never quite succeeded in overcoming its bad image despite the best efforts of its enthusiastic exponents. Around 1880, pigeon shooting began to be seriously criticised. It weathered the first attacks, but the criticism would eventually close it down in England.

It is notable that in 1905 the pigeon shooters at Hurlingham, who had founded the club and had once enjoyed pre-eminence, were out-voted by the non-shooting members. The matter went to law and the Polo 'party'—in a majority on the club committee—had their right to oust the pigeon shooters confirmed with costs awarded against the shooters. The pigeon is still the club's

A bird which numbered perhaps as many as 5 billion, the last passenger pigeon died in Cincinnati in 1914. Picture courtesy: Kalina White, Earlham College

symbol. And shooting continued at the Gun Club at least until the outbreak of the First World War and, no doubt, at some other venues.

In the United States, the decline in pigeon shooting (and the rapid rise of inanimate target shooting) may be attributed to similar pressures and, no less significantly, the decline and eventual extinction of the passenger pigeon, the preferred breed for trapshooting in that country. Flocks dwindled in the 1880s. A bird which had once been counted in millions—one estimate puts the mid nineteenth century population at 5 billion—suddenly disappeared because of the pressure of relentless trapping as a cheap food source (the number used for shooting contests, though great, was comparatively insignificant). The last wild birds were seen in the eastern states in the 1890s. The last wild specimen died in Ohio about 1900 and the last captive passenger pigeon expired in a Cincinnati zoo in 1914.

However much our late twentieth-century, politically correct sensibilities may now lead us to criticise the shooting of captive birds, the rules, practices and terminology of pigeon shooting have shaped the clay sports we know today. The layout of a live pigeon shoot was much like that of a modern Trap event and the guns we now use for clayshooting are the direct descendants of the live pigeon guns of the late Victorian era. These, typically, were heavier, more tightly choked and longer barrelled than those used for gameshooting. The flat, machined and raised rib and non-auto safe were popularised by pigeon shooters as was the Monte Carlo stock. And, the need for an advantage, however small, was a significant spur towards the development of a reliable single-trigger mechanism. Stuart-Wortley notes of the Gun Club Notting Hill:

> Here every modern improvement in guns, powders, or cartridges has been brought to the test and there can be no doubt that the practical proofs supplied by pigeon-shooting have been of great service to the science of modern gunnery.

There is not that much difference today between guns and ammunition. In the 1870s and 1880s, the differences were hugely significant and live pigeon shooting matches provided a contained, closely observed, environment in which to develop the ever-improving guns and cartridges of the era. You might make moral objections to pigeon shooting and deny it the respectability of 'sport'. But, its significance cannot be disputed nor, I suspect, its excitement: the battle between Messrs Purdey, Boss and Churchill in the 1890s must have looked much like the rivalry between the Ferrari, McLaren, and Williams teams in the 1990s.

Modern pigeon shooting

PIGEON SHOOTING continued in Germany, France and Belgium until the 1970s, Portugal until 1999 and remains popular in Egypt, South America, Andorra, Spain and French North Africa. It is also seen in some states of North America and, until recently at least, in private clubs in Italy. I watched live pigeon shooting in Texas recently (and was amazed by the size of the wagers being placed).

I also know that there is a dedicated band of devotees in Pennsylvania, Florida and some of the states of the Deep South. Matches are publicised by word of mouth only and conducted with a watchful eye for unwelcome visitors. The costs involved are, as ever, significant.

Modern competitions at live birds take two basic forms: release from metal box traps of sophisticated design and columbaire, where the bird is thrown by hand and must be dropped by the gun within a definite boundary (often a 100-metre circle).

There is also a pseudo-columbaire where the poor pigeon, or occasionally a quail, is propelled into the air from a tube attached to the arm of something that looks much like a clay trap.

In a box trap competition, still the most common form of live pigeon shooting, the guns stand at an allotted distance (26-32m) and face five traps. Modern traps are made to various patterns, some encourage the birds upwards by means of a jet of air, some involve a wooden ball which rolls towards the bird as the trap opens and, the most popular type for larger competitions, utilise a sling system in which the bird is located in a canvas loop.

As far as guns are concerned, both side-by-sides and over-and-unders are employed and semi-automatics also have a dedicated following. World championships may last a week to ten days and are leisurely affairs where the food and socialising seem to be as important as the shooting. Pigeon shoots are still expensive. Even a pool shoot—typically consisting of less than half a dozen birds—may cost £100 or more to enter.

Simulated pigeon shooting

BUSSEY'S 'GYRO' pigeon (pictured) of about 1870 was the first more-or-less successful mechanical pigeon. It was a clockwork-powered device with a twin bladed steel propeller of figure-of-eight form. The prop was located on two pins on the top of a canister that contained the spring mechanism. On the bottom, there was a spike so that the device could be stuck in the ground. A string could then be attached to a simple ratchet trigger. Wound up half a dozen revolutions, a Bussey target could fly considerable distances, especially if launched into wind. Moreover, the Bussey system had the capability to launch multiple targets simultaneously by simply stacking extra birds up to a maximum of about half a dozen.

The Art of Wingshooting, an American work of 1895 by William Leffingwell, noted of what I presume is the Bussey Bird: 'Among the first inanimate targets was the gyro pigeon; it was so constructed that arms would revolve working in imitation of pigeon wings. It was thrown from a trap and sailed gracefully away, but there was a certainty in its line of flight and an uncertainty of its flying and of its falling when hit that soon did away with its use.'

Bussey's was a maker of sports equipment and shooting accessories. The

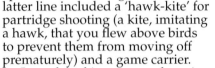

latter line included a 'hawk-kite' for partridge shooting (a kite, imitating a hawk, that you flew above birds to prevent them from moving off prematurely) and a game carrier.

It marketed its own products in England. In the United States, its gyro bird was sold by Henry Squires (specimens turn up occasionally in Canada, which may indicate an agent in that dominion too). The fact that Bussey's are comparatively common in collections today on both sides of the Atlantic seems to indicate that they were reasonably successful in their day.

My friend John Hargreaves is now developing his own version of the Bussey's target (of which his collection contains a number of original examples). Like the original, the Hargreave's gyro will have the capability for multiple launches.

At the time of writing, a prototype test day is being planned.

The original Bussey target is certainly challenging. It is highly unpredictable in flight and, when it goes off course a potential danger to the gunner and assistants.

ZZ/Hélice

ZZ SHOOTING was developed in the 1960s. It acquired its zippy name because the first targets were made of zinc and the name of the most popular breed of pigeon for live bird competitions on the Continent was zurito. It is now officially called Hélice, the French word for propeller. Other names for the discipline include: electrocibles—cible is the French for target—and robot pigeon.

The sport of ZZ developed rapidly as a serious alternative to live pigeon shooting. The man responsible was a celebrated live-bird shot of the post-Second World War era, the Belgian Chevalier David de Lossy who worked with a mechanic called Fernand Moinil to develop the original propeller target. This was twin-bladed and launched from the spindle of an electric motor. The first competition was at the test site—the Sart St Laurent shooting club in Belgium. It was introduced in Monte Carlo soon after. Legend has it that Princess Grace of Monaco had complained about the cruelty of live bird shooting much as Princess Alexandra once had.

ZZ has gained popularity rapidly in the last decade in England. Pat Lynch and Chris Potter have done much to promote this challenging discipline. Top clay shot Mickey Rouse is a fan of the sport, winning the world Hélice championship in Portugal in 2001. Howard Batt has also distinguished himself by winning the World Championship twice. Dionne Rogers has proven herself to be the world's finest female ZZ shot.

Hélice targets are made of orange plastic with a white central witness. Some 12in or so across and more expensive than normal clays, they look rather like an enlarged version of the helicopter toys once popular in breakfast cereal packets (you pulled a string wrapped around a spindle and it went whizzing off into the yonder). They are placed on the spindles of five upright but oscillating electric motors situated forward of the shooter. When the shooter—who stands at 27m (recently changed from 26)—calls for a target, a bird is released at random at an unpredictable angle from one of the five 'traps' and will zigzag in flight in an unpredictable manner. Two shots are allowed and the centre of the target must be detached from the propeller and be brought down within the boundary—21m from each 'trap'—to score a kill. Hélice is governed by FITASC. As with live pigeon shooting, Hélice championships are leisurely.

In the USA and occasionally in England, you may encounter 'American ZZ'. This uses a target which still has metal propellers but combines it with a plastic central witness. The prop may survive as many as ten shots and the witness unless fractured should be good for five according to the maker. Kenneth Gagnon of Quack Sporting Clays in the US has also experimented with vacuum-formed inserts inside a conventional clay to create a more cost effective ZZ-like discipline. James Lee of Sussex created something similar with 'Slapshot' or SLP (Simulated Live Pigeon). It used a conventional target with a white marker disc fitted under an ordinary clay bird. The disc had to be dropped within a perimeter boundary. The birds were launched from a conventional trap. A round consisted of twenty-one targets thrown at 10, 12.5 and 15m from the trap. A variety of targets have been devised over the years to drop a jack, or sub target, within a boundary to simulate pigeon shooting.

Glass balls

POTATOES, BOTTLES, wooden blocks, coins and all manner of other objects have been used as inanimate moving targets. One famous shooting match circa 1800 involved cricket balls launched by a fast bowler, another in 1804—concerning a bet between Ensign Burrows and Lieutenant Otto of the Sussex Militia—was settled by means of apples and a fowling-piece.[53] In 2004, top shooter George Digweed hit a golf ball struck with a five-iron.[54]

The most direct ancestor of the modern clay pigeon, however, is the glass ball, now a valuable 'collectable' with average specimens fetching £100 and rare ones as much as £7,000. This elegant if impractical form of inanimate bird probably originated in England but was developed in America. Details are sketchy, but glass ball targets appear to have been used in some form at country fairs in England in conjunction with a rudimentary catapult type trap. WW Greener writes in the second edition of *Modern Shotguns*, published in 1891:

> As a pastime, the shooting of glass balls or bottles has long been practised in this country, but was developed and made a fashionable amusement in the United States by Mr Ira Paine, Captain Bogardus and Dr Carver and other professional shots.[55]

Greener does not elucidate on the early origins of glass ball shooting. Most shotgunners, however, will have had the experience of shooting at a glass bottle tossed in the air at some stage in their shooting life (do not assume endorsement of the practice from this statement). We may guess that this is a fairly ancient practise—it probably pre-dates wingshooting. Bottle shooting was also a common practice in miniature rifle galleries. Some galleries used glass balls as well, typically as dangling or swinging targets, although they also were also put on chain-type conveyors and shot at much like metallic ducks. The Winchester gallery at Battersea Funfair, offered both ping-pong balls on water jets and glass bottles in the 1960s. I spent many happy hours there. The glass ball as a static mark has also been used by archers.

Although he is not mentioned by Greener, Charles Portlock of Boston appears to have introduced glass ball shooting into the United States. In 1866, he offered the American public ball targets and a trap for launching them as a mark for shotgunners.

The first recorded shoot took place at Boston's Beacon Park in 1867. The activity seems to have developed fairly quickly thereafter, but was initially impeded by the absence of an efficient trap. By all accounts Portlock's was inadequate. *The Illustrated Sporting & Dramatic News* for 15 May 1875 contains the earliest illustration of glass ball shooting with shotguns in England, as well as some historically significant words of description. The text reads:

> The engraving on the preceding page represents artificial pigeon shooting as carried out on the Downs at Epson between the station and the stand. The arrangements are remarkably simple. A catapult, formed of two pieces of indiarubber having a cup in the centre, is so adjusted that, by pulling a cord attached to a kind of trigger, the spring is released and a thin, coloured glass ball ejected some 50ft into the air. The shooters stand about 25 yards behind the catapult and to break the glass balls in the air requires some little knack. By attending to the following rule a decent shot may easily break the ball every time: 'Follow the rise of the ball with the muzzle of your gun, but wait until it is upon the turn before you pull the trigger.'
>
> At Epsom the odds are always against the gun, as the charge is only two pence per shot and, consequently, there is only a dram of powder in the cartridge and often no shot. Many really good shots have made terrible fiascos before their friends when shooting at the artificial pigeons at Epsom.

The accompanying line drawing to this story (above) is especially useful because it shows how glass ball shooting may have been conducted on both sides of the Atlantic in the early days. The target is launched vertically from a crude trap that may well correspond to that of Portlock. The location is interesting too—Epsom Downs in May. It supports the idea that glass ball shooting in England may have been associated with fairs. London's Agricultural Halls hosted glass ball shooting competitions in the late 1870s.

Ira Paine, first in Greener's list of the American shooting pros, was another early glass ball innovator. He produced both an improved trap (patented in 1876) and better ball targets, some filled with feathers to break with the simulated realism of a hit on a pigeon. Descriptions of the latter are hard to come by but DH Eaton states:

> It had an elastic spring causing it to throw balls farther and better, but it was hard to set up, heavy and cumbersome to move and too expensive to come into general use.[56]

It is possible that this is wrongly attributed, however and that the description may apply to the equally scarce Portlock machine.

Had he lived longer and written a book or two, Paine might be better remembered today. In his day, and as made clear by Greener, he was as famous as Bogardus and Carver. A brilliant pistol and rifle shot as well as shotgunner, Paine had a tragic end. He collapsed in Paris in 1889 after the performance of his shooting show at *Les Folies Bergères*. This may sound an elegant way to go, but his exit from the stage of life was none too pleasant. Having quaffed a cold beer after completing his act, he succumbed to twelve hours 'strangulation of the bowels' before expiring. *

The man who did more to popularise the glass ball game than any other, Bogardus. As well as being a great showman and show-off, he was also an

* My thanks to Ralph Finch for this rather macabre story which he gleaned from a contemporary obituary

inventor. At least, his name appears on the patent for an improved trap (US patent 188,333, 13 March 1877) and a better target (10 April 1877).

He may have taken the credit for someone else's design—he was that sort of man—but there is no doubt about his tireless efforts in developing and promoting the sport of glass ball shooting and his own fortunes with it. Apart from touring the country seeking challenge matches, giving exhibitions of pigeon and glass ball shooting—and later clayshooting—in the late 1870s and early 1880s. He also ventured into print with *Field, Cover and Trap Shooting*.

The book embellished his own achievements, while ignoring those of his rivals and also provided wingshooting instruction. The original, 1874, edition has no mention of glass ball targets, but the second, 1878 edition, significantly does. Bogardus noted at the end of the newly included section on the subject:

> Glass-ball shooting is destined to become popular, as a great many men who never care to shoot birds from a trap are becoming interested in glass-ball shooting and a great many sportsmen prefer them for sweepstake shooting, as they afford more even shooting and shooters have the satisfaction of knowing their opponents have no easy birds.[57]

Bogardus produced rules for glass ball shooting within this work. They are the first known to exist and were adapted by some clubs in the following decade for clayshooting. He stipulated the use of Bogardus equipment of course. His trap was certainly better than previous patterns—simple, effective and relatively cheap. It looked and functioned something like the ballista siege engine used by the Romans; the US patent office lists it under the heading 'Ball throwers for shooting practice'.

Bogardus's trap, unlike those that preceded it, allowed target balls to be thrown forwards and at considerable range. By projecting the ball in a parabolic arc up and up to 40 yards or so from the trap, it ensured the future of glass ball shooting as a competitive sport.

The design of Bogardus's trap had the merits of simplicity and relative economy. There was a launching cup on the end of a long carriage-style spring. The cheaper version cost US$6 in the USA.

There was also a deluxe US$8 model that allowed rotation by means of a pivot and a steering bar, to which two strings could be attached to turn the trap to one side or another. This could be achieved from behind the firing point and a third string released the trigger mechanism. Bogardus's preferred scheme of shooting put three traps 10 yards apart at 18 yards rise, trap one giving a bird to the left, trap two a straight-away and trap three a shot to the right. He noted, however, that good practice could be had from one trap, if it were hidden behind a screen.

His target balls were good but, at US$2 per hundred—around twice the price of smooth balls—it seems they were a bit too expensive to dominate the market. Their distinctive feature, one later much copied, was a corrugated or quilted surface. An advertisement of 1879 informed:

> Bogardus Patent Rough Glass Balls are made of uniform weight and thickness and have a corrugated surface that strengthens the ball for shipment to any part of the country, prevents the glancing of shot and thereby ensures the breaking of the ball when hit. Buy none but the best and patronise the man who has spent both time and money to introduce glass ball shooting to the sporting public, until it has become a national pastime.

Plain, moulded balls were the most commonly used in the US. Ball targets, in all their forms, were made in enormous quantity. One firm, the Bohemian Glass Works of New York, which is associated with Ira Paine, claimed it made more than a million balls in six months circa 1880.

Sears sold vast numbers too. And, glass balls are known to have been made in quantity outside the USA. Ball targets were manufactured in England,

Glass ball development

IN ITS earliest moving target form, the glass ball target was no more than a smooth, free-blown globe about 2½in diameter. It soon became more refined in form and the diameter was standardised at 2 5/8in. Smaller balls of 2in-2 1/8in were also made for shotgunning purposes and are sometimes seen in collections. Moulds were used for mass production. The glass was coloured amber, blue, green or amethyst to improve visibility and the surface was sometimes patterned or corrugated—a diamond pattern was typical—to improve breaking qualities. Balls were packed in barrels of sawdust for transport (as clays would later be). Very occasionally, one of these tubs is discovered with targets intact—an event which sends shudders through the antique glass market in case a rare and expensive ball should suddenly become available in quantity.

Ball targets were used in great quantity in the United States during the 1870s and 1880s and, to a lesser extent, in England. Glass ball shooting developed in parallel to live bird shooting, to which it became a cheaper and more politically correct alternative, as clayshooting would also become.

Although they had their shortcomings, ball targets continued to be made until the 1920s. They were especially favoured by exhibition shooters as they could be launched in relatively confined spaces. They might also be filled with powder, feathers or streamers for dramatic effect.

Sweden, Holland, France, Germany, Poland, Bohemia, Australia and Canada and collectors continue the search so that new countries might be added to the list.

When shows like Carver's came to London in 1879 or played in cities on the Continent, it is likely that they had local glass works produce targets for them. An act or production on extended tour would get through vast quantities of balls—more than it might have been practical to ship across the Atlantic.

Captain Bogardus's glass ball trap. Picture courtesy: Andrew Orr / Holt's

With millions manufactured in many locations and many subtly different patterns, it is not surprising that all manner of improvements were claimed for one product or another.

I have noted Ira Paine's and Bogardus's innovations. As well as corrugated Bogardus balls, there are a few 'hobnailed' ones with a stippled surface. The Standard Trap Ball (circa 1881) was covered with sand to prevent ricochets. Targets were often loaded with shredded paper, saw dust, wood shavings or flour to make breaks more interesting.

The problem with all balls made of glass remained the shards they left behind when shattered. This deficiency led to some practical and some odd inventions. Into the first category fall composition targets. They were made of

The Bogardus trap in action

Annie gets her gun

AN ACCOUNT of Annie Oakley shooting ball targets at the Chicago World's Fair 1893 by William Bruce Leffingwell:

> Then a vision appeared; a woman's form passed gracefully into the area, hundreds of hands clapped their applause and Annie Oakley, dressed in a tan coloured suit, smiled and bowed and modestly tipped her broad brimmed hat to admiring thousands. She stood in the presence of that assemblage the empress of her art—the most skilful exponent of expert marksmanship of her sex in the world. The rapidity of her shooting and her wonderful accuracy in hitting the objects fired at, astonished and captivated all. Round after round of applause greeted every shot. Then the audience was stilled by the announcement that she would break eleven balls thrown in the air, using five different guns in accomplishing the feat and this would all be done in ten seconds. The 12,000 people sat with bated breath; the crack of a gun broke the stillness; this was followed by repeated reports with astonishing rapidity and regularity, and, in the time announced, the last ball was flying into a thousand fragments, her smoking gun lay upon the table and she, the most expert shot of her sex in the world, stood for an instant bowing her appreciative thanks for this recognition of her skill and then she fled to the exit like a frightened deer, pursued by waving hats, handkerchiefs of those who paid such wonderful tribute to her skill.[61]

pitch or resin and a filler (the formula of which was usually a closely guarded trade secret just as the 'recipes' for composition clays today). They were used in great quantity and made commercially and also by users themselves. They certainly had obvious advantages for public display purposes because they left no shards. HA Thorn (Charles Lancaster) wrote in 1889:

> Pitch composition balls, as used by 'Buffalo Bill' at the American Exhibition [The Wild West Show was a feature of this exposition]—with an attendant standing ready to throw them from the side of the beginner in different directions—also afford good practice; moreover these balls cannot leave any objectionable pieces, likely to damage the feet of cattle, dogs, etc. as is the case with glass balls. The author supplies special gun metal moulds for casting these balls so that a gentleman having a mould can make balls at home thereby saving loss by breakage whilst in transit—which is always a difficult question to contend with.[58]

The great problem with the composition targets was to make them hard enough to break well in all ambient temperatures. This may explain why they did not completely oust glass targets (their development, however, must have shortened the R&D cycle on the composition 'clay' bird that would appear in the mid 1880s). Other ball targets were made of compressed paper and concrete; one was even designed to break down into fertiliser, though none of these appear to have survived to the present day.

There were some wonderfully named contrivances. For example, Belcher's Patent Paper Bird made by GF Kolb of Philadelphia was 'an oddly-shaped bit of stiff paper attached to a wire ball' which had some resemblance to a real bird and could be launched from a normal glass ball trap. And, there were Powell's Patent Puff Balls made by Henry Sears. These were a simple sphere made of paper and filled with dust. They puffed when hit and could be re-used allegedly. The Globe Flight, marketed by the Globe Shot Co of Saint

Louis (and patented in 1884), was a pasteboard disc 5½in in diameter with a small balloon of 2½in at its centre. It looked rather like a model of the planet Saturn and its rings. DH Eaton records:

> The claims for this invention were: that it was good until hit with shot; one pellet hitting the balloon, 'dead bird.' No rubbish and no disputes… The cost was $20 per 1,000 with a refund of $2.50 per 1,000 for pasteboards in good condition. The hand inflators cost 50 cents each.
> Apparently, the Globe was tried out at a shoot in Philadelphia and occasioned much mirth among the contestants. It never attained any measure of popularity and was soon forgotten.[59]

There were balls made of metal, too. In England, ammunition maker Kynoch & Co offered a thin, charcoal-filled, brass sphere in the 1880s. It was of 2 1/8in diameter and produced a satisfying dark cloud when struck. The company may have got the idea from Fletcher's Bell-Metal Ball, an American target made of heavy brass which—unlike the Kynoch—rang distinctly when hit. Later, Kynoch would make a similar stamped brass 'clay' in two versions. One was formed entirely of brass, the other had a card base, both had a powder filling and emitted a cloud when struck. Armitage of Manchester produced 'pottery' balls and impressed Basil Tozer with them. He wrote:

> Better than either [glass balls or metallic balls]… are clay balls manufactured by Mr Armitage… and possessing the following advantages: that the fragments are perfectly harmless and unless hit hard they will not break, which teaches the gunner to shoot in good style, whereas two or three shot are sufficient to smash glass balls. Both glass and clay balls can be filled with feathers… [60]

Some were even designed to explode, such as the Broughton and the Standard Clay Percussion Target Ball. This was made by Woeber & Varvig of Cincinnati and they cost US$15 per thousand in 1880. A contemporary description records rather optimistically:

> …It is so constructed that when penetrated by a single pellet of shot the composition in the interior, which cannot fail, emits a light flash accompanied by a dense cloud of smoke, which rends apart the earthenware shell composing the ball and shows up to everyone present an indisputable proof of a hit. The shot cannot glance from the surface of the ball. A heavy charge [of powder and shot] such as is necessary to break a glass ball, is not needed. The ball can be burst at 100 yards, where a glass ball only shows marks of shot. The balls are of uniform weight and furnished in any desired colour. The objection to the debris of glass is avoided in this ball, as the material is light pottery clay and burnt so that it will not resist the action of the weather. They are stronger than glass and do not break easily when striking the ground.

The earliest glass ball traps used a rubber band to catapult the ball vertically as we have noted. This was not much use for serious sport, but remained useful for exhibition shooting. The Bogardus trap used a flat metal spring and, later, there were more sophisticated 'rotary' or revolving traps such as the one made by the New York firm of Card in 1879. It threw its balls forward within an unpredictable arc that provided much more of a challenge than the leaf spring style trap. There were traps capable of throwing doubles, too. One of the first was the Davenport (also made in New York State about 1881). Card made a double that became well known in the 1880s, too. It is illustrated in both *Practical Hints on Shooting* of 1887 and in *The Gun and Its Development*. The latter work noted in its 1885 edition:

> The revolving is the latest American improved trap; it will project one or two balls in any direction (except towards the shooter), or it will rotate throwing balls in a direction impossible to foresee.[62]

The Pittsburg Rocketer (also circa 1880) could, it seems, hurl balls of various sizes. And, according to Eaton, was used by the Pittsburgh Gun Club which reportedly 'threw at least 20,000 balls on its grounds' using one. That's not much shooting by modern standards—many modern grounds throw more than half a million targets a year and large operations may throw a million-plus—but it is another indication that glass ball shooting achieved considerable popularity. It was not just an activity for exhibition shooters. America seems to have been the hothouse for glass-ball invention, as it would become for clay target and trap innovation. Eaton lists no less than 39 patents for ball traps taken out between 1876 and 1912.[63]

Practical Hints on Shooting, a work of 1887, illustrates single and double rotating traps and a single Greener stationary trap that looks like a more sophisticated and better made version of the Bogardus original. The 1896 edition of *The Dead Shot* by the Marksman records:

> There are several inventions of glass-ball traps by English manufacturers: among which are rotating traps which throw balls with great force in any required direction. But there are some which merely toss the ball a few yards perpendicularly in the air [the earliest ball traps were of this type as discussed]: such, however, afford but poor practice as anyone can soon acquire the knack of hitting every ball from such a trap.[64]

Albert Hockey of Bristol patented a most unusual magazine glass-ball trap in 1887. It appears to have been inspired by the American Adam's 'Self-Feeding Glass-Ball Trap' patented in the USA on 29 April 1879. A contemporary advertisement noted: 'Fifteen balls can be thrown in twenty seconds.'[65]

As with live bird shooting, there were many famous shooting matches. The stakes in competition could be vast. US$1,000 was not unknown—more like US$100,000 in today's money. There were invariably side bets too. The records for glass ball shooting stand with—who else?—Bogardus and Carver.

Bogardus once shot 6,000 glass balls for a claimed 6,013 shots expended. On another occasion he also managed to break 5,500 balls in 'a few seconds less than 7 hours 20 minutes' (missing 356). But things may not be quite what they seem, there may have been some skulduggery. A report in *The Spirit of the Times*, a sporting journal fond of controversy, suggested, after Bogardus had apparently hit 5,000 out of 5,156 balls during an earlier record attempt at Gimores' Garden, New York, that there had been a conspiracy. Some of the balls, they alleged, had been previously broken at the neck at Bogardus's factory in Brooklyn and secreted into the exhibition area. The decision over a hit or a miss was, they claimed, on many occasions made by a judge who would pick up a pre-broken ball and exclaim: 'See—the neck is broken; tally one for Bogardus'. The periodical fearlessly (or with malice) concluded:

Annie Oakley

> The unmasking of this gigantic fraud was an unpleasant duty and has been done without fear of prejudice. We know whereof we speak and if any of the culprits dare dispute our statements we shall be prompt to produce respectable and responsible witnesses who will swear to the truth. The 'trapper', Dr B Talbot, could not have been ignorant of the trickery. The scorer, TC Banks, at

least was not acute of perception. If Miles Johnson, the referee, was not party to the fraud, he is the phenomenal fool of the age and should have his head trepanned and brains injected with a syringe.[66]

Doc Carver, of whom no impropriety in this respect has ever been suggested, managed to break 5,500 in just more than eight hours. This does not appear to match Bogardus, until you remember that Carver was not using a smoothbore with shot but a rifle with single bullet.

Carver also had a famous glass ball match with W Scott in London in 1881. It was decided over 9,950 glass balls each. The scores were Dr Carver 9,737; Scott 9,735. It was evidently a close, as well as tiring, contest. Scott made one run of 640 straight. Out of the last 950 targets shot, Carver missed only two and Scott three. It was this sort of consistent, sometimes uncanny success under pressure that led Greener to note of the tall, quiet Westerner: 'His aim with the rifle is apparently unerring'. The native Americans in Carver's buffalo-shooting days had another way of putting it (if you believe the hype). They called him 'spirit gun'.

This is the report in *The Field* in 1879 of Dr WF Carver, 'the champion rifle shot', performing at the Crystal Palace in London with glass balls and even pennies thrown into the air—and mostly with a rifle:

On the 14th inst (Easter Monday) we witnessed Dr Carver's exhibition of rifle and shotgun shooting, in the grounds of the Crystal Palace. The weather was most unpropitious; a high wind causing many of the glass balls to rise most unsteadily and some snow and sleet, which fell by intervals, did not tend by any means to improve the shooter's chances.

The exhibition took place on the lawn at the north end of the Palace and the attendance, spite of the weather, was good at both the 12 o'clock and the 2 o'clock performances.

Dr Carver uses for his shooting a set of Winchester repeating rifles, half a dozen in number, which are handed to him ready loaded, when he is shooting against time. They are of the 1873 model, calibre 44, weight 9½lb to 10lb, octagon barrel, length 28in, open clover-leaf sights, loading sixteen central-fire cartridges, charged with 40 grains of powder and 200 grains of lead. The length of stock is 14in from the trigger to bottom of heel-plate and 13½in from the hammer to top of heel-plate; and the bend of stock is equal to 2in from the top of heel-plate to an imaginary straight line projected from the barrel. The heel-plate itself is much hollowed out, so as to give the shoulder a firm grip of the rifle.

The Doctor began (1) by firing ten shots, within twenty seconds, into a board and the whole of the ten bullets were within a 4in circle. He then (2) broke, with a single bullet, a glass ball swinging at the end of a string; then, (3) placing his rifle upside down on the top of his head, he smashed a glass ball placed on the ground. Another glass ball (4), similarly situated, he also smashed, holding his rifle sideways. The next performance (5) was the well-known one of shooting a glass ball, whilst standing with his back to the ball, sighting his rifle by means of a looking-glass.

Next (6), holding his rifle to his hip, he hit another ball placed on the ground. Then (7) came his attempted feat of breaking forty balls out of fifty, which were to be thrown in the air by hand. His black servant undertook, as usual, that part of the programme; and right well he threw them, but the wind was puffy and strong and in consequence thereof fifteen balls were missed.

When shooting against time, however (8), the doctor worked away right merrily. He wanted to break fifty balls—thrown into the air by his servant as before—within 3 min, but he actually performed the feat in 2 min 20 sec (in the afternoon, by the way, he broke forty-eight only in the 3 min, thus being two balls behind). Afterwards, five times running, he (9) purposely missed his first shot and smashed the falling ball with his second shot before it reached the ground.

Then (10), at balls thrown across the front of the shooter, he managed to score half his shots and was just equally successful (11) at balls thrown directly at him. How he arranged it, so that he should not 'bag' his servant at the same time when performing the latter deeds appears to us remarkably clever. We trust the negro Jem's life is insured; anyhow, he can certainly tell, from experience, whether a rifle ball 'bings' or 'whizzes,' as the bullets must all pass pretty close to his ears.

The trapshooting (12) proved a score of twelve broken balls to twenty 'pulled'. Not bad this, we should think, with a rifle. At pennies thrown in the air the average of hits was three to seven. This was not at all up to the doctor's form, it appears; but the atrocious weather we experienced readily accounts for it and for this reason he abstained from attempting his double shots at balls and also shooting a glass ball whilst lying on his back over a stool and holding his rifle upside down.

This concluded the rifle shooting part of the performance and the double central-fire 12-bore guns now came into action. The cartridges used by the doctor are WW Greener's, loaded with 1¼oz no 7 chilled shot. With these (1) he smashed ten single balls sprung from a trap in the usual manner; then (2) he fired double shots at five pairs of balls, two balls being sprung together from one trap. He only missed one ball out of the ten. Then, by way of a change, (3) he fired at single balls when they were actually falling and succeeded remarkably well. When firing from the left shoulder, (4) he broke half the balls. He then (5) turned his back to the traps and turning round only when they were sprung, he repeatedly broke single and double balls. Holding his gun with one hand, (6) he also scored most of his single and double shots; and (7) any balls thrown either very high in the air, or parallel to the ground, he ground to powder with the greatest ease.

He then mounted his horse (which he has used for buffalo hunting) and from its back, when at speed, he made an excellent average at thrown balls with the shot gun. Finally, he gave a short lasso exhibition, catching his horse and his servant with ease and this brought the affair to a most satisfactory conclusion. Our shooting readers should really see for themselves such a series of performances, which certainly stand unrivalled. The doctor will give his exhibition daily, at the Palace, until further notice.

Dr Carver went, on Easter Tuesday, to Sandringham, where he exhibited his skill before HRH the Prince of Wales and a numerous assembly of distinguished personages; and his visit proved a most complete success. The weather was everything that could be desired and the wonderful shot literally outstripped himself. The Prince of Wales himself kept the scores and most extraordinary results were obtained. For instance, when trying to break, with rifle bullets, 75 balls out of 100 thrown in the air, the doctor made a complete score of 100 consecutive balls without a miss. This was the first time he had ever made that record in a public exhibition, although in private he has broken 885 balls without a miss. He was equally remarkably successful in most of his other attempts and when he left Sandringham the Prince and all present were enthusiastic in their praise of the doctor's skill.[67]

In his well-produced and meticulously researched *The Royal Gun Collection at Sandringham*[68], gun historian David Baker notes that there are six Winchester model 1873 rifles—Carver's preferred gun—in the royal collection. One, originally, shipped in 1878 presents a mystery with regard to provenance. Could it have been ordered from an English agent by the Prince of Wales after watching Carver's masterly demonstration in the spring of 1879?

Mechanical alternatives to balls

THE FIRST 1881 edition of *The Gun and Its Development* mentions Greener's own 'Patent artificial flying pigeon machine'. This offered a variety of targets including a 'stiff pigeon to use with whitewash' and 'collapsing pigeons with hinged wings with valvular balloon body to fall to the ground when struck'. Sadly, there are no pictures and no known examples as far as I am aware.

In 1884, Jeremiah King of New York sought US patent protection for a target propelled by compressed air. The target itself was made of plaster of Paris 'or other similar material', with wings connected to an elastic band to make them spread. The 'artificial flying pigeon' of Messrs Mansell and Bartlet is illustrated in *The Gun and Its Development* in 1885. It was attached on a long arm that rotated above a stand. A human operator rotated a central axle by means of long strings attached to a turning handle at the operator's end and a hub at the main machine's.

To quote WW: 'A skilful driver is required to get good sport from the birds… for if the… handle be turned slowly and regularly, a slow, gentle sweep is given to the pigeon that no tyro could miss.'

Of the target itself he notes: 'The pigeon is either of iron, whitewashed, or of a wire cage, having inside an inflated india rubber balloon which keeps the two wings spread until caused to collapse by the penetration of the shots. Another pigeon with a balloon body is made which, when shot, falls to the ground.'

Greener further reports that the Prince of Wales had 'one fitted up and has expressed himself pleased with it.'

As well as his own glass-ball trap, Greener manufactured (and according to Graham Greener, patented) 'An Artificial Flying Machine'. This launched various artificial pigeons, including a 'Stiff Pigeon' to use with whitewash, a 'Collapsing Pigeon' with hinged wings and a pigeon designed 'to fall to the ground when struck'.[69]

A Mr Arbenz of Birmingham, England, created an even more curious propeller-driven device. 'The Eclipse Bird Flight Simulator' was offered in England in the 1880s and warranted a detailed description in Tozer's *Practical Hints on Shooting*:

> The propeller is a nickel-plated iron tube, 1ft long, in which is fixed a very powerful spiral spring, the end being covered by a metal cap. The projectiles are of different lengths, varying from 5 to 7in and made of thin sheet iron, in form resembling the Archimedean screw. Care is required in manipulating the apparatus, but with a little attention any child can work it. The propeller is nicely finished and weighs about 2lb.
>
> The distance to which it drives the projectiles depends on the wind blowing at the time. If there is a stiff breeze it will often carry them over 100 yards and some we have sent up to 150 and even 160 yards.
>
> This appliance possesses a single advantage over ball traps, namely that of being able to spring four or five projectiles together, which spin through the air like a covey of partridges and at about the same speed.

Another English invention was Jone's 'Snipe Throwing Trap'. This apparatus catapulted a metal bird 50+ yards. It was painted with a kind of blue poster-paint and, like steel 'clays' of later years gave off a puff of dust when hit. It could also be fitted with a rubber bladder—an idea that may have been copied by the Globe Flight ball target.

Thresher's 'Indoor Trapshooting Academy' (illustrated in *Trapshooting: The Patriotic Sport*, was, apparently, an American innovation. It might most easily be described as a greatly enlarged version of the moving duck galleries that used to be seen so often at fun fairs and on piers. The 'duck' in this case being a steel

Another kind of Bussey hand launcher

pigeon travelling on wires between two hand-cranked iron wheels. The system could be set up inside or out and it had a dedicated gun. This was not rifled as in the more modern .22 shooting gallery, but a smoothbore of .44 calibre. The only mechanical target to achieve a modicum of real success, however, was Bussey's Gyro Pigeon and, of course, the modern ZZ bird.

Invention of the clay pigeon

JUST WHO invented the clay target is subject to some controversy. By most accounts, the honour goes to George Ligowsky of Cincinnati, Ohio. He was granted US patent 231919 on 7 September 1880 for his bird and US patent 252230 for his trap on 10 January 1882. Legend has it that Ligowsky got the idea for a disc target while watching boys 'skimming clam shells across the water'. Another American resident, Nicholas Fischer, also laid claim to the invention—and was granted a US patent in 1883—but this went to law with Ligowsky's company winning a protracted battle and eventually being awarded costs.

Early disc targets, or 'mud saucers' as they were occasionally called, were not as similar to a modern clay as they might at first appear. The Ligowsky bird was a domed saucer and literally made of clay—terracotta—rather than the predominant modern mix of pitch and limestone; nor did the Ligowsky birds have the pronounced ridges of the modern bird. They left no glass shards and flew far better than the ball or any of the mechanical birds, but they were hard to break, ringing like bells when hit and fragile in transit.

Annie Oakley, who had a practical interest in breaking birds in front of her fans, noted this problem and observed that the early targets 'were made of a red clay and many of them were over-burned and hard as stone'. Consequently, she used 'no 6 soft shot, as the chilled shot would glance off'.[70]

Gun collector Glyn Jones tries out his Eley Expert trap from the early 1900s for shooter Ashley Vellacott in 2005

Another unusual feature of the Ligowsky birds when compared to modern targets, was that they were equipped with a small tongue of 'paste board' (card) glued to their edge. This projection was held by a pincer at the end of the trap arm (pictured bottom right) and allowed for the clay to be held more or less securely in the trap arm but in a completely different manner to a modern clay. Unfortunately, the protruding tab was fragile and could be damaged or become unglued in wet weather. The problem was partially rectified by including the tongue as a projection in the moulding. In later designs it was dispensed with altogether by improving the manner in which the trap arm gripped the bird.

The first generation traps had a small spring-loaded pincer, which operated in the vertical plane pinching the tab. The next generation had a larger claw-like pincer gripping the sides of the target as seen in the Cogswell & Harrison 'Swiftsure' (pictured bottom right) and Eley 'Expert'

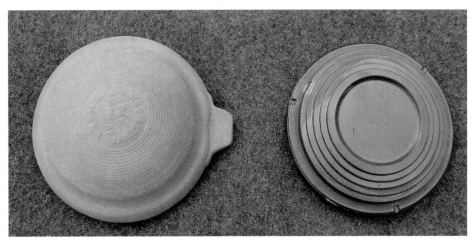

Ligowsky's original terracotta clay pigeon (left) next to a modern clay pigeon

(left). The modern manual trap typically operates with the bird sitting on the arm secured by a simple piano-wire spring, usually called a 'teal spring'.

Clearly, the early discs had a few disadvantages, not least their cost. At US$20 a thousand they were more expensive than plain glass balls, but they were far better targets. The frequent criticism of glass ball shooting was that it was too easy. This charge was certainly not levelled against the new clay birds. The shooting public took to them and the sport of clayshooting established itself at astonishing speed. Clays were not only more aerodynamically efficient—the dihedral shape ensured a much flatter and more realistic trajectory—but also much more challenging to shoot. And, they arrived on the shooting scene just at the moment the choked gun was being perfected. This was the ideal piece of equipment for engaging the new terracotta saucer. Shooting at clays without choke would not have provided much encouragement. With the combination of the muzzle constricted gun and the fast flying new target, an exciting discipline was created, something that really could compete with live pigeon shooting and which was significantly less expensive.

There had been an exhibition of the new pastime on Coney Island in Brooklyn, New York, as early as 1880 as a side-event to a major live bird championship organised by the New York State Game Association. The programme noted:

> The last contest is a shoot at flying clay pigeon. The pigeon consists of a clay disk and on being thrown from the trap sails a long distance with considerable speed. Only a small surface is presented to the shooter and it requires more quickness and skill than shooting at glass balls. They are to be shot ten birds at 18 and 15 yards rise.[71]

Sadly, there is no record of who won as far as the present writer is aware. There were a number of other fairly high profile matches in the early 1880s. The series of contests that ensured the future of clayshooting, however, was a clash of titans between Bogardus and Carver. This was a brilliant PR stunt conceived by Ligowsky or his associates using, of course, Ligowsky patent clays and traps. The protracted battle was played out in twenty-five different cities across the United States.

Bogardus was fifty at the time and he had already lost

A pair of Swiftsure traps

to the younger and hungry Carver three times—twice at pigeons and once at the novel clay birds. The first Bogardus-Carver contest had taken place at live pigeons at the Jockey Club, Louisville with stakes of US$500 a side in February 1883. The local press had taken much interest with *The Louisville Commercial*, for example, noting:

> Captain AH Bogardus, the champion shot, arrived in the city yesterday morning and immediately repaired to the Louisville Hotel, where his rival, Dr Carver, is stopping. Neither of them 'recognised' the other, although they met several times during the morning and dined at adjoining tables. Captain Bogardus [fifty at this time] remarked to a friend in a fatherly way that the young 'un appeared to be in fine form and Dr Carver was heard to say as he blushed before a plate of potato salad, that 'the old man was looking pretty well himself'. Once or twice they glared politely at each other… Thus did the champions dine… Later on they happened to come together at Griffiths & Sons establishment (a sporting goods store) and Colonel Joe Griffith stepped forward and introduced them. The Doctor bowed low and acknowledged the presentation and Bogardus returned the compliment and for the first time in four years the two champions spoke to each other. [72]

Bogardus lost by one bird, 82 to Carver's 83. Both men then went to Chicago. There they shot another match at live birds—Carver beating Bogardus again and by a larger margin 82 to 79. They also shot their first clay match, Carver winning that as well and by a large margin, 72 to 63. At this point, both men received a similar telegram from George Ligowsky. Carver's read:

> We herewith make to you and Captain Bogardus the following proposition.
> You and the Captain to shoot twenty-five matches at the Ligowsky clay pigeons. One hundred clay pigeons each, five traps, 18 yards rise, use of both barrels, English rules, same conditions as in the recent match in Chicago.
> Should you or Captain Bogardus, on any occasion, break eighty-two or more birds the winner, or if both of you should accomplish the feat, to receive $100 extra and the winner of the match to receive $300 for each match. The first match to be shot at St Louis during the present week; the second at Cincinnati March 10; and the balance to be shot in the principal cities in the United States before the 1st of May.[73]

Over the seven weeks that the serial contest took, US$7,000 was at stake, nearer US$½ million in modern money. Carver won nineteen of the matches and tied three. Bogardus won only three but gave Carver a run for his money on more than one occasion. Here are the results, with Carver's score shown first:

Chicago 72-63 (the first clay match in Chicago was incorporated in the 25)
St Louis 85-69
Cincinnati 89-74
Kansas City 91-69
St Joseph 92-63
Omaha 94-90
Leavenworth 85-63
Des Moines 100-97
Davenport 95-89
Council Bluffs 96-96 (tied)
Burlington 99-99 (tied)
Quincy 100-92
Peoria 99-92
Terre Haute 99-95
Indianapolis 98-97
Dayton 94-94
Columbus 76-93 (Bogardus win)
Pittsburgh 94-95 (Bogardus win)
Philadelphia 96-95

Doc Carver (left) and Adam Bogardus after completing a match at Des Moines, Iowa, in 1883. Carver may have just shot the first 100 straight at clays

Jersey City 98-94
New Haven 96-82
Springfield 96-91
Worcester 99-86
Providence 92-94 (Bogardus win)
Boston 93-91[74]

Carver's win by a fairly wide margin of seventy birds in the 5,000 clay contest is worthy of note. His total was 2,328 to Bogardus's 2,163. Their respective averages were 93.1 per cent and 86.5 per cent. Carver's 100 in Des Moines, probably shot in the last week of February 1883, was likely the first 100 straight ever shot officially at clays.

Carver remains, arguably, the greatest exhibition shot of all time. He went on to start 'The Golden West' with Buffalo Bill (putting up the capital, a claimed US$29,000 from his winnings at shooting matches), which evolved into the Wild West Show.

Bogardus would also work with the Wild West Show, but only for one ill-fated season in 1884. He had his own problems with Buffalo Bill. Like Carver, he lent him money and did not get it back.

Carver's favoured rifle was a Winchester '73, his favoured shotgun was a hammerless Greener 12-bore weighing 7lb 13oz (a point of some pride to WW). His ammunition choice was 1¼oz of no 6 chilled shot. Bogardus, on the other hand, favoured a hammer-actioned W&C Scott and preferred a heavy gun—10lb or so when rules allowed, though in their famous twenty-five-match contest, it appears he used a 7lb 6oz 12-bore. He preferred smaller shot for clays, no 8 in his first barrel and 7s in the second.

There was another interesting difference between the two: Carver shot with both eyes open and Bogardus with one eye shut.

Bogardus had complained of recoil injury that he attributed to using a lighter gun than normal in their matches. This smacked of an excuse; Carver retorted with uncharacteristic cheek that the Captain would have had no problems if he had kept both eyes open.

Carver may well have been wrong, though. The decision to shoot with one eye or two must always be made on the basis of an accurate diagnosis of eye dominance. It is only good advice to shoot with both eyes open if it suits your eye dominance. It is the right thing to do, for example, if you are a right-hander with a right master eye. A significant minority of men and most women are not well advised to shoot with both eyes open.

Ligowsky also sponsored the 'First International Clay Pigeon Tournament'

American clayshooting organisations

THE FIRST national clayshooting organisation in the States, the American Shooting Association, was created in 1889*. It was set up, funded and controlled by interested businessmen in the arms and ammunition trade. This early commercial involvement is worthy of note. The example was later copied in the UK when members of the gun trade started the Inanimate Bird Shooting Association and when, for many years, British clayshooting was effectively run by 'Nobel's Clay Pigeon Shooting Department' which funded the CPSA—and continued to do so until a generation or so ago.

The American Shooting Association changed its name to the Interstate Manufacturers & Dealers Association in 1892. Membership included the Remington Arms Company and Union Metallic, Winchester, Western Cartridges, Parker Bros, Peters Cartridges, the Chamberlain Cartridge & Target Company and many others—a *Who's Who* of the US shooting world.

In 1895 there was another name change to the Interstate Association. This was based in Pittsburgh, becoming the American Trapshooting Association in 1919 and moving to New York.

An American Amateur Trap Shooting Association had also been formed in 1916. Its president was the famous musician and keen amateur trap shot, John Phillip Sousa. The AATA was, apparently, 'disbanded and absorbed' by the newly formed American Trapshooting Association. The Amateur Trapshooting Association, the governing body of trap shooting in the USA to this day, was formed in 1923 (replacing the earlier ATA). Now the ATA is best known for its annual logistical miracle—the Grand American Trap Shooting Festival. It does much other work, of course, not least maintaining a trapshooting museum and Hall of Fame and supervising the rules for ATA-style Trap Shooting.

---

* Hinman also notes a US Inanimate Bird Shooting Association as the first organisation 'of record,' but not 'of influence'. I have been unable to find further details of it. Clearly, it did not survive for long or prosper

in May of 1884 at Chicago with modified English Ranelagh Club Rules applying. Just how international it really was beyond this is a matter for conjecture. We know from the advertising flyer that the intention was to present ten birds single rise at 18 yards rise and five doubles at 15 yards rise, which may illuminate the precise nature of the Coney Island shoot of 1880 as well. Five screened traps were place three yards apart and the prize to the winning team was US$750—a large sum even without adjustment for the massive inflation of the last 125 years—with a diamond badge valued at US$250 for the highest individual score.

The first national open tournament was held in New Orleans on 11 February 1885. It was also won by Carver, defeating Bogardus once again and many other top shots including JAR Elliot and Rolla Heikes. All things considered, Ligowsky's brilliant promotion had worked almost too well. It attracted the sort of attention normally reserved for heavyweight boxing matches. Once the clay dust had settled, he soon found himself with all sorts of competitors who wanted to cash in on the clayshooting boom and, meantime, with an inability to supply the huge new demand for his saucer style targets. To make matters worse, the terracotta clay would soon be ousted by the better-breaking composition bird. Considering his efforts and innovation, poor old Ligowsky did not have much luck. There must be a moral here for inventors.

The clay arrives in England

THE FIRST mention of the clay pigeon in the English sporting press is in *The Field* of 18 March 1882:

> An improvement upon the gyro pigeon and glass ball has recently been brought to our notice, which has attained a considerable amount of success in America, where numerous clubs have been formed for Trap shooting by its means. It consists of a simple saucer-shaped piece of brittle crockery, to which a pasteboard handle is cemented and by this handle it is projected from a spring trap and made to skim for about 40 or 50 yards with considerable velocity, somewhat resembling the flight of a partridge and especially in alighting. With the gyro pigeon the shooter only has to wait until it begins to hover in the air, when it is readily hit and the shot marks tell whether the blow is hard or soft; but here it is necessary not only to hit, but to hit hard, for success is only reached by breaking the clay, which, unlike broken glass, is unattended by subsequent danger to cattle or sheep. The clay starts at a great pace, and, with the trap at 21 to 25 yards rise, must be hit very soon after it has started, or the braking necessary to a score is not effected [sic].
>
> In America, we understand that the usual rise is 10 yards [if true, it is worth noting that it soon became longer] and even at that distance the 'kills' are not more than 75 per cent. No boundary is required and there can be no dispute about the fracture in the air of the shooting as on the grass, for the clay is strong enough to bear a fall without breaking, unless it is over hard ground.
>
> This appears to us the best plan hitherto brought out of affording the tyro a cheap method of learning to shoot either in public or private. The invention is that of Mr Ligowsky of Cincinnati, whose agent in London is Mr L Loeb, 50 Aldermanbury, EC. The price of the trap will be about 2 guineas and of the clay birds 1s 3p a dozen: but we understand that the stock in England is only sufficient for experimental trials.
>
> Specimens of the trap and pigeons may be seen at Mr H Atkyns, 18 Oxendon Street.

Not much more is heard of the clay in *The Field* for a year so. Then, in February 1883 it becomes a subject for considerable discussion, most notably in the form of a long letter from the well known live pigeon shot H Cholmondeley-Pennell who had just attended a demonstration of the new target being used in London:

> Sir—Your editorial notice last year of the 'Ligowsky patent clay-pigeon' probably called public attention to this latest ingenious Yankee 'notion', and I understand it has been since tried on various occasions in this country, both in public and in private, with considerable success. A trial of the latter description took place to-day on the lawn of the Ranelagh Club, at Fulham, in the presence of several well-known members of Hurlingham and a considerable gathering of ladies and gentlemen; and as it appears not improbable that a substitute will ere long have to be found for the real pigeon in shooting-matches, a short account of the 'habits and ways' of its clay rival when actually under fire may not be altogether without interest.
>
> The 'pigeon' may be described in two words—as a Terracotta Saucer. The saucer is stuck into the arm of spring trap which, when released by the 'puller', sends it flying with great velocity right, left, or straight forward, according to the angle at which the trap has been previously set.
>
> Let us imagine, then, five of these traps, set as for ordinary pigeon-shooting in a semicircle of twenty-five yards; a small green linen screen (of which more anon) in front of each and a well known knight of the trigger, celebrated as being one of the quickest shots in Europe, facing them at a distance of 21 yards. With gun almost at his shoulder and prepared to dash down his 'bird' the very moment it emerges from the trap he gives the word of command. 'Pull!' But alas for our gallant Captain Snap-shot! In vain his practised eye takes

Swiftsure trap

a lightning and well-nigh ubiquitous glance as he gives the signal. There he stands, finger on trigger, watching in blank amazement for the customary flash of the falling trap, or glimpse of the departing pigeon which, in the present case, neither he nor anyone else can see at all till it has got 'well away'—say 10 or 15 yards from the screen; and it has evidently become a question of 'game'—rather than of 'trap'-shooting. But the 'plunger' whose unerring tubes have so often dealt death at the very verge of the Hurlingham boundary, is not to be defeated without an effort and, pulling himself together, he takes a vicious and deliberate 'pot' at the little reddy-brown object now rapidly vanishing into space. Bravo! bravo! the terra-cotta saucer flies into fifty pieces. There is much clapping of hands and the successful performer retires meditatively from the post, internally revolving, no doubt, whether, in the 'goody time' coming, he will be able to make anything like sure of killing his five Ligowsky clay-pigeons out of six.

Another shooter presents himself at the mark—12 yards only. Surely he must kill at that handicap? But no; the pigeon, as our American friends would say, takes steps to place at least 50 yards between himself and the gunner before the latter can bring his piece into action and a clean miss is scored against him. The fact is that, close as the handicap is, the starting flight of the pigeon is so rapid—to say nothing of the intercepting screen—that the quickest shot in the world would fail to 'get on' his bird under 15 yards and much more frequently the first barrel could not be effectively fired until it is from 35 to 45 yards distant from the gun.

But let us see what this gentleman will do, who is handicapped at scratch—21 yards. He has been the victor of many a well-fought field in the tournament of doves and curiosity is strained to see how the clay pigeon will suit his well-known 'form' of shooting. 'Are you ready?' says the puller. 'No,' says the shooter; 'I've got to say that, not you. Now, then, are you ready?' 'Yes!' 'Pull!'

No doubt or hesitation this time—not for a moment. The veteran game-shot puts up his gun as coolly as if he was covering a partridge, or a pheasant on 1 October and at precisely the proper moment knocks the clay pigeon to 'immortal smash'.

And so the game goes on with varying success, until, towards five o'clock, a general move is made in the direction of the club-house and an examination of the score shows that a hundred clay pigeons have been shot at and that of this number fifty-five have been hit and forty-five missed, giving the odds as very little more than even on the gun.

'And what is the verdict,' some of your readers will ask 'on clay versus real pigeons for match shooting?'

I asked the same question myself of those best qualified to give a judgement and the general consensus of opinion appeared to be—'Well, we have had capital fun. Quite as good, I dare say, as we should have had at pigeon shooting and we have not got a bill of £3 or £4 to pay for it!'

My own judgement I reserve till further experience; but what I have seen convinces me that the clay pigeon is far superior to anything of the kind brought out hitherto (glass balls, gyro-pigeons, &c) and that for the purposes of practice, or for a *dies non* in a country house, when a 'rest' must be given to turnip fields or pheasant coverts, they would afford a most agreeable diversion from the smoky billiard room or the interminable round of inspection of the squire's stables.

London, Feb 17

H Cholmondeley-Pennell

PS—I think the screens in front of the traps are a very questionable advantage—not to say unquestionable disadvantage—making that still more difficult which is already difficult enough, as the 'score' conclusively shows; and I am not surprised, therefore, to learn that in America, where the invention is best understood, holes or trenches, in which the traps can be sunk nearly or quite to the level of the ground, are substituted for screens. This improvement it is also, I understand, intended should be introduced in future shooting matches at the Ranelagh, whose proprietor, Mr Reginald Herbert, was one of the most successful pigeon shots at Hurlingham and the Gun Club and therefore understands practically what is really required.

The EC powder again scored a triumph, the shooter who used it having won or divided the lion's share of the spoil during the afternoon; and the most brilliant shot of the day—an extraordinary long double-rise kill—having been made by another gentleman who used the EC powder for this final coup only. His cartridges were loaded by Messrs Alfred [sic] Lancaster, who have invented a very ingenious machine for compressing the EC powder much more firmly and regularly than can be done with the hand and arm.

The Ranelagh, England's first recorded clay club, was an upmarket

'Terracotta pigeon' shooting demonstration at the Ranelagh Club, London, 10 March 1883

establishment with a reputation for innovation. Polo, pony racing, pigeon shooting and tennis were all conducted there in the 1880s. Like its neighbour, Hurlingham, it was on the banks of the Thames in Fulham. Founded in the 1870s—soon after Hurlingham—it went through the financial doldrums before one Reginald Herbert bought the lease in 1878. In 1882, the committee list was headed by two Dukes (Beaufort and Portland) and a Viscount (Castlereagh).

The Ranelagh was a smaller establishment than its more famous neighbour with 300 members on its list circa 1880. On 16-17 June 1879, Doc Carver had demonstrated his awesome rifle skills there in front of the Duchess of Teck and her children, together with 'a large and fashionable company'. In the following year, a polo match was conducted under electric lights with the Prince and Princess of Wales, the King of Greece and Prince Louis of Battenburg attending.[75]

On 10 March 1882, *The Field* editorialises on the Anderson Bill to ban live pigeon shooting. It wrongly predicts the probable closure of the pigeon shooting clubs but, most interestingly, qualifies 'except those which may follow the example of the Americans, by shooting at the clay pigeons that have for some time past taken the place of live birds on the other side of the Atlantic.'

In the same issue of the influential sporting journal, there is indication that clayshooting has, meantime, made some progress in Britain. There is another piece on clay sport entitled 'Clay Pigeon Shooting' at the Ranelagh Club:

> *Each Saturday* [my italics] shows an increased number of entries in the sweepstake shooting at this club, and, as the shooters include some of our best known sportsmen, both as game and pigeon shots, Mr Ligowski's [sic] ingenious invention must be allowed to have made a very successful debut. The same gunners would not, of course, be seen every Saturday facing the traps if they did not find this sort of competitive trial of skill both amusing and exciting enough, in the long run, to sustain the interest.
>
> To judge by the 'score', the inclination at present seems to be to make the conditions of these matches more difficult than ordinary pigeon-shooting contests. When there are two or three 'misses' to every 'kill', it would seem to indicate that the handicap generally might be reduced with advantage.

Various advertisements for Ligowsky traps and birds from the 'Anglo-American Clay Pigeon Company' appeared in the periodical during 1883. We learn from the correspondence pages that the cost of the trap circa March 1883 was now three guineas and the birds were fairly pricey at 15s a hundred. Nevertheless, clays, though relatively expensive, were still much cheaper than blue rocks.

There is another important source: *The Illustrated London News* of 10 March 1883. Within it, there is an engraving of 'Terracotta Pigeon' shooting at the

Ranelagh Club (which relates to *The Field* story of 24 February). This is the first pictorial reference to clayshooting in England of which I am aware. The text that accompanies the picture notes:

> An interesting experiment was made at the Ranelagh Club on Saturday afternoon last, when several well-known shots tried their skill on the American Flying Clay Pigeon. The 'bird' is simply a clay saucer with a pasteboard tag glued on the side...

A British patent for flying saucer targets was lodged in September 1883—some six months after the Ranelagh club demonstration—in the name of CJ Barrett, Secretary of the Anglo-American Clay Pigeon Company from designs transmitted by JE Bloom of Cincinnati, Ohio.

Apart from the Ranelagh, there are few records of early clay pigeon clubs in Britain. One does, however, appear to have been formed at Botley in Hampshire in 1880s. A reference to it is contained in the first edition of Lancaster's *An Illustrated Treatise on the Art of Shooting* within an advertisement for Ligowsky clays and traps:

> The 'Ligowsky' Standard Patent Clay Pigeons and Traps
> Ready for the healthy entertainment of guests at a moment's notice
> Lt-Colonel Kennedy (Hon Sec of Botley Clay Pigeon Club, Hants) says: 'The Club was established in 1884 and has derived great amusement from the use of Clay Pigeons, they afford excellent sport at a very moderate price. The Club will always be willing to speak in favour of Clay Pigeons.'—Royal Albert Yacht Club, Southsea, 16 February 1888.

In 1885, Greener gives his imprimatur to the new sport in the third edition of *The Gun*:

> …All [other types of inanimate target] have been superseded by the Ligowsky Clay Pigeon-Trap and Pigeons. The 'pigeons' also called mud saucers… are very thin, concave below and convex above and are skimmed from the trap with a most irregular flight…
> For officers in the army and sportsmen in the summer months they offer a never-ending source of amusement.[76]

Greener appended Bogardus's rules for the benefit of newly formed clubs and notes that inanimate target shooting had already superseded pigeon shooting in the United States, 'which in several states is strictly prohibited by law on grounds of cruelty'.[77]

In 1887, Basil '20-bore' Tozer confirms (incorrectly if you consider H Cholmondeley-Pennell's letter to *The Field* which notes some previous but less publicised trials) in *Practical Hints on Shooting* that clays were first tried at the Ranelagh club and noted the new sport had:

> ...been highly spoken of by Mr Reginald Herbert and Mr Cholmondeley-Pennell—two of our finest shots and straightest riders—Sir Ralph Payne-Gallwey and many other celebrated sportsmen… The 'pigeon'… is in reality a thin clay saucer, 5in wide and weighing 2oz, the convex surface being roughened or fluted to prevent the shot from glancing off. To one side of the bird is affixed a short pasteboard tongue. Brass pigeons [a Kynoch product as previously noted] are sometimes substituted for terracotta, but the latter are preferable… As clay pigeon shooting promises to become such a popular pastime, we reproduce full instructions for fixing and managing traps, from the Clay Pigeon Company's circular'

Like *The Field*, Tozer also notes that clays might become an alternative to live birds 'should pigeon shooting ever be prohibited'. The same year as this was published, 1887, Annie Oakley demonstrated her shooting skills in London using both ball targets and clays. She is also known to have gone to Charles Lancaster's shooting school in 1887 and 1888 for both gunfitting and instruction[78]. And, she gave shooting lessons to ladies of fashion at Lancaster's ground at a guinea a session. These would almost certainly have involved

Inanimate Moving Objects

FROM CHARLES Lancaster's *An Illustrated Treatise on the Art of Shooting*:

> I know of but one really serviceable appliance for this work and that is the now celebrated Ligowsky trap and clay pigeon used from same. I certainly think it advisable to caution sportsmen against buying worthless imitations, which will only cause them much inconvenience and annoyance.
>
> The beginner can place the trap so that the clay pigeons will be thrown forward, to the right or left, high or low, or can have the trap worked by an attendant from behind a wall or shot-proof fence—somewhat after the flight of driven birds or even for high incoming shots.[80]

HA Thorn (aka Charles Lancaster) was involved in litigation concerning 'worthless' imitation 'clays' only a few years after he wrote this. In 1894, he sued the Herculite & Electrical manufacturing company for manufacturing clay pigeons that were not actually made of clay. He had acquired the sole UK and German sales rights to the real thing (probably from Ligowsky). Don Masters notes in his excellent history of Churchill gunmaker that several witnesses, including EJ Churchill were called to give evidence in the ensuing case. The latter unfortunately stated that he sold all sorts of 'clay' pigeons in his shop and that any disc target might be referred to as such and even glass and brass balls on occasion. 'Other well-known gunmakers of the day gave similar testaments. Since this terminology has existed for more than a century, we must assume that Mr Thorne [sic] lost his case.'

the trendy new clay target. As well as her other activities, Annie occasionally accepted challenges. One of her most interesting was brokered by Buffalo Bill and the Prince of Wales. She was asked to meet the Grand Duke Michael of Russia in a 'friendly match' using clays. The venue was Earl's Court in London. Courtney Ryley Cooper writes in his biography *Annie Oakley: Woman at Arms*:

> The Grand Duke bore the reputation of being one of the best shots in Russia. But from what Annie Oakley and her husband had heard of him he got his best results on clay birds which flew about 40 yards from the trap... 'We'll just make it a good test,' she said and ordered the traps screwed down to 65 yards. 'That'll be something to shoot at'.
>
> The contest began, the winner to be judged by the best score out of fifty targets… By the time the first ten targets had been sprung Annie Oakley had moved into the lead. When thirty had been reached the Grand Duke Michael was fighting hard, but with a handicap which seemed impossible to overcome. And when the end of the match arrived it brought a result by which Annie Oakley had missed only three targets out of fifty, while the Grand Duke of Russia had failed on fourteen.[79]

There is a reference to clays, Buffalo Bull and Annie in the seventh 1896 edition of *The Deadshot*. After describing composition balls, the author notes:

> Clay pigeons may also be had and are much used now in preference to the glass balls. The clay pigeons afford excellent practise from a trap called 'The Ligowsky Trap'; the same as that used by Buffalo Bill and Miss Oakley in their feats of skill in shooting, at the Wild West Exhibition in London in the year 1888.[82]

We can speculate that she had probably been using disc targets in America sometime before she arrived in England in 1887. The Wild West Show's effective endorsement of the Ligowsky system, and the interest generated by the activities of Annie Oakely and Buffalo Bill in the 1880s and later, must have had significant consequences for the growth of British and American clayshooting.

Manufacture of early clays

THE EARLIEST clay targets—ie those of Ligowsky's terracotta saucer pattern—were baked, much like bricks, in moulds in an oven. Their manufacture was, evidently, complex and required more capital expenditure than glass balls. The American DH Eaton, author of *Trapshooting: The Patriotic Sport* writes in 1920:

> The [early] birds were made entirely of clay, cast iron moulds being used. An iron plate was laid in a long narrow furnace, at one end of which was the fire and on this plate the moulds were placed to be heated. The clay was ground very fine and mixed with water to a consistency very little thicker than water. Each mould was filled with this mixture through a hose; after the mould-filler came a second man who, by means of suction, removed from each mould as much of the mixture as had not hardened. A third man removed the dry clay from the moulds. The birds were then placed in a kiln and burned like bricks. The result was an extremely hard target, ringing like a bell when hit and almost impossible to break. It often happened that a quartering target would be knocked completely off its course without breaking off the smallest chip, an examination of the target showing the marks of the shot plainly visible.

Composition targets of the new disc type—as opposed to composition balls which preceded them by a few years—were introduced in the United States in about 1884 and in England by Cogswell & Harrison around 1888. These were easier to break than the original terracotta birds and quickly superseded them. The names usually associated with the improved targets are McCaskey ('an Englishman'), Charlie Stock and Fred Kimble. The latter was a famous American market hunter, often erroneously credited by himself and others as the inventor of choke bore. *

McCaskey's targets, made of limestone and pitch, were marketed as 'blue rocks'. Stock's and Kimble's were a mixture of river silt and plaster of Paris and became famous as 'Peoria Blackbirds' because, instead of a paste board or moulded tongue, they had two moulded ears. Sharp sand and ash were also use as fillers for composition targets and resin could be used instead of pitch in some formulas.

As with ball targets, there were some bizarre variations on the discus theme. The Lockport clay of about 1886 had a piece of wood running right through it, with part of it projecting (so it could be gripped by the pincer of a Ligowsky-type trap arm). The Best 'Tin Pigeon' was made of metal and had a disc within it attached by a small chain. In theory at least, both were released when the target was hit (Parker-Hale marketed a similar bird in the 1920s and 1930s under the trade name 'Collapso'). The Atlantic Ammunition Company of New York offered the Blue Rock Bird in 1887. It was similar to a modern target save for the groove that went all round its base. The Blue Rock Bird and trap of 1889, however, is notable in that it looked quite modern.

By the end of the Victorian era, the development of the clay target and basic manual trap was just about complete. In the USA, magazine-fed traps appeared in the 1890s, though there had been earlier patents for magazine fed ball traps. One of the more interesting patents was that of Albert Davis in 1894 for a 'magazine adapted to take a vertical column of targets'.

The first automatic angling trap was introduced by the Chamberlain Co in

---

* Choke in shotguns dates back more than 300 years. It was re-discovered in the nineteenth century and used by certain American gunsmiths in crude form. William Rochester Pape laid claim to the invention in England. WW Greener, who, rightly, contested Pape's claim, perfected modern methods of choke boring and may be accorded the honour of being the father of the sophisticated forms of choke seen in modern sporting guns

1897. The same firm offered a practical lever trap in 1903—a style which would soon become very popular with American trapshooters. This type of trap was not seen in any significant number in the UK until the 1920s. The 'Dickey Bird' bicycle magazine trap—a device that might well inspire zany film director Terry Gilliam—was put on display at the Grand American trap tournament of 1902. A trigger-operated hand trap was marketed in the same year by the Mitchell Manufacturing Company and similar devices would appear in Britain in the new century such as the 'Blanton' and the 'Mitchell-Henry' portable target thrower. Simpler flingers such as the 'Perfect' and the ICI-Eley hand trap became more popular in later years, though. There was also a 'Midget' hand flinger.

Developments in England had followed those in the US, albeit less dynamically. In the late 1880s, the English firm Cogswell & Harrison offered an improved trap, the Swiftsure. And, according to Cogswell & Harrison historians Graham Cooley and John Newton, this was tested by the London Gun Club on 28 March 1889. The company also began manufacture of composition clays as noted above. Their advertisements noted of these targets: 'Travel well. Fly well. Break well'. They cost 15 shillings for a barrel of five hundred or 5 shillings for a box of a hundred circa 1890.

In 1900, the firm published a small book *Shooting with Game and Gun Room Notes*. It included the official rules of the Inanimate Bird Shooting Association which it evidently aimed to promote. Rule number three—'Challenging Guns, Etc'—noted:

> The gun or cartridges of any shooter may be challenged by a competitor as not being in accordance with rule two [maximum calibre 12, maximum payload 1.125oz], and if found on examination to be in breach of the Rule, the holder of such a gun or ammunition shall pay a fine of 10s 6d to the Club funds, and be disqualified from the competition; but if the gun or ammunition be found correct, the challenger, except it be the Referee, shall pay 2s 6d to the Club funds.

Cogswell & Harrison's products did much to popularise clayshooting in England, but there were other innovators. Kynoch offered its metal pigeons filled with charcoal dust. There was indeed a plethora of similar inventions in this era and most, of course, sank without trace. Survival of the fittest left the Cogswell-style trap and the composition bird as the most popular. Organised clayshooting was yet to become a major sport (circa 1890), but an improved trap and clay target were attractive to the new shooting schools that were then becoming fashionable. These establishments combined the use of mechanical target plates and clays presented in natural surroundings with the release of captive birds and rabbits. From this strange, ethically questionable start, modern Sporting Clays would eventually develop. *The Encylopaedia of Sport*:

> One of the most remarkable results attendant on the introduction of artificial target shooting has been the establishment of shooting schools, where the young gunner is quickly taught to handle his weapon in a workmanlike manner, and errors of fit are discovered and rectified by the try-gun and other means. It is now also admitted by the most conservative sportsmen that clay bird shooting is excellent practice for field shooting generally, and that a season at the clay birds will enable the average shot and novice to render a far better account of himself at "fur and feather" than would otherwise be the case. The same result would, of course, be obtained by pigeon shooting, but the cost is many times greater.[83]

Shooting schools in Britain sometimes manufactured their own targets to reduce costs and ensure availability. Both the West London Shooting Grounds at Perivale and Churchill's ground at Crayford are known to have done this, in the case of the latter on site manufacture continued until well after Second World War. Don Masters, an ex-Churchill employee, writes of his firm's production:

These clay targets were made in two big old vats in a corrugated iron shed behind the visitors' pavilion. The shed could be opened on three sides to let the yellow fumes from the pitch escape and for this reason, the targets were usually made on slack days or at the end of the day after all the shooting clients had departed. The shed, in which the clay pigeon targets were made is identical to the one used previously at the West London Shooting Grounds.

After the Second World War, Len Summers was initially in charge of clay pigeon production at Crayford. Later the clays were made by Leslie and Midge Garrood. The two basic ingredients were pitch and sand. Sand was found on-site—the land had once been used for extracting sand and gravel. The silver sand was dug out of the cliffs behind the Gun Club and was spread out on a concrete floor to dry.

The first step in making clay targets was to light the fires underneath two big old galvanised vats, known as 'coppers' because they were lined with copper. Similar coppers were used by housewives all over Britain for their weekly wash. Next, big chunks of pitch were put in the coppers and stirred with large shovels until the mixture became a soft, tar-like substance. After this the silver sand was stirred in. When the pitch and sand had been stirred to a smooth consistency, a measure of the mixture was poured into a tray containing four separate base moulds. The male half of the saucer-shaped mould was swung down on top, together with a weight. This compressed the mixture and most of the excess was forced out. When the mixture had set hard, any excess pitch around the edges of the mould was broken off and carefully dropped back into the vats to be used again. The two vats and four presses were worked in rotation to allow the first batch to cool down so that the solidified clay targets could be removed. The finished clay-pigeon targets were finally stored in *papier-mâché* cartons.[84]

The first clayshoots

IN THE EARLY days in the United States, one man would stand centrally behind a row of five traps in imitation of a live pigeon contest. Five birds would be presented 'unknown traps and unknown angles'. Later, a squad of five shooters would stand behind the traps with the man on no 1 shooting at the no 5 trap, no 2 shooting at no 4 etc.

The 'walk-round system' or 'continuous fire' as it was later called in England, speeded things up with six men at the firing point. Each—save for a spare man standing behind position 1—would fire a single shot from the five positions before walking to the next, the sixth man occupying no 1 when it became vacant.

The 'Sergeant system' as invented by WG Sergeant of Joplin, Missouri, reduced the number of traps to three, with the traps placed 4ft apart, at 16 yards rise—unknown trap, unknown angle. The shooters stood, as today, on positions placed on the arc of a circle of 16 yards radius from the trap

Although a modified Sergeant system would later be adopted in Britain, in early competition, five, ten or fifteen traps might be used. In the case of ten and fifteen trap layouts, the traps would be positioned in five banks of two or three respectively at 18 yards rise (the standard British distance until about 1920). Only one person would shoot at a time. This was called 'single fire'. The traps would be shielded from view by sackcloth or something similar.

After the firer—who stood on the centre mark of the firing point—had shot his birds, the trappers would run forward and re-cock and load the machines. Traps would be released by pulling strings behind the firing point. The release of the traps was determined by the referee drawing shuffled cards 1-5, 1-10, or 1-15. Competition could be slow and ten birds, single rise, was the standard event.

First English internationals

IN MAY 1893, the Inanimate Bird Shooting Association was formed after a meeting at Anderton's Hotel in Fleet Street, London, and, within a few weeks several affiliated clubs were created[85]. As was the case in the United States three years before, those responsible for the IBSA's birth were all members of the gun and ammunition trade. Representatives of Eley, Westley Richards, Joseph Lang, Cogswell & Harrison, Moore & Grey, the Schultze Powder Company and the Smokeless Powder Company were in attendance.

The IBSA—which in 1903 was to become the Clay Bird Shooting Association—appointed a professional secretary (a Mr W Keep of 4 Lincolns Inn Fields) and elected Mr Dougall of the Smokeless Powder Company chairman. He noted in a speech that was evidently slanted to his audience's aspirations: '…the oftener guns are used the oftener they will have to be replaced. The constant use of guns means the use of an increased number of cartridges and upon these two simple propositions stands the Inanimate Bird Shooting Association.'[86]

The IBSA held its first clay pigeon championship at Wimbledon Park. Few shooters turned up at the appointed hour (noon) and those that did, took one look at the wet weather and immediately broke for lunch. Happily the weather cleared, more shooters arrived—forty-four eventually presenting themselves— and the IBSA's first championship went ahead.

It was shot over ten single targets at 18 yards rise; ten Cogswell & Harrison Swiftsure traps were employed, arranged in five banks of two. Each bank was screened with cloth, so the shooters could not see in which direction the birds might be angled. W Ford shot well from the start, breaking the first seven straight. He missed his eighth and tenth birds. AH Gale, soon to become a major figure in British clayshooting, also scored eight but with more intermittent success. Frank Izzard of the Wealdstone Club missed his first bird but then straighted the rest, taking the championship and a silver cup with a score of nine. It was no flash in the pan. He went on to win in 1894 and again in 1896. *The Field*, which had first drawn attention to the arrival of clays in England a decade before, speculated:

> In America the amusement of shooting at these inanimate birds has attained to a popularity of which the average Englishman has no conception. Clubs exist everywhere; shooting takes place constantly and, as a consequence, the consumption of ammunition is on a large scale. What degree of favour may be in store for these clay birds over here remains to be seen. They are not, of course, an absolute novelty, having been in use for some time; but until recently, scarcely any attempt has been made to introduce them to the attention of the general public, to whom they may prove a convenient and cheap means of practising.[87]

In 1894 the constitution of the IBSA was changed after concern was raised over the excessive dominance of the gun trade. A system of proportional representation was introduced giving affiliated clubs one vote for every twenty-five members. *The Young Sportsman*, an encyclopaedia of 1900, noted: 'This change has worked well and the subsequent advance has been rapid…'[88]

It is clear that, even in the early 1890s, a number of clubs were in existence. It is hard to determine which were dedicated to clays alone. It certainly seems that members of the firm of Charles Lancaster started a dedicated clay club in 1893 with a subscription of a guinea a year and clays seem to have been high on the agendas of the Surrey County Gun Club, the Wealdstone Club, the West Kent, the St Georges Club and the Park Gun Club around this time.

The Ranelagh at Fulham lasted well into the twentieth century as a venue for gymkhanas, but what its later associations were with clayshooting (if any) I have not been able to determine.

The Dougall Memorial, here won by Eric Horlock in 1950

In the second annual IBSA Championship meeting in 1894 (an event which took up two days—compared with the few hours required for the first), *Shooting Times* put up a Tantalus, usually a wooden holder for matched decanters as a trophy. In the June 1895 championship at Wembley Park—a shooting festival which by then attracted more than 500 entrants competing over three days in a variety of competitions—the now famous periodical offered a magnificent mock-gothic clock for the winner of the handicap event. This was won by Harry Churchill, the seventeen-year-old son of the proprietor of EJ Churchill, 'Ted' (Edwin), who himself came fifth.

'Harry' (in fact Henry) was, of course, using a gun made by the family firm. He received his magnificent prize from the Marquis of Lorne. *

The first recorded international match in Britain was held at the IBSA championship of 1895 as part of the third annual championship. It appears to have been arranged by FW Moore who would go on to captain the British squad in the 1908 London Olympics. Eleven men each represented England, Ireland and Scotland. The competition was for the '*Rod & Gun*' shield (called the 'International Shield' by *Shooting Times*[89] and later generally called that). Each team member shot at thirty targets—an unusually high number for the era. England won, Ireland second and Scotland third. *Shooting Times* noted sincerely: 'It must be remembered, however, that inanimate bird shooting is a comparatively new sport in Scotland and there is little doubt in our minds that the Scottish team will require to be seriously reckoned with at the next meeting.'

These words notwithstanding, England retained the shield under FW Moore's captaincy until 1901. That year and the next, an 'All Comers' team captained by D O'Conor took the shield. FW Moore and friends won it back in 1911. The comments of *Shooting Times* concerning the development of the sport in Scotland did eventually prove prescient, however.

The Nobel magazine *Clay Target Shooting* has a cover story in its issue of April 1927. It is headed (misleadingly) 'First International Clay Target Match' and refers to a memorable dual between England and Scotland in Carlisle that was held on 24-25 March 1927. Scotland was victorious by a margin of seven points, in a contest that saw both teams of twenty score, most curiously, 1,779 kills, but with the proportion of first barrels just favouring Scotland. The team had 1,619 first barrels to England's 1,612. Percy Stanbury was high gun on 98 ex 189, two birds clear of the Scot JW McCrick, on 96 ex 185. The first barrel scoring two points at that time, the second barrel, one. Clearly, the 1927 tournament was not the first international, but it deserves its place in clayshooting history.

The Dougall Cup—now the Dougall Memorial and one of the premier events in the DTL calendar—was first put up at the 1896 IBSA championship. A gift from the IBSA's first chairman it was first won by Frank Izzard, one of the crack shots of the era. The Dougall contest was unusual in that it was a twenty-birder to be shot in one stage. 1896 was also a key year for women shooters because a competition for ladies only was held at the Middlesex Gun Club. It was ten birds single rise at 10 yards rise. Five entered, the winner scoring two. It appears the rest of the field did not score at all. **

---

* Tragically, Harry Churchill died of pneumonia in 1902 leaving his younger cousin, Robert, to promote the shooting honour of the family—a task which he accomplished with aplomb becoming not only a famous gunmaker, shooting instructor and author but an expert for the Metropolitan Police and subsequently something of a TV star. Robert died an OBE in 1958

** It was not until 1912, however, that a Ladies Challenge Cup was introduced at the CBSA's annual championship. It was first won by Mrs FJ Wright and, in 1913, by Mrs F Davey

The CBSA Championship meeting 1900

TAKEN FROM *The Field*:

> Saturday, 9 June. The eighth annual championship meeting was brought to a conclusion this afternoon, when Sir John Hutton distributed the prizes to the various successful competitors. The attendance on the final day showed little improvement on those that had preceded it, although the weather was all that could be desired. The arrangements, under the charge of the committee, with the able assistance of Mr Paul, from America, could not have been better, the trapping being carried on with a regularity and freedom from mistakes and 'no birds', that left little room for improvement. It was a subject for general comment that the number of competitors was the smallest for several years, there being an almost total absence from both Scotland and Ireland. The association has now been in existence for eight years and it must be admitted that the methods recently adopted have not conduced to the popularity of the pastime. The [Boer] war accounted for some absentees and Whit-week also is an inconvenient time, but the date was specially fixed
> at the suggestion of shooters not resident in London who, however, did not put in an appearance. For the vice-presidents' prize a keen contest was witnessed between Messrs Fryer and A Leeson, the latter eventually winning with a run of no less than twenty straight. Mr Merrill, a visitor from America, secured *Shooting Times* trophy, also *The Field* prize and the Dougall Memorial Cup. The English team won the International Shield by the narrow majority of one point. For the Championship Cup thirty-six entered, Mr Ellicott, a well-known Bisley shot, eventually winning. Mr Ellicott broke five out of six from the tower and six straight unknown traps and angles; Mr Palmer was second, Mr Williams third and Mr O'Conor fourth.[90]

The success of the Americans at the 1900 Championship may have inspired a larger contingent for 1901. The first known international between England and the United States took place in London in that year at a series of matches at the Middlesex Club. Captain Money, by then sixty-two, acted as referee. The American team also went to Glasgow to compete against the Scots. It wiped the board south and north of the border. *

By the end of the Victorian age (1901), the British landed classes had been exposed to clayshooting in some number via the increasingly popular shooting schools. These had taken off in the 1890s and no gunmaker worth his blacking salt could afford to be without such a facility if he wanted to retain the custom of the carriage trade. In addition, *The Young Sportsman*, an English encyclopaedia of 1900, reports that there were no less than 6,000 clubs in active existence.[91]

The schools had evolved in some cases from cruder practice or testing grounds, but the invention of inanimate targets and of the try-gun (a late Victorian contraption) ensured that such establishments evolved and their numbers grew.

There was also a social imperative. The late Victorians and Edwardians were great ones for knowing the 'right form'. The emergence of the shooting school may be seen as a symptom of their style of thinking. A gentleman might not admit to going to one, but it might save him—or those who aspired to be gentlemen—from the social calamity of being 'sent off the field' for incompetent gun handling, or the simple embarrassment of being a duff marksman.

The upwardly mobile could also ensure that their offspring were properly trained in much the same way as the socially ambitious attended dancing and drawing classes.

---

* A report of these matches, including a description of the Middlesex Club, appears in the appendix

Charles Lancaster (HA Thorn)'s North Western Shooting School off the Harrow road, a couple of miles from Willesden Junction, was one of the first and most successful of the modern schools opening in the mid 1880s. Holland & Holland's ground, first at Kensal Green off the Harrow Road, was also a leader of fashion, opening some time after 1883. It moved to its present site at Duck Hill in 1932. Westley Richards had two grounds circa 1900, one at Edgbaston in Birmingham, the other at Hendon near London at, or near the site of the old Welsh Harp, as did Cogswell & Harrison, with one at Colnbrook 'The Cogswell & Harrison Shooting Park' and the other, The Blagdon Shooting Grounds, at Malden. There were also independent grounds such as the London Sporting Park of Mr Watts, also at Hendon; from 1901, Mr Richmond Watson's West London Shooting Grounds at Perivale, which moved to its present site at Northolt in 1931; and the Albermarle Shooting Ground at Worcester Park on the south-western outskirts of London.

Throughout this era it seems that the primary commercial push to sell clayshooting in England was to those who already shot game regularly, as is made clear by a cursory reading of contemporary periodicals. This is to be contrasted with the situation in the United States, where clayshooting quickly established itself as a sport in its own right because of a quite different marketing approach and, perhaps, because of the more egalitarian culture. There was, meantime in England, considerable criticism of clayshooting as 'unrealistic'. The typical moan, sometimes still heard, was that clays slowed down too quickly and dropped while live game accelerated and rose. There is, of course, some truth in this but not enough to detract from the merits of clayshooting as a sport in its own right or as an effective means of practising field shooting.

Not all were prejudiced against the saucers. In 1905, King Alfonso of Spain, a keen shot, came to England to meet his bride-to-be, Princess 'Ena'—actually Victoria Eugenie of Battenberg—King Edward's niece. This took him to the Isle of White, where he entered the local clay pigeon club's competition with much enthusiasm. George V, one of the best royal shots, was also a clay pigeon fan and an early patron of West London Shooting Grounds.

Circa 1912, Irish clubs included The Caven (sic) and Leitrum (sic), County Wicklow, King's County and Queen's County[92]. In Scotland, Edinburgh, Glasgow and Perth had successful clubs. The Glasgow Gun Club, moreover, produced the winner of the 1904 Clay Bird Shooting Association Championship, Mr J McAuley.

As far as English clubs of the time were concerned, those in and around London predominated. The sport also appears to have been popular in the West Country and the Home Counties. Clubs in London and the Midlands often operated from the grounds of commercial shooting schools. The St George's Gun Club at Neasden was one of the first formed, the Ealing Gun Club with grounds near Park Royal and the London and the North London at New Southgate were also famous, but the pre-eminent clayshooting club of the era was the Middlesex at Hendon. It produced no less than ten winners of the IBSA/CBSA championship 1893-1912.

FM McFarland, author of the *Shooting Times* Library volume *Clay Pigeon Shooting* notes of the St George's Club: 'The club shot every Saturday. The rules said traps must throw the birds forty yards and cartridges used in competition had to be purchased on the ground. If a member introduced a friend, then the member was responsible for this friend's behaviour and all his stakes. In early IBSA rules, a shooter who closed his gun with the trappers in front was immediately fined 1s.'

McFarland also comments that there was an ongoing debate concerning the gun-up, gun-down rule and that the secretary of the Eastbourne Club (another well-known club of the era) had declared that only game guns should be used in

'Methods of shooting'

TAKEN FROM the second edition *The Encyclopaedia of Sport* of 1912, a comprehensive work that might best be described as a sporting *Encylopaedia Britannica*:

> The minimum equipment for club shooting on the single-fire system (that is, in a way similar to that adopted for pigeon shooting) consists of three traps. This battery allows of birds being thrown quartering to the left, straight away and quartering to the right. The shooter is kept in ignorance of which bird he will receive. The full equipment for a first class club consists of three traps arranged in five groups of three each. These traps are fixed on the ground level and behind them a trench is dug. The earth from the trench forms a bank, which hide the traps from the shooters. In the trench, completely screened and protected by the bank, are the trappers. Their duty is to re-fill and set each trap the moment after it has been released by the puller. The puller has his station behind the firing line. He releases the traps, in the order shown by the indicator, the shooters kept in ignorance of the angles at which birds will be thrown. There are five firing marks, each fronting a corresponding group of traps and the ordinary distance is 18 yards [which by 1920 had been reduced to 16]. In shooting 'Down the Line' the competitors are made up in teams of six men. The first five in order take their places at the five marks and the sixth man stands 'in waiting' behind no 1. Each competitor fires at one bird in turn. When the fifth man has fired, no 1 moves to no 2 and so on. No 5 leaves his mark and becomes the competitor 'in waiting'. There is thus no delay between the rounds. A competition usually consists of ten birds, but may be extended to any number desired. With the full equipment of fifteen traps, single-fire shooting may also be conducted. One competitor then stands at the centre mark (no 3) and may have his birds from any one of the fifteen traps. A modification allows two men to on the line together, standing at no 2 and no 4. Handicaps by distance can also be arranged.[97]

After the First World War, Nobel Industries introduced the automatic angling trap to England. This greatly simplified shooting as it meant that only one trap was required—albeit of a more expensive and complex type.

competition. He sounds a bit of a reactionary.

AH Gale, who worked for Westley Richards in London, was secretary of the St George's and went on to run the Middlesex. The latter appears to have operated on the same ground at Hendon as the firm's shooting school. It closed down in 1907, due to what McFarland calls 'pot hunters canker' but opened again in 1908 as a limited company on another site funded by Westley Richards. Gale is one of the pre-eminent figures in early British clayshooting, he chaired Willesden District Council and was a JP. A history of his firm noted in 1913:

> So long ago as 1895 he founded the Middlesex Clay Bird Shooting Club, of which he is still the honorary secretary and leading light and it is owing to his indefatigable perseverance that its success has continued to this day. The killing of caged live birds released from a trap is a wanton and brutal amusement. The humane substitution of the clays birds or inanimate targets for practising marksmanship deserves every encouragement and Mr Gale for the past twenty years has devoted an abundant energy to the establishment and furtherance of a sport which can offend no susceptibility.[93]

The CBSA's twenty-first annual championship was held in June 1913 at the grounds of the Middlesex Gun Club, with Herr H Goeldel of the Hamburg Gun Club taking top honours. He was the first foreigner to take the individual championship and received his much-coveted prize from Sir Thomas Dewar Bt.

Goeldel and a Mr Fesingher of the Brussels Gun Club also received 'Gold Stars' (an award instituted in 1909 for outstanding performance in the 'Grand Aggregate') for their scores of 92 per cent. There had only been three previous recipients: W Ellicott , an English crack who had won the championship five

The Holland & Holland Pavilion in the 1890s

times by 1913, received two Gold Stars, one for a score of 89 per cent in 1909 and another for a score of 94 per cent in 1910. Captain Van Tilt of the Brussels club had received a gold star in 1911 for a score of 93 per cent and WP Grosvenor of the Middlesex Club had got one in 1912 with 89 per cent.

I also have the programme from the 1914 'British Championship' (a treasure from Chris Cradock's collection that has passed to me). The venue was the Middlesex Club and the event was held over four days on Wednesday-Saturday 24-27 June. Tickets for entry were sold at a shilling each. There was a large list of events with many prizes. The Championship programme specifically invites ladies to attend (on its cover) and states the object of the association as the promotion of 'the pastime of Shooting at Clay Birds.' Maximum shot payload was 1 1/8oz, maximum shot size was 6. All sorts of competitions were on offer as well as the main CBSA championship. The Duke of Somerset, who was president of British Olympic Council, gave away the booty on the final day, as contestants, organisers and onlookers were entertained by the band of the Ninth Battalion of the Duke of Cambridge's Own Middlesex Regiment. In envisaging this pleasant scene as the contestants gathered, you cannot help but consider the momentous events that would soon engulf them. The Archduke Ferdinand was assassinated in Sarajevo the day after the championship finished, the Austro-Hungarian empire declared war immediately and Britain was at war with Germany within five weeks. But none of that marred the *Shooting Times* handicap on the opening day. It was shot over ten birds down the line with a chiming clock as first prize, a silver goblet for second, a Webley & Scott single-barrel full-choke Trap gun for third and 'a best silk hat' for fourth. The entry fee was 5s. The London Gunmakers' Cup, a handicap by distance event was also contested on the first day. It was 'to be shot for at THREE birds from three sets of traps', with a Charles II silver-gilt cup to the winner. The latter being 'a reproduction of one made for George Villiers, second Duke of Buckingham, dated 1680, the original now being in the possession of the Corporation of Oxford'. You are lucky to get a cheap metal trophy today.

The Automatics, another preliminary event, involved ten birds down the line, 'one barrel only' with a first prize of a Browning A5-type semi-auto 12-bore in a brass bound canvas case and second prize of a Browning .22 'sporting and saloon rifle', both provided by Fabrique Nationale d'Armes de Guerre. Third prize was five hundred 'Double Demon' 2¾in pigeon cartridges 'loaded to the instructions of the winner and delivered to his order'.

Thursday started off with the Middlesex Gun Club competition at 10am. The Rottweil Prize (first prize a Rottweil over-and-under valued at £47 5s and donated by the United Cologne-Rottweil Powder Factories of Berlin) was scheduled for noon but appears to have been cancelled. A Ladies' Challenge Cup offered a glittering array of prizes headed by the 105½oz silver cup, a ruby and diamond silver brooch and other prizes down to twelfth place. The norm competitions was four. The Dewar inter-club shield at 3.30pm, a scratch event inviting teams from clubs 'whether in the United Kingdom, India, South Africa, Ceylon or elsewhere, if duly affiliated to the CBS Association.'

The Field 'Single Fire, Gun Down' event is also interesting. Not because of its prizes—which were as extravagant as the others mentioned—but because it was shot over five pairs with one bird from each being 'thrown from the tower and the other from the trench, so that both are in the air at once'. The competition, was 'single-fire' meaning only one person shot at a time and the gun had to start 'below the elbow' until both birds were in the air. It is evident that this style of proto-Sporting shooting had been around since at least 1901 as a similar event at the Middlesex Club is described in *Trapshooting: The Patriotic Sport* on the occasion of an American team visiting Britain.

Friday at the 1914 Championship began with the RSPCA competition 'Trovers and Tyros', shot over ten birds down the line, single barrel. The Perrier Goblets competition at 12.30pm was billed as a gun-down handicap, shot at five pairs each, though subsequent research appears to indicate it was a competition for partners with each pair facing four birds in the air[94]. The Westley Richards at 2pm on the Thursday was a handicap event with a detachable lock gun as first prize. The main event of the day was the still famous Dougall Memorial Trophy, first shot for in 1896, a handicap-by-distance event shot over no less than twenty targets straight 'not in lots of ten' down the line. The Dougall Cup, value 80 guineas, had been presented to the CBSA in 1896 by its founding chairman Mr JD Dougall for annual competition.

Saturday began as every other day with practice shooting and moved on at 10.30am to the *Country Life* Competition (handicap, ten birds down the line).

Trapshooting from aeroplanes

TAKEN FROM *Trapshooting: The Patriotic Sport*:

> Trapshooting from aeroplanes seemed to appeal especially to women shooters. Annie Oakley (Mrs Frank Butler) tried hitting the inanimate clays from one of Uncle Sam's [air] ships while flying over Atlantic City, NJ, at the rate of a mile a minute and later Mrs Ada Schilling, of Portland, Ore, attempted to annihilate a lot of clay targets while in an aeroplane crossing the Willamette River. Mrs Butler discovered that she had to shoot very quickly, much quicker than on the ground, for the airship and target going in the same direction did not give her much time to raise the gun and aim. Mrs Schilling, too, had difficulty in breaking the 'Blue Rocks'. She found that the airship, going so fast in the same direction as the target, sometimes passed the target before she could get perfect aim. She modified this somewhat by rigging up the trap so that two targets would be thrown into the air and a trifle to one side but, no matter how the targets are thrown, they are difficult to hit when the airship is moving along 50-60mph.

Clayshooting with the pistol

THE AMERICAN shooter Walter Winans notes in his book *The Art of Revolver Shooting*:

> My way of shooting clay pigeons is either to have them bowled down-hill from beside me, which give very good practice for shooting at with a bullet—it is too easy for shot—or else to have a trap which throws discs straight up.
>
> One of my traps has a horizontal cylinder which contains clay discs; these are pressed close against one end of the cylinder by a spiral spring. A lever, which flies up by a strong spring, is kept down by a spring held tightly by an assistant who stands behind me. When the word 'Pull!' is given, he loosens the string, the lever is released and flies upward through a slit in the end of the cylinder, throwing the disc straight up in the air, to the height of about 10ft, out of an opening at the other side of the cylinder. The end of the cylinder is towards you, so that the discs also are thrown with their flat sides towards you. This gives one a nice shot for the bullet, as it has to be taken just at the highest point of its flight and teaches one to 'snap'…
>
> Another way is to have the old-fashioned Bogardus trap, which throws glass balls or, better still, composite balls, as these do not mess the lawn up so. These are rather harder to hit than the objects I have just described, as they do not come up quite vertically, but in a parabola. They are therefore more suitable, perhaps, for the shot revolver.
>
> The advantage of 'saucers' for practising quick revolver shooting is that there is no cruelty in it: although there was an old lady who said that the poor clay pigeons suffer just as much as any other breed.

The scratch International Challenge Shield followed after lunch (it was first presented to the CBSA in 1895 by the magazine *Rod & Gun* 'for competition by international teams at each yearly Championship Meeting'). It was followed by the Vice-President's prize, another handicap over ten birds down the line and the Championship event thereafter. This scratch event was shot over thirty birds straight down the line and a final at ten birds from 'unknown traps and angles on the single fire principle, five birds from no 2 and five from no 4 mark, three sets of traps'.

While the Americans preferred the Sergeant system and 18 yards rise, the English favoured something more like a modern Olympic Trap layout with five banks of three traps. In early days, they were at ground level shielded by sackcloth. Quite quickly they were put in a trench that might protect the trappers. Each competitor shot 'down the line' at one target from each bank of three traps. After five shots, the trapper ran forward and reloaded and cocked the traps. Because of the screens, the shooter did not know which trap of the three would be released or what the angle his bird would be.

Among the results of this championship meeting reported in *The Field*, Mrs Grosvenor, wife of member of the British Olympic clay squad in Sweden in 1912 WP Grosvenor, won the Westley Richards competition; Mrs Jurgen, the wife of the secretary of the Hamburg club, won the Vice-President's Cup; Herr Goeldel who had done so well in 1913 won another Gold Star with the highest championship aggregate of 93 per cent (a score shared with a compatriot J Luttich); and the Germans also won the International Challenge Shield.[95]

A sad little notice appeared in *The Field*, 29 May 1915:

> The Clay Bird Shooting Championship. The Clay Bird Shooting Association announces that, owing to the war, the championship meeting will not take place this year. Twenty-two annual meetings have been held consecutively up to the present time and last June, Belgian, French and German competitors were amongst those attending the very successful meeting at Hendon.[96]

CLAY
TARGET
SHOOTING

No. 4   *Issued by Nobel Industries Ltd., London, S.W.1.*   APRIL, 1925.

THE AUTOMATIC TRAP FIXED IN POSITION WITH TRAPPER PROTECTED.

THE PULLING LEVER WORKING THE TRAP FROM A DISTANCE OF 23 YARDS.

The two Illustrations represent a Complete Outfit for a Clay Target Shooting Club.

Birth of the CPSA

AFTER A FEW hiccups at the dawn of the new century and a suspension during the war, the sport of clayshooting boomed in Britain in the 1920s. New clubs were formed and it became a less select activity than it had been before. The first two decades of the twentieth century also saw the sport expand massively in the USA, though it was already a major sport in that country by 1900.

Nobel Industries did much to promote the sport in England and Scotland in the 1920s and 1930s and sponsored the creation of the CPSA in 1928. Between the CBSA and the CPSA came the British Trapshooting Association (BTA).

In 1926, the BTA listed its headquarters as 23 Conduit Street, London W1, subscription was 2s 6d per annum and a guinea for trade members. Its precise relationship to the early CBSA is now unclear. It is a reasonable assumption that it may have evolved from it after the First World War. From its advertisements, we know that it existed for the purpose of 'promoting, managing, supporting and encouraging the holding of a championship meeting' and published

Major HG Eley

comprehensive rules for Trap shooting (including single and double target events) and for handicapping. It certainly looked like the work of a governing body, or, at least, one intimately connected with the organisation of the sport.

The 1923 'revised' BTA rules note the following classifications:

Class A. 90 and over.
Class B. 80 per cent and under 90
Class C. 70 per cent and under 80
Class D. 60 per cent and under 70
Class E. Below 60 per cent.

There is little mention, however, of the BTA in the early copies of *Clay Target Shooting*. Nobel appeared to be doing its own thing from 1925 onwards. It certainly put considerable effort into promoting both Trap and Sporting clay pigeon shooting and, from 1927, Skeet shooting. Maybe Nobel bosses thought that the BTA was not up to the job or needed re-organising. The firm was particularly active in promoting the 'automatic' trap in this era. This meant a manually-loaded but auto angling trap. Today, of course, it refers to a carousel magazine-fed electric trap.

The 'automatic' made DTL competitions fairer, as the angle of flight could not be predetermined by the trapper or read by an experienced shooter. One of the first clubs to install them in England was Bisley, where McFarland notes two being in place by 1921. F Martin was club secretary at this time, with Major Northover a leading light in club affairs.[99]

Clay Target Shooting issue no 1, January

CLAY
TARGET
SHOOTING

No. 6.   *Issued by Nobel Industries Ltd., London, S.W.1.*   JUNE, 1925.

ARRIVAL OF THE "GUNS."

DRIVEN GROUSE.

The First Sporting Amateur Clay Target Shooting Championship of Great Britain.

Shooting under lights

ACCORDING TO DH Eaton, the first recorded use of artificial light for shooting inanimate targets occurred in the United States in 1880, when the Orion Gun Club in Philadelphia used large calcium carbide lamps. They were followed by the Jacksonville Gun Club of Illinois. However, it is reported that Doc Carver was shooting glass balls by experimental electric light in Pittsburgh as early as 1878. He ordered the lights switched off at one point for dramatic effect and shot fourteen balls straight by sound alone.[100]

I have been able to dig up no other records until 1915, when the Salem Yacht Gun & Rod Club used artificial light for trap shooting. This led to many others copying them. In England DTL was shot under artificial light at the White City Stadium in February 1933 using white targets. McFarland notes that nothing much came of it. In the USA it became commonplace (which is not to say that clayshooting under lights did not occasionally occur in England after 1933—the present writer has happy memories of shooting DTL style birds at the excellent Little Clacton Gun Club of Andy Riva in the 1990s).

1925, quotes only ten automatics being in place by January 1924 and 29 by January 1925. Thereafter, the numbers appear to have accelerated rapidly. By December 1926 there were 123, 182 by December 1927, 220 by 1928 and 238 by December 1929. The story behind this initiative and the clear determination to make clayshooting a major sport in England, as it had already become in the United States, may explain the desire to sponsor an entirely new organisation.

In 1927, Eley installed its own range at Witton, Birmingham, with Major Henry Gerard Eley, grandson of one of the original Eley brothers, directed by his firm 'to give a lot of attention' to the increasingly popular pastime. The same year, Eley's parent company, Nobel, published a seventy-two page illustrated *Handbook on Clay Target Shooting*, which included sections on both Trap and 'game' (Sporting) shooting. It also gave considerable information on the 'automatic' trap.

In February 1928, Nobel invited clubs to send details of their fixtures to 'The Clay Pigeon Shooting Department, Nobel House, Buckingham Gate, SW1'. And, on 14 June of the same year at a meeting at the Stadium Club, London, the Clay Pigeon Shooting Association was formed as a 'Governing Body' with £50 promised towards 'preliminary expenses' from Nobel. Major Eley became the first president. Nobel's sponsorship of the organisation lasted until the early 1970s. The CPSA remains the governing body for clayshooting in England, while Scotland, Wales and Northern and Southern Ireland have their own associations—the SCTA, WCTA and ICPSA.

The February 1925 issue of *Clay Target Shooting*—later *Clay Pigeon Shooting Monthly*—included a growing list of grounds where auto-angling DTL traps were being introduced. In addition, on the back page, there was an advertisement for the final of the Scottish Medal Competition at Gleneagles Hotel. The success of Eley Trap shooting cartridges in the past season was noted, with honourable mention of Mr HV Larsen's recent feat—147 straight kills. The cover story in March was the auto-angle trap. On page three, there is a pleasant photo of the Nobel cartridge display at Cruft's Dog Show, where the auto trap was also displayed.

'Automatic Angle Trap'—How It Works', from the front page of *Clay Target Shooting*:[101]

> The trap is set by a bar connection, worked by a puller 23 yards to the rear, operating two ratchet wheels which swings the trap to different angles. By means of an ingenious

Clay target shooting in 1924

THIS REPORT was published in *Shooting Times*[102] and reprinted in the first issue of *Clay Target Shooting* by Nobel Industries in the same year and month.

The year just closed has witnessed a considerable advancement in the popularity of clay target shooting, not only in the United Kingdom, but in the Irish Free State. At the beginning of 1924 it might have been said that the pastime had 'caught on' in and around London, in Norfolk, Yorkshire, Lancashire and intermittently in Wales and Scotland. Today the position is very different. The sport is now stabilising itself in the Principality, while its development at one-day meetings among gamekeepers north of the Tweed and in Lancashire has been one of the outstanding features of the past year, although in this respect the place of honour must surely be accorded to the West of England, where the progress made has greatly exceeded the expectations of the most optimistic.

Until within the last six months clay target shooting was practically an unknown quantity in that part of the globe, whereas to-day automatic traps have been installed at Bristol (two), Honiton, Okehampton, Taunton, Higher Shutescombe (near Barnstaple), Torr, Liskeard, Newton Abbot, Launceston, Minehead, Highbridge and Tiverton; while the formation of clubs in Exeter, Wadebridge, Yeovil, Dorchester and other towns can practically be considered as an accomplished fact.

Many times in the course of history the lads of Cornwall and Devon have shown the way and in this instance they are not lagging. The first county to form an association (Cornwall Clay Target Association) was Cornwall and a great deal of the success of the movement must be attributed to Mr AG Creber, of Torr; but even he would be the first to admit that the task would have been impossible but for the enthusiasm and support of many of the leading sportsmen in the county.

The example of Cornwall has been followed by Devon (Devon Clay Target Association) with an association under the presidency of Lord Sidmouth and, with the backing of the Otter Vale Beagles, its future success is assured.

Already two inter-county meetings have been held and, with the large accession of towns to the list of those possessing automatic traps, it can be taken for granted, from the scores which have been put up by several of the competitors that, in the field of sport, England can depend on the men of Cornwall and Devon, just as she did in the days of old when sport had to take second place in the grim struggle for King and Country.

The visit of the American and Canadian teams en route to the Olympic Games at Paris infused additional interest in clay target shooting in the Metropolis during the past year. Both of them were treated right royally by the London clubs and right royally did they shoot. Never before have such a fine exhibition of shooting and of endurance been witnessed as when at Waltham Abbey Mr Etchen of the American team succeeded in defeating Mr Montgomery of Canada at the two-hundredth attempt in a sequence of kills which to the lay mind must have been seen to be credited [Etchen, the Captain of the US Olympic team, shot 200 straight].

The meeting at Bisley, held under the auspices of the National Rifle Association was a

arrangement the pulling of the connecting bar automatically changes the angle of delivery and not even the trapper can determine the angle at which the target will be thrown…

A supplement to July 1927 issue notes further:

With it more targets can be thrown per hour than with the ordinary hand-set trap and at much less cost, since one automatic angle trap will do the work of four hand traps, thus making the running of competitions a simple affair. In Great Britain and Ireland, the automatic angle trap has undoubtedly been the chief factor in the revival of clay pigeon shooting.

The auto-angling trap is also the cover story of the April 1925 issue. All of page 2, however, is dedicated to an advertisement for the first Sporting Clay Target Shooting Championship, which was due to be held at the Albemarle Shooting Grounds, Worcester Park, on 20-21 May 1925. Much of the June edition is also devoted to the now historic Championship won by great success and it is evident that the events contested during 'the fortnight' are each year attracting a larger number of competitors from all parts of the country. In this connection advertisers should carefully consider the possibilities there are in encouraging clay target shooting among the public school boys, by some of whom very creditable scores were put up. One point which calls for attention is the increasing number of meetings organised by various regimental messes, one of which was patronised by HRH the Duke of York.

Another feature of the past year's work has been the introduction of clay target shooting on some of the large liners making extended trips, such as the 'Belgenland' and the 'Laconia'. The Cunard Co was probably the pioneer in this innovation, although a complete equipment was fitted up on HMS 'Renown' when our popular Prince made his visit to India a few years ago.

Nobel Industries Ltd has introduced a Medal Competition on a large scale in Scotland and, if the writer of this article has the opportunity of compiling a review of another year's work, it is hoped that it may then be possible to make a more flattering reference to the development of the sport in the 'Land o' Cakes'.

As already announced, Gleneagles, which is undoubtedly one of the most up-to-date hotels in the country, has been selected as the venue of the final in Nobel's Medal Competition in May 1925 to be followed by the Scottish Clay Target Shooting Championship (Open) in June or July. The proprietors of the hotel are to be heartily congratulated on their enterprise as it is confidently expected that these two meetings will draw together the largest gatherings ever seen north of the Tweed. The programme of the Championship Meeting is in course of preparation and the latest information from Buckingham Gate tends to show that the prize list will be prepared on lines which will offer an inducement to sportsmen from all parts of the country to take part. Full particulars will no doubt be published in the columns of this paper immediately they are available.

We now turn to that delightful but 'distreshful' country—Ould Ireland. For the first time since AD 1169 the Tailteann Games were held outside Dublin and, in the programme, were included several clay target shooting competitions. While possibly the meeting was not conducted on lines which would have met with the approval of our American friends, an eyewitness has stated that the events drew together a gathering such as had never been seen in that country or, for that matter, in any part of the world. Some of the competitors used guns which had been buried in the bogs for years, for reasons best known to the owners; but still, as is characteristic of the country, the fun went fast and furious and, given better conditions, it is hoped the sport will continue for ever and a day.

There is no doubt that, encouraged and fostered by those in authority, it will flourish and some of us may yet live to see a championship meeting, reminiscent of the good old days at Wembley and Hendon. Some of the old brigade are still with us and it might be permitted to make special reference to Mr JH Butt and Mr W Ellicott, who can still hold their own with the best; and Mr AH Gale, for many years so closely identified with the Middlesex Gun Club, who is now enjoying in good health a well-earned retirement in the South of England. These memories conjure up names such as Izzard, Black, O'Conor, Cave, Moore, Maunder, Back, Coopmans, Pike and others. Those who survive must one and all have pleasant and happy recollections of days spent in the pursuit of the elusive 'Saucer'.

CW Mackworth-Praed on a score of 63 ex 80. FG Horne came second on 61 and Percy Stanbury was third on 60.

The following year, 1926, the result was similar—Mackworth-Praed would win (71), GS Horne would come second (68) and 'Stan' third (66). FG Horne—who had been second the year before and was brother to GS—came fourth (65) and a CE Horne came twelfth (57). The Hornes were evidently quite a force with which to be reckoned; 1927, saw GS win the Championship (67), with FG taking second (65) after a shoot-off with FN Horne; CE came fifth (63) and Stanbury sixth (62).

Stan had some consolation that year, however, winning the Third Annual Grand Open Clay Target Shooting Tournament—the Down the Line Championship of Great Britain—at Cheshunt in 1927 and the Dougall Memorial Trophy. In 1928, he won the Grand Open again (but this time at Lune Valley in Lancaster) and his first Amateur Sporting Championship. This was an unusual, go-as-you-please, part-handicapped competition split between the West London Shooting School at Perivale and the Albermarle Shooting School at Worcester Park. The legendary West Country shot carried a handicap of minus-two birds—with Mackworth-Praed burdened with minus-five and FG Horne minus-three. In 1929, Stanbury pulled another national sporting victory at a more conventional contest—the Fifth Annual Amateur Sporting Championship held at the Albermarle grounds. His score was 69.

Clay Pigeon Shooting Monthly reported:

> Mr P Stanbury the splendid Devon shot again excelled himself and won the Silver Cup for the second time in succession with a score of 69 points out of 80. It will be observed… that the scores were not so good as they might have been, but one had to remember that the shots are difficult and entirely different to ordinary 'down-the-line' shooting.[103]

There is also an interesting letter published in the September magazine from C Lucas, then chairman of the Clay Pigeon Shooting Association. He states his apologies for the unexpectedly high turn out for the fifth sporting championship and consequent logistical problems and he notes the intention to form a London Sporting Clay Pigeon Shooting Club:

> Looking through the list of names, I see a very large percentage came from very near London and therefore I can only conclude that this [Sporting] clay pigeon shooting appeals far more than the ordinary down-the-line stuff and that being so, I am going to suggest that we form a new club to meet on at least one day per month throughout the whole year… We could no doubt arrange with Messrs Harrison and Hussey to shoot at Worcester Park and I would suggest that we shoot from the same stands, only cut down the programme to, say, fifty birds. We could charge quite a small entrance fee and give first, second and third prize at each meeting. I suggest winter as well as summer, as there is no shadow of a doubt that this kind of practise improves one's gameshooting tremendously. I am certain that if I can start this club I shall gain the approval of every pheasant who has an objection to walking about without his tail feathers.[104]

Royal clayshooters

WHEN KING George V, a first class game shot, went to shoot clays at the West London Shooting Grounds. *The Daily Express* reported:[105]

> The King showed himself to be one of the finest shots in the kingdom yesterday, when he fired about three hundred rounds at different kinds of 'game'—clay grouse, partridges and deer [sic]. He spent yesterday morning at a West London Shooting School, practising for the 'Twelfth'.
>
> The King was received at the entrance by Mr Richmond Watson, the proprietor of the school, with who he shook hands. He went straight to the butts and, receiving a gun from one of the attendants, began firing at swiftly moving clay birds.
>
> He practised under the field conditions that he will find when he goes north for the season. He also fired dozens of rounds at 'deer' with his rifle and much impressed onlookers with the accuracy of his shots. The practice lasted nearly two hours.

King George V

George V's son, Edward—later King Edward VIII and later still the Duke of Windsor—had traps fitted to the battleship Renown so that he could shoot clays while on imperial tours. Before his abdication and exile in 1936, the Prince came to know Robert Churchill's innovative Crayford shooting grounds well.[106] He was given an early specimen of the Browning Superposed gun in 1930. The gun must have been one of the first of the B25s— the last creation of John Moses Browning, who died at his Herstal workbench perfecting it (his son Val took on the task of perfecting a single trigger). Edward's brother, Prince Henry was also an occasional clayshooter. In 1926, *The Daily Mail* reported from Bisley:[107]

> At the clay bird and revolver ranges a slim young officer arrived during the afternoon. 'Give me a ticket, sergeant.' He said. 'Name, Sir, please,' asked the NCO. 'Lieutenant Prince Henry,' was the reply and His Royal Highness, who belongs to the Tenth Hussars, took his ten cartridges and with them made six 'kills'.

This may well have been tabloidised, as Nobel's *Clay Target Shooting* for September 1926 notes that Henry attended the day before the eighteenth annual 'Aldershot Command Rifle Meeting' on 4 August and, with General Sir Phillip Chetwode GOC Aldershot Command, had ten shots 'walking up'. HRH Prince Henry killed seven birds and the *Clay Target Shooting* reporter noted: 'Other notable shots attending were Lord Gough, Lord Stratheden and officers of the Guards Regiments. Among the onlookers were Japanese officers and officers from Iraq. The latter were very interested in the working of the automatic trap.'

Whether this refers to same shoot as described in *The Daily Mail* or not, the royal family's interest provided critical support for the then relatively new sport of clay pigeon shooting in Britain, just as their support for driven gameshooting had helped establish that sport, which indeed they had actually been instrumental in introducing to England. Their interest in clay pigeon shooting persists to this day.

Prince Philip at Bisley

Clayshooters at war

DURING BOTH World Wars, clayshooting was used as a means of training. Robert Churchill, who would do much to promote clayshooting in the Second World War, notes its practice in the First World War as well. In his first book *How To Shoot*, for example, he writes: 'Its educational value is so great that it was adopted during the war as part of the essential training of the fighting branches of the Air Forces of Great Britain, America and France.' [108]

As far as Second World War is concerned, there is much more detailed information available. Sport clayshooting ceased on the outbreak of war in the UK, however, clayshooting was used by the RAF, US Air Force and Navy and various other arms, as a means of teaching personnel—aerial gunners and pilots predominantly—how to shoot a moving target. Both Trap and Skeet fields were often used for this. As far as Britain was concerned, some well-known clayshooters were enrolled in the RAF as specialist instructors. CPSA chairman C Lucas became commanding officer of a specialist unit. FM McFarland writes:

> Quite senior officers were very soon sure that the results of this training were profitable. Amongst these instructors was Arthur Turner of the West Country. Turner was probably every Commanding Officer's nightmare. Discipline meant nothing to him if he did not want it to![109]

McFarland also informs that the well known Bisley shooter Major HR Northover—one of the greats of British clayshooting—was occupied in clay production for the services during the war and made no less than 40 million targets for them. Ever inventive, he also designed the 'Northover Projector' for the Home Guard, a crude tripod-mounted weapon designed to launch grenades and Molotov cocktails at the invading Hun.

The wartime role of honour on this side of the Atlantic also included Percy Stanbury and Robert Churchill. A first class clay shot who gave Stan a run for his money on occasion, Churchill instructed the Home Guard in methods of engaging German paratroopers using shotguns firing cartridges into which wax had been dripped to form a solid projectile. He drilled his LDVs—Local Defence Volunteers—on the importance of keeping the gun swinging and their 'eye on the ball' or Fallschirmjäger. 'I showed them,' he later wrote, 'how, in picking off a paratrooper, the secret was to hold… fire until he lifted his knees to land.'[110]

This ' other' Mr Churchill seemed to have had an especially 'good' war. Apart from a vast increase in work as an expert witness in murder cases, he undertook a secret mission to Brussels, became the armourer to MI6 and—according to his own unconfirmed claim—shot down a doodlebug using the bren gun that he had fixed on mounts in the orchard of his Crayford home. I wonder if he gave it conscious lead or just kept his eyes on the target?

My favourite wartime clay story, though, is a rather more gentle one from Jack Eveleigh, a former Lancaster gunner, who recently recounted memories of his RAF training:

> I liked clay pigeon shooting. It showed you the action of actually going through the target. Most of the boys had never handled a shotgun. Well, I was a country boy and I had used one. So, I had a little advantage. We put a bob each into a kitty and usually I managed to make a few bob.[111]

RAF pilots practising. Picture courtesy: Imperial War Museum

As for guns, just about anything that would shoot was pressed into service in England. I have heard rumours of Webley & Scott side-by-sides with War Department arrowhead marking but I have been unable to track one down. Photographic evidence suggests a wide variety of guns. In the United States, the most popular shotgun for wartime clay service was the Remington Model 11 long-recoil semi-automatic—the Remington-made version of the famous Browning A5—the first successful auto-loader.

John Glenn

As well as being shot at clays in the normal way, the USAF and Navy modified some guns to be more like anti-aircraft machine guns. They removed butt stocks and replaced them with twin vertical grips with machine gun-style triggers; they added large metal sights to the barrel and attached the gun to a cradle by means of pintle mounts. In an article in *Gun Digest* in 1988, Eric Archer quotes USAF Lt Gen KE Pletcher:

> Shotguns were mounted on an apparatus resembling the machine gun mount used on bombers and training was conducted by running the mount around while clay targets were thrown at various angles. The very poor record of aerial gunnery employed by bomber gunners against attacking enemy aircraft would indicate that the training was not very effective, perhaps due to bad simulation. Skeet shooting to train fighter pilots was considerably more effective since the movements of the airplane through the controls was reasonably simulated by body movement in shoulder firing.[112]

As in Britain, the USAF and US Navy sought the services of civilian shooting instructors during Second World War. D Lee Braun, who is arguably one of the greatest instructors of all time, and the actor Robert Stack—a champion Skeet shot of the 1930s, who would later star in the famous 1960s TV series *The Untouchables*—were both put into uniform to act as trainers. While a trainee fighter pilot in Second World War, Ed Scherer was introduced to the sport in which he would later excel as a competitor. Similarly, astronaut and former Second World War air ace John Glenn (pictured above) is among many who believed that clayshooting helped them master the principles of forward allowance so necessary to win in aerial combat.

Post Second World War

OLD EQUIPMENT was dusted off across the UK and old clubs and a few new ones started. It was an austere time, however—meat rationing continued until the early 1950s—and progress was slow. Albert E Browning, 'The Govnor', held two shoots near Blandford Forum in Dorset in 1946. Browning was one of the greats of British clayshooting in the mid twentieth century and his were amongst the very first shoots to take place after the war.

The forty-third English Championship, under the auspices of the CPSA, was held in 1947. In 1948 the international match between England, Ireland, Scotland and Wales returned. It was held in June in Eley Park, Cardiff. In July, there was an English, European and World Championship meeting at Bisley, shot over three days and three hundred birds. The first hundred counted for the English Championship, the second added to the first for the European and the combined total for the World Championship. FM McFarland records:

> The first was won by Mr H Aasnaes of Norway, the European Championship by Stan Rimmer and Mr Aasnaes again came into his own and won the World Championship with a then record score for his country of 291 out of 300.[112]

When the London Olympics restarted on 29 July 1948, there was no clayshooting. It would not return until 1952 in Helsinki. The sport of shooting seems to have passed through the doldrums in the years immediately after Second World War. It was relatively expensive and people at that time were not flush with cash, contrasting with the 'you've never had it so good' times of the 1950s and 1960s when there was far more disposable income.

There was much tinkering with rules post war. This appears to have been motivated by the CPSA's desire to get interest in the sport back up to pre-1939 levels. It caused some confusion initially. However, as McFarland explains:

> …Within about ten years [1946-1956] matters had steadied down and the trapshooter was still using both barrels but scoring two points for a first and one point for a second barrel kill. The Skeet shooter had edged closer to the American style of shooting, stood away a little and finally came back half way. So that now a round of Skeet was twenty-five birds and not twenty as previously. Doubles were thrown instantaneously but instead of taking the shots at station eight—right between the traphouses—we, being different, decided that we would shoot a pair from station four.[113]

Prince Philip visits Bisley on 9 July 1954. He is seated in the front row

Major Northover and 'Skut'

MAJOR HR Northover OBE MC was among those who dominated British clayshooting in the first half of the twentieth century. He was an excellent shot himself—featuring frequently in the prize lists of the 1920s at the highest level—a selector for English and British international teams for many years and extremely inventive. He founded the Bisley Gun Club in 1923 having 'been to Germany and seen aircraft gunners being trained to hit moving targets by practising on clays.' * He was also a frequent visitor to the West London shooting grounds where he was involved in the manufacture of targets. Many of his evidently numerous contributions to British clayshooting have been lost, but one that survives is 'Skut'.

Back (l-r): Teddy Fear, Stanley Bamber, Eric Horlock. Front (l-r): Major Northover, Charles Lucas and Paul Catteral. Taken at Bisley and note the clock tower in the background which is there today

This was introduced to the world at a meeting of the Bisley Gun Club in September 1950. It was conducted rather like a DTL event with five-man squads. But, instead of a traphouse to their front, they were placed 18 yards behind a 50-yard track with traps placed at each end and a 'blind' half way. Five 'drives' were shot. LB Escritt, a contemporary shooting man, explains:

> In drive no 1—running 'skuts'—the squad stands with guns loaded but open and in the gun-down position. When no 1 closes his gun, the 'skut' target is released (being secretly signalled as in Skeet) to run as a rabbit along the track. When no 1 fires, no 2 closes his gun and a skut is released from the opposite trap and so the shooting continues, until every member of the squad has fired at two targets, one released from each end of the track. Then they change position as in Down the Line.
>
> In the second drive the traps are adjusted to throw their targets into the air, otherwise the procedure is as before. In drives three and four, both ground and bird shots are taken in various combinations of doubles and the fifth drive is confined to 'birds' only. As in Skeet, the second target of a double is released on the report of the competitor's gun.
>
> At the time of writing, the traps for this new game are not yet on the market and it is likely to be some time before they are available to the general public.[114]

The Major's new shooting game did not take off—perhaps it would have had he not died in 1952—but the Skut target remained as an improved rabbit. There had been clay rabbits before this, but of a cruder, thicker, pattern as illustrated in some of the ICI pamphlets before the Second World War.

---

* You can find a little more at www.bisleygunclub.org.uk

'Stan'

The remarkable record of Percy Stanbury:[115]

1925	Third place, first Amateur Sporting Championship of Great Britain
1926	Third place, second Amateur Sporting Championship of Great Britain Championship Of Devon (twenty-five birds DTL, five walked-up, twenty Double Rise)
1927	Open Championship of the British Isles
	Sixth place, third Amateur Sporting Championship of Great Britain
	High Gun International
1928	Open Championship of the British Isles
	High Gun International
	Amateur Sporting Championship of Great Britain
1929	Amateur Sporting Championship of Great Britain
1930	Open Championship of the British Isles
	Championship of Gloucestershire
	Championship of Devon
1931	Devon Championship Cup
1932	Championship of Devon
	Championship of Southern Counties
	Championship of the British Isles
1933	Sporting Championship of Devon
	Championship of Devon
	Championship of Southern Counties
1934	Devon Open Championship
	Devon Skeet Championship
	English Open Championship
	High Gun International
	British Open Championship
	British Skeet Championship
	British Sporting Championship
1935	Championship of the West of England
	High Gun International
	Championship of the British Isles
	Sporting Championship of the British Isles
1937	Skeet High Gun in the Coronation Shoot
	Championship of Devon
	Double Rise Championship of Devon
	Skeet Championship of Great Britain
1938	Skeet Championship of Great Britain
	Sporting Championship of Great Britain
1946	Dorset Open Championship
	Championship of Shropshire
1947	Dorset Open Championship
	English Open Championship
	British Open Skeet Championship
1948	Championship of Great Britain
1949	Championship of Great Britain
1951	High Gun International
1952	British Open Championship
1953	Middlesex County Championship
	London and Middlesex Championship
	English Open Championship
	English Championship

Part II

Registered shooting

OF THE 700,000 or so certificated shotgun owners in England, Wales, Northern Ireland and Scotland, only about 23,500 are members of the CPSA—the national governing body. Although some join for insurance or other benefits, such as the Association magazine *Pull!*, most sign up in order to get 'classified' for registered competition. The list of recognised disciplines is now quite large and includes:

- DTL (Down the Line)
- Single Barrel
- Double Rise
- English Skeet
- Skeet Doubles
- English Sporting
- Sportrap
- Automatic Ball Trap (ABT)
- All Round
- Olympic Trap (OT)
- Olympic Skeet
- Double Trap
- Universal Trench (UT)
- FITASC Sporting

Nearly 14,000 shooters have classified in one or more disciplines. The usual classes are AA, A, B or C in domestic disciplines. In FITASC Sporting, Olympic Trap and Skeet, Universal Trench and Double Trap the classifications are A,B, C and D. The CPSA also announced at the end of 1999 that, in imitation of the system used in the USA, a triple-A class (AAA) would henceforward operate at the English, British and World Sporting Championships:

A cut-off point will be established and all shooters above that point will be promoted to AAA class for those events. The AAA class will not need to be used at any other registered events and will not appear in the 'Classification Book'.[116]

AAA has also been introduced in some Sportrap events. All the classifications used to be published annually in a book. The last one (no 23) was effective from 1 January 2002. Now, like much in life, everything is on disk.

International shooting in the UK

AS FAR AS international shooting is concerned, there is a British International Clay Target Shooting Federation (BICTSF). It evolved from the English CPSA's 'British International Olympic Committee', which was replaced by—via an argument over Olympic selection—into the CPSA's British International Board, which developed into the British CPSAs (English, Ulster, Scottish and Welsh) International Board and finally became BICTSF.

One of BICTSF's main tasks is to select those clayshooters who will represent Great Britain in major competition abroad. The federation is also involved with the International Shooting Sports Federation (ISSF), formerly known as UIT (Union Internationale de Tir) and sometimes, unofficially, as the International Shooting Union or ISU.

The ISSF is the organisation that governs all Olympic disciplines in the shooting sports. The *Fédération Internationale de Tir aux Armes Sportives de Chasse* (FITASC) is the controlling organisation for International Sporting Shooting (known as *Parcours de Chasse* in France), Universal Trench and Hélice (ZZ).

The Grand American Handicap Championship

EVEN A BRIEF consideration of clayshooting organisation in the United States would be incomplete without a mention of the ATA and its Grand American Handicap, the world's greatest Trap event.

The Grand began as a live bird shoot in 1893 in Kansas City, Missouri. In 1900, the competition moved to the Interstate Park, Long Island, New York. The usual live bird shoot was held there in April of that year but a clay event was added and a new Grand American contest at inanimate targets was held for the first time in June 1900. Seventy-four attended and the winner was a Remington professional, Rolla Heikes, who came to England the following year to shoot in the first Anglo-American International. The ATA's excellent Trapshooting Hall of Fame website www.traphof.org (which supplied much of the detail for this section)— notes that Heikes 'was the first and last professional to win the Grand American Handicap at clay targets.'

The clay pigeon Grand became the sole event in 1903. As noted, live bird trapshooting was by then under considerable pressure on both sides of the Atlantic. The Grand went to Vandalia, near Dayton Ohio, in 1924, where it would remain for more than eighty years. There it evolved into a ten-day extravaganza with 5,000 or more participants and many trade exhibitors.

The shooting line is 1½ miles long and competitors have to learn to ignore the large jet aircraft, which taxi on runways immediately in front of the firing points.

Because of expansion of the airport, however, the Grand is about to move to the newly constructed World Shooting Complex at Sparta, Illinois, about 50 miles from St Louis. The first Sparta Grand American is due to take place in 2006. The facility will be run by the Illinois Department of Natural Resources and the idea is to attract other shooting sports, including cowboy-style action shooting. A few will no doubt shed a tear for the good ol' real old days.

BICTSF is affiliated to ISSF and FITASC. There is also an International Clay Pigeon Shooting Council (ICPSC) of the United Kingdom and Ireland which oversees home international events in Ireland, Ulster, England, Scotland, Wales, the Channel Isles and the Isle of Man (although the Channel Isles and the Isle of Man do not sit on the council).

Another body worthy of note is the Great Britain Target Shooting Federation (GBTSF) which co-ordinates the flow of money from the Sports Council towards various shooting organisations.

American clay pigeon associations

IN THE UNITED States there are separate associations for domestic Trap and Skeet shooting: the Amateur Trap Shooting Association (ATA) and the National Skeet Shooting Association (NSSA). The latter body has branched out into sporting clays and also runs the National Sporting Clays Association (NSCA), which is now the dominant sporting association—though it had some rivals in the early days. The National Rifle Association (NRA) maintains an interest in all firearm sports and, until 1994, was specifically responsible for the international Skeet and Trap disciplines. It passed this responsibility on to a new governing body, USA Shooting, in 1995. USA Shooting is also responsible for the selection and training of the US shooting team.

The modern clay

THE MODERN clay target is made with a limestone filler and a binding agent of petroleum products—bitumen, coal tar pitch or petroleum pitch. The standard UIT target used in the UK for all disciplines is 110mm (4 5/16in) in diameter, plus or minus 1mm, with an overall height of 25-26mm (about 1in). The base height—ie the height of the widest ring at the bottom—is 11mm (plus or minus 1mm). The rotating ring height (the next ring up) is 7mm (plus or minus 1mm) and the dome height—the part above the rotating ring—is 8mm (plus or minus 1mm). The target weighs 105 grams (plus or minus 5 grams). *

For UIT competitions, the target must be 'clearly visible against the background of the range under all normal lighting conditions'. The colour of the target 'may be all black, all white, all yellow, all orange; or, the full dome may be painted white, yellow or orange; or, a ring may be painted around the dome in white, yellow or orange'. In addition to standard targets, there are:

- Midis, which are 90mm wide and notable for their speed
- Minis, which are 60mm wide and notable because they slow quickly
- Battues, which are about 100mm wide, thin and cut through the air much faster than a standard target
- Rabbits, which are much more solid than a standard clay since they need to bounce along the ground
- Rocket clays, a thick and heavy battue developed for use in auto traps and used in FITASC Sporting competition.
- 'Flash' targets—birds which have a quantity of coloured powder above or below their dome—are sometimes used to make a more spectacular and visible break in shoot-offs or other special occasions.

In the United States, the dimensions of the standard target are different from those in the UK. This clay is narrower (4¼in) and marginally higher.

A new petroleum and pitch-free biodegradable target, which decomposes when in contact with moisture, was offered in the USA in 1999 by White Flyer Targets. This important innovation has been in development for more than a decade and is now perfected, according to the maker. The target flashes white when broken because of its entirely new composition. The firm is still keeping the exact recipe secret because the patent has not yet been granted.

It is not the first eco-friendly bird—though it may well be the most developed. A Dutch biodegradable target, the Lireko, is in existence and, I am informed, available in pink and brown. The Finns, too, are experimenting with the use of natural resin as a binding agent.

There are at least three bio-birds which pre-date all these developments: the Victorian ball target which broke down into fertiliser; the original terracotta disc target; and the 'ice birds' of the 1960s, made from dyed and frozen water. The ice bird was a brilliant idea, but did not catch on because of the need for a freezer for target manufacture next to the trap house. It might well be reconsidered as it sounds an ideal plan for large grounds.

From the sublime to the ridiculous: parachutes, confetti, feathers, a variety of powders, explosives and all sorts of other unexpected things (including

---

* In practice, clay targets are subject to wide variation. Dimensions and weight may fall outside specifications; some targets fracture in certain traps; some are too hard to break consistently, which can cause big problems in serious competitions. It is always good advice to test targets in your own equipment and also to sound out friends or colleagues on their experience with a new or untried bird, before ordering a large quantity. The use of pick-ups—which may have hairline fractures—and poor storage are both common causes of problems. Damp is not a specific problem, save in winter when it may cause targets to freeze together. Heat, however, can cause targets to buckle in the summer if they are stored in direct sunlight

exotic ladies underwear) have been secreted in clay birds by pranksters, or those looking for dramatic effect. Commercial novelty targets have been created with streamers contained within them and, among other things, spring-loaded, accordion-like 'Jacks'—a type of target which achieved a modicum of popularity in England in the 1930s. Manufrance of Saint Etienne once made a clay with a washer attached to its belly by means of a metal clip. The purpose of this was to create a competition where the washer had to fall within a certain boundary as in a live pigeon shoot. The idea seems to have been copied from the Best Tin Pigeon of 1889 and a similar idea was also pursued in Slapshot.

Lireko marketing material: 'a clay pigeon really made of clay!'

A number of imitation 'clays' were made of metal—brass or steel—in the Victorian era and two patented steel birds were still being offered in England in the late 1920s. One of them, the Steel Inanimate Bird, was an outward copy of a conventional clay painted with a special blue powder mix before use and which emitted a cloud of dust when hit. It is listed, for example, in the AG Parker catalogue of April 1928:

> This invention consists of a steel bird of the form of ordinary clay or composition birds… they are practically indestructible and may be used an indefinite number of times… previous to use they are painted with a fairly thick mixture of blue powder mixed with water and allowed to dry. Hits are plainly visible in mid-air by the emission of distinct clouds of dust when the bird is struck, even with the shot from both barrels, or, by a single pellet and the shot marks may be clearly discerned. There is very little trouble in gathering them as the blue powder may be seen at long distance.

The other, the 'Collapso', had a steel 'mother' target with a disc about the size of a midi nesting inside it which was attached by a small chain to the larger target. The disc was held in position by a spring attached to the rim and by an adjustable peg. It was released by shot striking any part. The manufacturers noted that feathers or paper might be added to give it 'a very realistic appearance'. The Collapso, which bore upon it the legend 'specially adapted for use abroad' seems to have been a rip-off of a very similar product sold in the United States in the early days of clayshooting. DH Eaton writes in *Trapshooting: The Patriotic Sport*:

> The 'Best' tin pigeon, made in Chicago about 1885, was called the 'worst' substitute for live birds yet offered to shooters. The inventor claimed that a pellet of shot striking the target would release a sort of flange, which, hanging down, would retard the flight of the 'pigeon' and gradually bring it to the ground like a wing-tipped bird. The theory was fine, but it did not always work out in practice. Some of the birds would be found perforated by shot and the flange still in position, while in other cases, the catch was so sensitive that a jar of the trap would release the flange. An improvement on this target was placed on the market in 1889.[117]

Targets have also been made from wood, plastic and aluminium. I know of one batch of alloy targets that was turned by a mischievous sporting machinist solely to confound his regular shooting companion. He painted the birds black and arranged for them to be launched at a driven stand when the friend shot. The latter apparently became increasingly frustrated, exclaiming to the shooting party (co-conspirators):

A modern battue target

'I know I hit that, didn't you hear it.' The shaking heads, repeated calls of 'no visible chip—bird lost' and glum expressions all round led him to pause, change chokes (to full) and try again. This time the clay was not broken but sent hurtling skywards. Broad smiles broke on his companions' faces. The penny dropped, as did the target eventually. 'You b*st**ds!'

Enthusiasts might be advised to get an example of all the more usual targets—and some ancient ones, if you can acquire them—and mount them on a display board, together with pictures of the basic types of trap. For instructors, I also recommend turning up a few copies of the mini clay from wood or plastic (or you can mould them in resin). This is not a scheme to confound your clients, but to give you an invaluable teaching aide. They are especially useful in explaining the barrel-bird relationship to beginners.

Trap shooting

Scenes from the English DTL championship meeting at Harrogate in 1950

THE MOST common Trap disciplines are:

Down the Line (DTL): this is the most popular trap discipline in the UK. The trap is placed 16 yards (15m) in front of five shooting positions situated along an arced firing line. The trap oscillates in the horizontal plane only. On calling 'pull', a bird is released anywhere within an area bounded by an angle of 22 degrees each side of an imaginary centre line. This means that the extreme angle left-hand bird looks like a straight away shot when viewed from position 5 and the extreme right-hand bird looks like a straightaway from position 1. Targets are thrown a distance of 50-55 yards (45 to 50 metres). Two shots may be fired at each target in DTL, but the first scores 3 points and the second only 2 which, historically, is known as the Scotch or Scottish system of scoring. Shooters, firing alternately, are presented with five single birds from each position before moving to the next station. A round consists of twenty-five birds (maximum possible score: 75 points). Competitions are usually shot over 100 birds. Cartridges must be loaded with no more than 28 grams of shot, maximum shot size no 6 (no minimum specified). Ported barrels are allowed but not 'attached ventilated recoil reducers' (ie ported chokes).

Single Barrel: essentially DTL with only one shot permitted. Sometimes seen in Britain, it is the predominant form of Trap shooting in the USA, where it is simply called American Trap and governed by the ATA. The same five-position arced firing point is used. A round consists of twenty-five birds. Competitions may be shot over any multiple of this, although hundred-bird events are the most popular. Cartridge and gun rules are as for DTL. In the USA 1 1/8oz loads may be used and the maximum pellet size is US no 7½ (British no 7).

Double Rise: this is an interesting and challenging form of clayshooting which dates back to the Victorian era. Two targets are released simultaneously on predetermined angles but, because shooters move position after two pairs, effectively the angles change. You score 5 points for killing both targets, 2 points for killing one bird of a pair. A round consists of twenty birds. Competitions are usually shot over eighty or sometimes a hundred targets. A good piece of advice with Double Rise is to shoot the target going straight away first. It is also worth noting that both targets should be scored lost if the second barrel is shot at the first target. Cartridge and gun rules are as for DTL. In the United States, this event is known as Trap Doubles. The scoring system is different, with one point per target killed.

Percy Stanbury shooting at the Double Rise competition, CPSA championship meeting, West London Shooting School, 27 April 1957

Handicap by Distance: another variation of DTL, rarely seen in Britain, but popular in the USA. In this discipline, competitors shoot from different distances

RJH Cooper of Sleaford, Lincolnshire, at the 20th Annual Open Sporting championship of Great Britain combined with the eleventh Open Skeet championship of Great Britain, held at West London Shooting Grounds

AJ 'Jack' Foster at the eighth British Open Skeet, 23 September 1949, West London Shooting Grounds

A British grand prix for OT at North Wales Shooting School, in the late 1980s

depending on their registered handicap. In the United States, the best shots retreat to the 27-yard line which is a real test of skill—and still they manage 100-straights on occasion. In Britain, the best shots go back only to 23 yards, with A class shooting from 21, B from 19 and C from 17 yards. Each squad is formed from the same class. Scores are not registered for averages but the handicaps are based on the current classification. In Britain, Handicap is a two-shot discipline; in the United States it is always a single-barrel event with a more complex handicap system involving increments of 18in (half yards). A round consists of twenty-five birds. Competitions may be shot over any multiple of this, although hundred-bird shoots are most common. Cartridge and gun rules are as for DTL in Britain, in the USA as for ATA trap.

Olympic Trap (OT, also called Olympic Trench and International Trap): in this challenging discipline, which has full Olympic status, there are five firing points but they are placed in a straight line rather than in an arc. There is a concrete trench 15m in front of the firing points, in which the fifteen traps are concealed and grouped in threes in front of each individual firing position. The traps are set on fixed angles (maximum horizontal angle 45 degrees to either side of the centre line) with varying trajectories. These are set according to a predetermined plan. On the command 'pull', the target may be launched from any one of the three computer-controlled traps. The shooter does not know which of the three traps for his firing point will be released or what the trajectory of the bird will be. Ultimately, everyone gets the same birds in a different order. It is perfectly fair (unlike ABT which has an element of chance).

OT has been developed from the early, high level clay competitions where fifteen traps in five banks of three were hidden behind a screen, later put just below ground level and eventually put in a purpose built trench. OT is demanding shooting, with fast targets being thrown as far as 76m. * Target speeds can exceed 100mph. The discipline offers fifteen speeds, fifteen heights and fifteen horizontal angles. A point is scored for every broken target, two shots may be fired at each and there is no penalty for second-barrel kills.

Competitors in squads of six (one more than in the domestic disciplines discussed above) take it in turns to shoot at targets from each position, before moving to the next stand. A round consists of twenty-five birds. Large competitions may be shot over 125 targets plus a final of twenty-five, or 200 birds plus a final. In the Olympic event, the course of fire is now 125 targets over two days, plus a final. For women, it is seventy-five targets in one day, plus a final. Cartridges may be loaded with no more than 24 grams (with a variance of 'plus 0.5 grams'). Shot size is 2.5mm maximum. Ported barrels may be used only if original to the gun. Olympic Trap is governed internationally by the ISSF.

---

* There have been some changes, most notably, when 24-gram loads were first introduced. Up until 1996, target distance was 75 metres, this changed to 80 metres up until 2000 and went down to 76 metres in 2004

The table of trophies at the 48th annual English open championship. Left-right: Mrs C Lucas, CPSA chairman Charles Lucas and CPSA secretary Peter Page

Universal Trench (UT, also known as Five Trap): this is a simplified version of Olympic Trap but still difficult. Sometimes, the central traps of an OT layout are used for UT. It requires five fixed-trajectory traps and offers five bird speeds, five heights and fifteen angles (corresponding to the five firing positions). 28-gram loads are still permissible. Shot size is 2.5mm maximum. Ported barrels may be used only if original to the gun. FITASC is the official governing body.

Automatic Trap: this discipline, governed by the ISSF, was invented in the early 1970s. It uses a single horizontal and vertically oscillating trap placed 15m in front of the firing points. The targets are thrown within an area bounded by angles of not less than 30 degrees and not more than 45 degrees left and right of the imaginary centre line. There used to be a crescent-shaped firing line similar to DTL but now a straight line is employed, so Automatic Trap and Double Trap may be conducted on the same range—the trap may be locked down to provide one of the Double Trap birds.

A round consists of twenty-five birds and competitions are usually shot over a hundred targets. Both Automatic Trap and UT may be pursued as sports in their own right or used as a cheaper form of training for Olympic Trap. Maximum squad size, as in OT, is six. Cartridges must be loaded with no more than 24 grams in France. Maximum shot size is 2.5mm. Automatic Trap offers good sport because the trap oscillates in two planes. Some criticise it because, unlike OT, there is variation in the targets presented to shooters and consequently an element of chance that cannot be controlled. I think that this is its particular appeal, however. Automatic is a fast and exciting Trap discipline.

Automatic Ball Trap (ABT). This is, essentially, the same discipline as Automatic Trap but governed by the CPSA in the UK. The CPSA has now adopted the ISSF plan for a straight firing line. The only significant difference is that you may use 28-gram loads for the CPSA version, but 24 grams for ISSF's original.

Double Trap is one of the most demanding forms of clayshooting. It was developed by Konny Wirnhier for the UIT as a means of making Olympic shotgun shooting more interesting for the cameras. His first version had one fixed and one oscillating trap. This did not prove popular with shooters because it resulted in some odd combinations and hence low and inconsistent scores. A Grand Prix was, nevertheless, conducted under this system at the Montecatini ground in Italy—and it was won by Kevin Gill with a score of 80 ex 100.

In Double Trap today there are two fixed traps in front of a straight OT style firing point. Normally DT is shot on an OT layout utilising the centre group of traps—7, 8 and 9. Shooters have to hit a pair of clays thrown simultaneously—they know what birds they will face. Maximum squad size is six. Competitions are shot over 150 birds with six competitors entering a fifty-bird final (making a total of 200). Fifty targets are shot using the left trap and centre traps, fifty using the centre and right traps and final fifty using left and right traps. The fifty-bird final is conducted using right and left traps—the wide pair.

As with Olympic Trap, loads are limited to 24 grams, shot size no larger than 2.5mm. Recently, a variable delay (0-1 second) has been introduced to prevent shooters spot shooting the first bird of the pair. Ported barrels may be used only if original to the gun. The ISSF is the international governing body. While straight rounds have been recorded, there has never been a perfect score in international competition. The best to date is 149 ex 150.

Hunting Clays (sometimes known as Nordic Trap) is a form of Trap shooting popular in Scandinavian countries and is essentially DTL from a gun-down position (as live pigeons were once shot). However, Hunting Clays allows two shots at each target with no penalty for a second barrel kill. I have tried it and enjoyed it. We could make an interesting new game merely by shooting DTL (or ATA trap) with a FITASC start position.

Skeet shooting

ANOTHER POPULAR form of clayshooting is called Skeet. It was developed in about 1915 by three enthusiastic American game shots: Charles E Davies, proprietor of the Glen Rock Kennels in Andover, Massachusetts, his son Henry and friend William Foster. They sought a way to practise their shotgun marksmanship out of season and came up with the idea of shooting 'round the clock' by positioning a single clay pigeon trap on the edge of a 25-yard radius circle, divided into hours like a clock face. The trap was at twelve and threw its birds towards six. The game was to move positions and thus 'shoot around the clock', firing two shots from each 'hour' and leaving one cartridge for a shot from the middle (the genesis of station 8). In doing this, a wide variety of angles were encountered and any flaw in the shooters' technique revealed.

Good idea though this was, the development of Skeet was not without problems. The story goes that the chicken farmer next door complained of shot falling on his birds (although a new property development nearby is also sometimes mentioned), so Davies together with Davies junior and Foster cut their full circle in half and added an extra trap, thus reducing the danger area considerably. When one trap was subsequently raised to increase the variation, Skeet almost as we know it was born. In 1923, the radius of the circle was reduced to 20 yards.

However, the game still lacked a name. This was provided by a Mrs Gertrude Hurlbutt, a Montana housewife. Foster was a contributor to *The National Sportsman* magazine and, in 1926, wrote an article describing the rules of the new game. The magazine sponsored a major competition to finally give it a name. Mrs Hurlbutt came up with Skeet, a Scandinavian word for shooting. Hers was the best of 10,000 entries and earned her US$100, a handy sum in 1926. With a catchy name and a sound basic system, the sport took off.

The first straight round was recorded in 1926 by Mr HM Jackson Jr, of Garner, North Carolina. In 1931, a rule was introduced (later withdrawn in the United States and Britain) insisting on a gun-down starting position. The rules, as revised in January 1934, stated:

> The shooter shall not raise his gun to his shoulder to shoot until the target is seen in the air. When ready to shoot he shall take his position at the shooting station in an informal field position. This position shall be defined as one in which the referee, standing at least 10ft directly to the side of the shooter, from which he shoots, can see some part of the stock of the gun below or behind any part of the shooter's arm; and that in which no part of the stock of the gun shall be closer to the shoulder of the shooter than the width of the referee's hand. Shoulder in this case is construed to mean the area covered by the butt of the gun when the gun is in actual shooting position.

The rules added that, on calling for the target the bird might be released anytime 'within an indefinite period not to exceed seconds'. This was another rule later withdrawn from American and English Skeet but which is still a feature of the Olympic discipline.

In 1936, after some lobbying, both traps—the high and low house, as they are called—were set to throw their birds at a slight outwards angle for safety reasons (with a crossing point 6 yards out from station 8). Previously, shooters had been showered with bits when shooting stations 1, 7 & 8. The locations of stations 2,3,4,5 & 6 were moved inward in compensation. These changes created the game we shoot today and allowed layouts to be easily place together to form a line of Skeet fields, as might be wanted in a large club or for a major championship.

Joe Wheater in action at the British Open Skeet in 1949. He went on to win the Lord Chesham Cup

The first national championship, under the old rules, was held at Cleveland, Ohio, in the summer of 1935. There were 113 entrants. The new system was adopted at the Great Eastern Championships at Lordship, Connecticut, in the summer of 1936 and officially confirmed at the national championships in September of the same year. The original National Skeet Shooting Association held its last tournament in Syracuse in 1942. The war intervened, but Skeet shooting as a means of training pilots and gunners continued. Many famous shots signed up and spent the duration passing on their skills. In 1946, a new NSSA was formed with money borrowed from the NRA. A championship was held at Indianapolis that year and there has been one every year since.

This is taken from Bob Nichols' *Skeet And How To Shoot It* published by Greenberg, New York, 1939:

> Skeet has come a long way since a relative handful of us started shooting the game back in 1926. In that year, a small group of us living in the metropolitan New York, started the Valhalla Skeet Club—the third Skeet club organised in the United States. To show any interest at all in Skeet at that time meant that you were a field shot, a hunter. We came out to shoot Skeet dressed in hunting clothes. We used the same guns that we carried in the field. At the time there was no such thing as a so-called Skeet gun. Curiously enough, though we didn't suspect it at the time, the game of Skeet was to considerably revise and improve the American field gun.
>
> …the special Skeet gun of today can be as weighty as a duck gun without interfering with the shooter's skill. We are called upon to bear the weight of the heavier type of special Skeet gun only during the shooting function. Therefore, added gun-weight is no particular disadvantage. Indeed to the shooter who might otherwise be sensitive to recoil, the heavy gun noticeably absorbs recoil that otherwise might result in bruised flesh and battered nerves.
>
> Compared to the modern Skeet club, we were a motley crew back there in 1926. Our equipment was almost Spartan in its crude simplicity. Two flimsy traps threw targets, one mounted on a rickety platform 10ft above the ground, the other slightly above ground level. The traps were entirely exposed, enclosed by no such structure as the modern trap house and the trap loader was protected only by a sheet of corrugated iron nailed up in front of him. Incidentally, we took turns at functioned as 'trap boys'. Also, the trap loader was the puller… Skeet shooters still call 'Pull' for the hi-trap and 'Mark' for the lo-trap target. It was necessary, of course, to have two different calls back in 1926. This was the only way the 'trap boys' could understand which target meant to be thrown.'[118]

Skeet in Britain

SKEET WAS brought to this country only a year after it was officially named in the States. Its introduction on this side of the Atlantic coincided with a revival of interest in clayshooting. Robert Churchill was an early enthusiast and may have been one of those responsible for bringing it here. He had watched and been impressed by Skeet at Alton, Illinois, in the 1920s.[119] The first documentary reference to Skeet in England that I can find is in the *Shooting Times* of 1 October 1927.

In a letter written by the Secretary of the Waltham Abbey Gun Club, CB Bass, the basic principles are brought to the attention of readers. The Rules of Skeet are published in 12 November issue and, on 19 November, Bass goes into more detail in another letter to *Shooting Times*. This was immediately reprinted in the Nobel Industries publication *Clay Target Shooting* and indicates the determination of ICI to popularise the sport:

> Dear Sir, Since my letter appeared in your issue... it has been interesting to read the various comments from other correspondents. From the nature of the inquiries it would appear that further information is sought after and, in this connection, I understand that the Clay Pigeon Department of Nobel Industries Ltd will shortly be issuing some instructions and advice on the subject. In the first place it should be clearly understood that this form of shooting is distinctly different from that obtained with the automatic trap... 'Skeet' provides sporting shots in a confined area, which is a good substitute for those shooting men who are unable to pay a visit to some of the well-known shooting schools. Competitions can be arranged, but the shooting is naturally slower than under automatic trap conditions. Two trappers are employed and these go forward and reload the traps while the shooter with the gun open moves to the next station. Two shots are fired from each station, 'A' trap being released first in each instance. Only one cartridge is allowed in the gun at a time. It will be remembered that a few years ago Mr R Kelland introduced something of a similar nature [see Sporting]... This differed from 'Skeet' chiefly in two ways, namely the side traps were continually being swung to a different angle by the trappers, while the firing marks were those used for firing over the automatic trap. Where an automatic trap already exists a 'Skeet' ground can be laid out in practically the same area... Positions nos 1 and 7 undoubtedly provide the easiest shooting and no 8 the most intricate. In fact, at the moment, we do not recommend the use of the no 8 mark. The experienced shooting man will appreciate that shots taken from the no 4 mark are difficult, as the bird from each trap presents a direct crossing shot and a fair amount of practice is necessary before the correct allowance is made... most shots are taken at fairly close range... the ordinary field gun is ideal for this sport... from the interest already shown it seems fairly safe to assume that 'Skeet' will appeal to the game shot for 'out-of-season' practice and many Skeet fields will undoubtedly be laid out during the coming year. As suggested by Mr [Robert] Churchill, we hope that the movement will develop so as to justify the formation of a 'Skeet' league.[120]

FY Moore of Twickenham, winner of the British Open Skeet in 1936

In the summer of 1928, ICI began to distribute a pamphlet entitled *Practise Shooting on Private Estates*, which included instructions on setting up a Skeet layout. It even offered to send representatives to choose sites and help set out Skeet fields. This early propagandising continued well into the 1930s. In July 1935, for example, the company took out a double page spread in the then popular periodical *Game & Gun*. The headline was: 'Skeet—the Sporting Practice for GAME SHOTS'. It says:

> Skeet is a form of Clay Pigeon sport especially designed for those who feel that gameshooting is the only worthwhile type of shooting. Until now, the inanimate bird has made little appeal to the man who is used to shooting at live game, but many game shots who have tried Skeet have been impressed by the fact that the same skill is required for it as for gameshooting. This advertisement appeals to game shots to try Skeet, in the firm conviction that they will find it a splendid auxiliary to gameshooting, an excellent form of practice and a good sport in itself.

The advertisement describes the equipment and layout required:

> Two single rise traps, 40 yards apart, one of them 10ft above ground level and the other 3ft above, so that the birds are thrown over the opposite trap-house to fall 15 to 20 yards beyond (the birds would be outwardly angled as in the USA soon after). Seven firing stands at points round a semi-circle, of which the line between the traps is the straight side, provide the shooter with incoming, going-away and crossing birds in singles and pairs at varying heights and angles. Real practice is provided under conditions similar to field conditions but in a restricted area.

Game & Gun also gives a valuable list of the venues for Skeet shooting in England circa 1935. These included Waltham Abbey, Barnet (Boss & Co), Crayford (Churchill's), Northwood (Holland & Holland), Ruislip (James Purdey & Sons), Barnet Gate (Westley Richards), Greenford (West London Shooting Grounds), Salisbury, Hull, Bristol (George Gibbs), Chapel-en-le-Frith in Derbyshire, Birmingham (Westley Richards), Oxford (J Venables), Bridge of Cally in Perthshire, Glasgow (Alex Martin) and Lancaster (W Atkinson & Sons). It is notable

Nigel Foster, 12, of London, who was the youngest competitor in the colt's event at the Open Skeet Championship and Annual Open Sporting in 1952

that so many gunmakers were involved and I suspect that they must have seen Skeet not only as interesting game but as a means of boosting business.

A diagram of a Skeet layout was also included in the 1938 ICI publication *Gunning Without Game*. The old English rules as published in the same booklet make interesting reading. For single targets only one cartridge was allowed. The shooting position was a 3ft circle immediately behind the firing point. The starting position was gun-down with the toe of the butt 'below the elbow' of the trigger arm. By assuming this position, the shooter signified his readiness and the bird would be released within three seconds. I still think this a good rule—more interesting than gun-up shooting and not as awkward as the artificially low Olympic start.

No definite distance was laid down within which birds should be shot,

Courses of fire

English Skeet
- Station 1: high house single, low house single, double (shooting high house first)
- Station 2: as station 1
- Station 3: high house single, low house single
- Station 4: high house single, low house single, double (shooter must nominate first target to be shot, ie 'high' or 'low')
- Station 5: high single, low single
- Station 6: high single, low single, double (low house first)
- Station 7: low single, high single, double (low house first)

The first target missed must be repeated (whether it is a single or one of a pair). This is called the option target. If all targets have been shot, the final bird is an 'option' from station 7, the shooter choosing 'high' or 'low' by nomination before calling 'pull'.

American Skeet
As English Skeet, except no double is shot at station 4. Instead, the centre station, station 8, is employed. The high house bird is shot first, then the low house. If all the targets have been broken, the final bird is a repeat from the low house.

Olympic Skeet
- Station 1: high house single, double (high house first)
- Station 2: as station 1
- Station 3: high house single, double (high house first)
- Station 4: high house single, low house single, two doubles (high house first, then low house first)

although it was suggested 'that all targets should be shot at when nearly over the midway point between the two houses'. A round was twenty birds, fourteen singles on stations 1-7 and three doubles taken from stands 2, 4 and 6.

Yet another interesting early English reference to Skeet—and one reinforcing the idea that the activity provided practice for game shots—is contained in the Holland & Holland catalogue for 1936, which notes in a feature section on its 'New Badminton School of Shooting' at Duck's Hill, Northwood, Middlesex—the location of the Holland & Holland Shooting School since 1932:

> 'Skeet' Shooting—is a form of clay bird shooting very popular abroad, especially in America. It enables the shooter, by moving a few yards to fixed positions on the arc of a circle, to practise a variety of shots coming from different angles.

This was sensible enough, but it is notable that the British seemed to find it much harder than the Americans to accept clayshooting of any sort as end in itself. It was often seen as a poor relation in influential quarters. FM McFarland made the point in the 1960s that he thought that the policy of pushing clayshooting to those who had gameshooting was mistaken. 'Are we trying to sell bicycles to Rolls Royce owners?' he noted, 'and clay pigeon shooting to those people who have plenty of the proper stuff to shoot at instead of trying to interest the artisan and town dweller who may possibly never shoot at game in their whole lives, but who could make extremely useful clay pigeon shooters?'[121]

Today, Skeet is shot to a variety of rules, including those of the English CPSA and the American NSSA. At the time of writing, there are more than 1,000

- Station 5: low house single, double (low house first)
- Station 6: low house single, double (low house first)
- Station 7: double (low house first)
- Station 8: high house single, low house single

Olympic Skeet (men): targets are released to a total of twenty-five per round. Targets are launched from high and low houses on fixed trajectories at fixed speeds. Shooters rotate through the eight stands. The target is released within three seconds of the command and only one shot is allowed per target. The gun can be shouldered after the call is given and the target has appeared. There are 125 targets over two days.

Olympic Skeet (women): as for men, save that the course of fire is seventy-five targets that may be shot in one day.

Maximum loads
The maximum load for English Skeet is 28 grams. For NSSA Skeet, 32 grams are allowed. Olympic Skeet stipulates a maximum 24-gram payload. Both Olympic and English Skeet now allow shot sizes up to no 6 to be used—though why anyone should want to use no 6 shot for Skeet shooting is a mystery to me.

Skeet Doubles
This is Skeet but with pairs shot on each station. Doubles are shot to both English and NSSA rules. A round of Skeet Doubles usually consists of fifty birds. The first 'half round' being twenty-four (twelve pairs) and the second, twenty-six (thirteen pairs) in that order. First half:
- Station 1,2,3 & 4: double high bird first
- Station 5,6,7—and returning—6,5 & 4: double low bird first
- Station 3 & 2: double high bird first
- Second half: As above plus final double on station 1

Skeet shooting facilities affiliated to the NSSA in the United States, with an estimated two million shooters participating in the sport annually; there is also an Olympic version of the sport.

English and American Skeet are similar. The gun may start pre-mounted or not. The main difference between English and American Skeet is that, in the latter, the centre station, station 8, is used. American Skeet also has special competitions for small gauge guns (20, 28 and .410) and combined events for 12, 20, 28 and .410.

In Olympic Skeet (formerly known as ISU Skeet), the birds are significantly faster than the American and English domestic disciplines and the gunstock must start in a low and, until mastered, awkward position. A cloth band 30mm by 250mm must be positioned so that the bottom edge is level with the crest of the hip bone. The gun must touch the body, with the toe of the stock on or below this band. Just to make it even more interesting, there is a delay of up to three seconds after you call for the bird. As with American Skeet, station 8 is used. Maximum squad size in Olympic Skeet is six. There are a few other quirks. With the exception of stations 1 and 8, the gun may not be mounted for a pre-shot trial mount. During single-target shooting, when the gun is loaded with two cartridges, the gun must not be broken between shots (also a rule in English Skeet).

Like Olympic Trap and Double Trap, Olympic Skeet is governed internationally by the ISSF. The first person to score 200 straight at this discipline and be formally recognised to have done so by the international governing body was N Durnev of the USSR in October 1962.

Sporting

CHALLENGING AND popular though Trap and Skeet are, the most popular and arguably the most challenging form of clayshooting in Britain is Sporting clays. This sport—now spreading all over the world—developed from the type of shooting that was offered at the great English shooting schools of the late Victorian and Edwardian eras as a means of perfecting gameshooting skills. At first intended just as means of practising, it gradually established itself as a sport in its own right.

By the end of the nineteenth century, when most of the great gunmaking firms had their own shooting schools or practice ranges, they were already offering what we would recognise as Sporting targets. Cogswell & Harrison's 'Shooting Park' at Colnbrook had Sporting targets as early as 1888. In 1896, in *The Badminton Magazine*, Sir Ralph Payne-Gallwey reported on 'A visit to a modern shooting school', Holland & Holland, where birds were shot at single and double rise, pheasant and partridge were simulated and even a mechanical rabbit was on offer.

Although there was some proto-Sporting shooting previously, such as the occasional event at the Middlesex Gun Club that combined a trap bird with a crosser from a tower (a format that may well have been repeated elsewhere), serious Sporting clay competition did not take place in Britain until well after the First World War.

In 1921, Nobel Industries produced a booklet entitled *The Versatile Clay Bird*, which set down the system of simulated gameshooting then in use at the West London Shooting School. Although not specifically concerned with competition, it included sections on running rabbits (which were shown being bowled down a path by hand), driven partridge, driven grouse, pheasants and 'variations'. It explained these as follows:

Top Sporting shot Countess Orssich in action at West London Shooting School

Rabbit trap from Skeet tower

Early mechanical rabbit trap

There are many directions of bird flight which are extremely puzzling to the shooter and most of them can be imitated by a blend of ingenuity and patience. The skimming bird, closely hugging the ground on a down-hill course, is one of them. The bird doing the same up-hill is another. The pheasant starting from ground level and climbing to the tree-tops is yet another… A fourth is the high overhead bird which has passed the line and must be shot at after a right about turn has been made… The use of the second barrel when the first has missed presents a pretty problem in gun manipulation…

It goes on to talk of 'registering progress':

There is much to be said for standardising whatever conditions the private individual may decide to reproduce at home, because, apart from the interest attaching to friendly competitions, the whole thing can be better held together by observing some system embodying formality and order. Wherever firearms are concerned, discipline of some sort is desirable. The various grades of skill can be brought into harmony by allotting free kills by way of handicap and also by varying the distance of the shooting position from the trap.

The first English Amateur Sporting Championship, organised by *Shooting Times*, was held in May 1925 at the grounds of the Albemarle Shooting School at Worcester Park, near Wimbledon. It was confined to amateurs only. No member of 'the gun, ammunition or allied trades' was eligible to compete and a gun-down rule was enforced. Seventy-two attended on the first day, which was considered a great success. The competition consisted, amongst other stands, of a ten-bird 'walk-up', five 'driven grouse' doubles, twenty 'rocketing pheasants' and ten birds from an automatic (auto-angling) trap. The laurels and the very large *Daily Telegraph* Championship Cup, a miniature replica of it and a silver cigarette case, were taken by CW Mackworth-Praed (63 ex 80). FG Horne of Reigate was second on 61, with Percy Stanbury third on 60.

On 15 August 1925, *Shooting Times* published a detailed article entitled 'Clay target shooting for game shots'. And, the following month, *Clay Target Shooting*, the magazine issued by Nobel Industries, noted on page 2:

The bold and highly successful venture of holding a competitive meeting at a fully organised shooting school is well-nigh certain to be repeated in the future, probably in more places than one, following the happy experiences of the initial attempt. The idea certainly does not confine itself to the highly equipped metropolitan establishments, since every country gunmaker's practice ground contains traps so mounted as to produce the conditions of driven game. Towers, partridge platforms, ground traps set amidst rough covert, grouse

West London Shooting School today

Sporting in the USA

AMERICANS TOOK an interest in the style of shooting seen at British shooting schools in the late Victorian era. Annie Oakley attended Charles Lancaster's establishment in the 1880s and was impressed by it. The members of the US international team of 1901 participated in a form of Sporting contest at the Middlesex Gun Club as noted earlier. They found it interesting and challenging. There were, moreover, a number of early attempts to introduce Sporting-like shooting, or features of the shooting school such as the 'walk up', to the United States. Sometime circa 1914, for example, the Rumson Country Club of Red Bank, New Jersey, installed a walk up. The man responsible was the club's golf professional, Mr WW Green. The facility was described thus:

> Real brush shooting is indulged in by means of a pathway about 60 yards long through the scrub oak, young pine and bushes of all sorts, with traps concealed in the brush that throw clay targets unexpectedly at a great variety of angles. As in field work in England and Scotland, the gunner has a beater, but he follows the gunner instead of preceding him and springs the trap as he walks behind the marksman down the pathway. The targets can be sent up in singles, doubles and coveys and the traps are set so that the gunner gets a full variety of shots—straightaway, incomers, quartering, crossing, high, low, in fact every possible direction. Another innovation is the placing of a series of traps in the top of the water tower, near the club-house, from which the clay targets are sent whirling down after the manner of wild ducks coming into decoys and the speed of these targets furnishes a real test of the gunner's skill.[123]

Abercrombie & Fitch, the famous New York City gun shop, opened a shooting school along British lines at Bayside, Long Island, after the First World War. The facility included 'several hundred' traps, a 120ft high tower, a number of other towers and a walk up. Lawrence B Smith wrote in 1938:

> When a tour of the school has been completed, one has the chance to fire at practically every type of shot to be met with in the field. It is evident that such practice is invaluable, but unfortunately beyond the reach of most American gunners. Thus one must fall back on the more orthodox types of trapshooting which may be made to serve the purpose if intelligently and purposefully pursued.[124]

butts, and in sundry favoured spots true hillside shooting—whatever is available can be mosbilised on competitive lines. Favouring such a use of existing establishments is the fact that during the early summer months the additional business would be welcome; moreover, such meetings would extend the list of regular patrons.

Not surprisingly, the English Amateur Sporting Championship was repeated in 1926 and became an institution. In 1927, Nobel published its *Handbook on Clay Target Shooting*, which included the Kelland system of Sporting as first tried on the ground of Westley Richards by Mr R Kelland, secretary of the Edgbaston Gun Club. The handbook noted: 'Until recently it has not been possible for sportsmen to obtain this style of shooting except by paying a visit to a shooting school'. The Kelland system—the progenitor of Compak Sporting—was designed to be set up on a DTL style, five-place firing point. It consisted of 'an auto [angling] trap positioned at 16 yards in conjunction with eight single rise traps'. Two of these were positioned 35 yards to the left and two 25 yards right—and concealed by corrugated iron sheet—to provide Skeet-like crossers. Two more were placed left and right, 60 yards forward, to provide driven birds. The idea was to give the Guns unpredictable targets. The handbook continues:

> It is not suggested that attempts should be made to throw targets from all these positions

Sporting re-crossed the Atlantic in about 1980. It had notable help from the Remington Arms Company, Bob Brister, the Dryke family, English clay guru Chris Cradock and Orvis. Remington—which appears to have been the first company to express a serious interest in Britain's favourite shotgun sport—produced a 'Shooting Development Proposal' in March 1980. It considered how the interesting and, to Remington, new discipline of Sporting clays might be promoted in America. In April, Remington circulated another discussion document. This one considered more specifically how Sporting might appeal to US hunters. In July 1980, US shotgunning guru Bob Brister wrote an article in the immensely popular periodical *Field & Stream* entitled 'At last, a clay game for hunters'. This attracted great interest. In the same month, Remington came up with a 'three-year plan' to get Sporting started in America. At the end of August 1980, it announced the first invitation competition, at the Lordship shooting grounds in Connecticut. Things moved quickly from this point on. In September, Bob Brister departed for England, where he had arranged to meet Chris Cradock. The first Sporting shoot in the USA, sponsored by Remington, also took place in September 1980. It was a modest thirty-target event with ninety participants including US Shooting Team members Matt Dryke and Dean Clark. Other notables were Dick Dietz, Ted Burke, Fred Collins, Ed Vieux, Dan Lytle, P Therault, Alex Stott and Don Bratger. Shortly afterwards, at Brister's suggestion, Remington invited Chris Cradock to visit its own 'Remington Farms' shooting ground to advise on setting up a British-style Sporting layout. He arrived there in April 1981 and, as he noted in several conversations with me, had a great deal of fun. On his return home, Chris arranged for two Farey SC traps to be shipped to Remington. In May 1981, the firm printed 'an information sheet' on 'Sporting clays'. In June, it approved a sixteen-page 'brochure' written by Bob Brister.

According to Brister, the first major US tournament was the North American Field Shooting Championship at the Sunnydell Shooting Grounds in Washington State in 1980. Chuck Dryke, father of Olympian, Matt, set this up. Matt, however, kept up his interest in the new sport, an interest he maintains to this day. Brister and others have also noted the major role of the Orvis company in establishing Sporting Clays in the US in the early 1980s.

in one competition, as this would entail too many operators, but at least three positions could be used on each occasion and changed round from time to time, so as to give the whole variety of flights and angles.[122]

The Sporting Championships remained at the Albermarle ground for five years, save in 1928 when it was split between the Albermarle and the West London Shooting Ground, which was then at Perivale. It moved to the new West London Ground at Northolt in 1932. In 1938, it became a hundred-bird event and, the same year, ICI produced its booklet *Gunning Without Game*. This extended the formal discussion of what we would now call Sporting and also provided an interesting section on early English Skeet shooting which, it suggested, fell somewhere between DTL and the type of shooting offered by shooting schools.

Sporting clay pigeon continued after the Second World War, but it did not really begin to take off again in the UK until the 1960s. As late as 1964 FC McFarland wrote: 'At the time that this… is being written, clayshooting is progressing throughout the United Kingdom and Ireland. It is not possible to say that it is booming. Unfortunately we have still not found the right recipe to make it boom.'

Trapper at the 1948 British Open Sporting Championship, Northolt, Middlesex

Happily, clayshooting—and Sporting in particular—expanded rapidly throughout the 1970s and 1980s. During these years, a huge number of small weekend shoots appeared as well as major sponsored events offering rich prizes, including guns, watches and even motor cars.

In Sporting, a wide variety of targets are presented to the shooter. The basic idea, not always adhered to, is that they should simulate the flight of live quarry species. Thus, on a typical Sporting layout, you might be confronted by 'crossing pigeon', 'springing teal', 'driven grouse', 'driven partridge', 'high pheasant' and, the bête noir of many a Sporting shot, 'bolting rabbit'.

In competition, nearly all the targets will be presented as pairs. These may be simultaneous pairs, where both birds are released simultaneously from one or two traps; report pairs, where the second bird is only released after the first shot is fired (again one or two traps may be used); or following pairs, where the second target is released from the same trap as soon as possible after the first has been launched. Pairs are an even greater challenge when the timing required for each bird is grossly or subtly different.

Although the great majority of birds in competition are presented as pairs, occasionally a hard single is offered with 'full use of gun' meaning that two shots may be fired at the same bird without penalty.

The fun of Sporting shooting is that the targets are so variable. Sporting is one of the most demanding clay disciplines; runs of 100 straight are fairly common at Trap and Skeet but rare indeed at Sporting. As yet, Sporting is not an Olympic discipline as Skeet and Trap are in some of their forms. It is not beyond the bounds of possibility that it might become one.

The three most common forms of Sporting are English, American and International (or FITASC). English Sporting allows any start position for the gun, as American Sporting now does. In International, the stock must be 25cm below an imaginary line drawn along the top of the shoulders along their axis.

Miss June Horsfall at the Sporting Championship in May 1948 at Northolt

I have heard this described by one FITASC referee as equating to a starting position with the 'stock below the nipple'. Another feature of FITASC is that there is greater target variety than in English Sporting.

As far as cartridges are concerned, you must use 28 grams or less in English Sporting. Permissible shot sizes are nos 6-9. American rules allow 32 grams and those for International permitted a whopping 36 grams, although a change to 28 grams was brought in January 2005. This may not go down too well with hard-shouldered French competitors who, traditionally, have favoured heavy loads.

A registered English Sporting competition might consist of anything from twenty-five to a hundred targets. Registered events—competitions at which scores are centrally collated by the CPSA—are usually shot over a hundred birds. A shoot might present any of the targets already mentioned. At official events, no more than 30 per cent of the birds can be non-standard clays. The trend in English Sporting is to make targets harder and to reduce the number of birds shot at each stand.

Not so long ago, you could be assured of being presented with five pairs at each stand, with the possible exception of the high tower. Today, there is greater variety and frequently you will be called up to shoot only three or four pairs at a particular stand. The best course designers know that they do not need distance to fool a shooter. Angles, deceptive speed, and variety are the best way to make things more interesting, not 60-yard midis.

Pool Shoots are a popular event at many English Sporting shoots. Typically, this will consist of ten really hard targets (often long crossers) in simultaneous pair or on report presented from one firing point. There are variations on the theme, however. The number of targets may be reduced or increased. Sometimes there may be a number of firing positions. Payout—and pools are all about cash prizes—may be paid 'on the sheet' or as a percentage of call entries (typically 50 per cent). The most imaginative pool I have seen—'the rat shoot'—involved mini targets being rolled down a bank propelled by nothing but gravity. All entrants had to use the same .410. The hardest was a long bird shoot in the States where the target was presented nearly 100 yards from the firing point.

Flushes and flurries are popular events at major shoots and country fairs. A flush may involve one or more shooters being presented with a sequence of driven targets. Reloading quickly is a required skill (as is teamwork, when applicable). In a flurry, one or more shooters are presented with a predetermined number of clays sent out in any order. Again, fast reloading is all-important.

Walk ups, called 'quail walks' in the USA, are never seen in competition in the UK today. Walk ups were either competitions in themselves, stages in a competition, or merely an interesting form of practice for the gameshooter. In a walk up, the gun walks up a path and is presented with targets of opportunity. One of the most famous walk ups used to take place at the West London Shooting School. It was a facility of the school but also used in the British Open Sporting competition when it was held for many years at West London. It was about as close as you could get to shooting in the field. The trap pullers would always try and catch you on the wrong foot and you always finished thinking what an interesting Sporting challenge it was.

Walk ups have disappeared in competition in the UK for two reasons. They are slow to operate (a major factor when a large number of entries must be processed). And, it is hard to ensure that each participant gets exactly the same shots in a walk up. These comments notwithstanding, many would welcome their return.

International Sporting or **FITASC** (*Fédération Internationale de Tir aux Armes Sportives de Chasse*) is a 'squadded' discipline which typically involves shooting rounds of twenty-five birds over a number of different layouts with the same group of shooters (the squad). Smaller shoots may take place over 150 targets but, at major events, 200 targets are presented to each competitor over two or three days. More birds may be shot in a final as well.

There are two systems for shooting FITASC. The traditional system—which is still popular in Britain—involves six guns shooting a round on a layout to which no-one else has access. They shoot their targets from three or four posts (stands) with four or five traps in operation. As the squad moves from post to post on a layout, they shoot at the same targets but the angle presented to them is different. Each layout will involve twenty-five targets. The new system for FITASC has been designed to speed up competition and allow for more shooters. It is used in selection shoots in the UK, most notably in the European and World Championships. It is more like English Sporting—and has been criticised as such. In this case, there are four layouts, each with four stands in line but positioned about 150-200 yards apart. Again, there might be four of five traps but the big

The 1952 British Open Sporting champion, ET Peacock

Three-time World FITASC champion and owner of High Lodge Shooting Ground in Suffolk John Bidwell, using a Blaser F3 shotgun, with a stock designed according to pinciples laid down by my book Gunfitting: The Quest for Perfection

difference is that four squads may be in action at once.

The procedure for shooting the targets is similar with both systems. From each stand you shoot the birds as singles with full use of gun. After every squad member has done this, the same targets are presented in combination as pairs. There are no shooting cages in International Sporting. Because of this, the typically challenging targets and because of the relatively the high cost of entries, FITASC is not to be recommended for novices. Nevertheless, many regard it as the ultimate form of Sporting.

There are also a number of more recently developed sporting disciplines.

Five Stand devised by ex-patriot Scotsman, Raymond Foreman, uses a similar firing point to Trap shooting but with cages. It is an official discipline in the USA where it is licensed to the NSCA and now called NSCA Five Stand.

Compak Sporting is similar to Five Stand but usually with four stands and slightly different rules. Compak is seen quite widely in Europe. It is governed as an international discipline by FITASC. There have been attempts to rationalise Five Stand and Compak at the time of writing. A recent championship in the USA was conducted under FITASC rules. The UK distributor for Browning and Winchester guns, BWM, also sponsors its own version of the Compak game, which it calls Browning Compact Sporting.

Pro-Sporting has a single firing point with multiple traps to the front, presenting twenty or twenty-five typically quite hard birds. It is often seen as a side event at larger events in the UK.

Sportrap came formally into being in November 1999 when the CPSA announced the creation of a new discipline based on a combination of Compak and American Five Stand. At each stand, a single, a report pair and a simultaneous pair are engaged. Full use of gun is allowed on the singles. Shooting cages must be 1.2m wide to accommodate wheelchairs—a thoroughly sensible rule for a Sporting discipline ideally suited to the disabled.

There were rumours some years ago that another Sporting discipline, along the lines of Five Stand and Compak, was being created by the UIT for introduction into the Olympics. Whatever final form the new discipline takes, there is much demand from shooters for this style of event. These disciplines have the great advantage that a very wide variety of challenging targets may be presented in a limited area.

Birdbrain is a computer-based shoot invented by Raymond Foreman. A Birdbrain unit might be used to present Sporting targets in unpredictable order to a line of guns arranged as in Five Stand or Compak. There are three levels of difficulty. In the first, only singles are thrown; in the second, three singles and a pair; and, in the third, one single and two pairs. Birdbrain is conducted much like Trap shooting. The clever thing about the Birdbrain computer is that it ensures each gun receives exactly the same combinations of targets in each position but in an order which the individual cannot predict. At the end of the shoot, the computer, aided by a human

Former England Sporting team captain Arnie Palmer

scorer, generates a score sheet. Birdbrain is the original form of Five Stand but the NSCA, who now control Five Stand, has dispensed with random target launching.

Make-a-Break is another discipline invented by Raymond Foreman. It involves eight autotraps and a single firing point. Each competitor shoots ten report pairs. The first target scores one point; the second, two points and so on. Targets become harder as their value rises.

This is a clay target game where a competitor can gain ground on his opponent. Intensity accelerates dramatically through the last four 'bonus' pairs. Quick thinking and a bit of gambling are required.[125]

Supersport, invented in the USA, is a sophisticated walk up that involves between fifteen and thirty automatic traps on a large course. A computer is used to control target release and degrees of severity may be selected before shooting. The shooter wears a transmitter, which fires the traps via sensors en route. In its most sophisticated form, a lifelike noise of the particular simulated species will precede its launch. Battues could present problems.

Trap House Sporting Clays (pictured, left) in the USA is a specially-built, two-tier trailer, making the shoot mobile, which incorporates fifteen manual traps and requires two energetic trappers. Thirteen firing points are set up around the 'trap house' unit, which offers a surprising variety of angles in a limited space. I tried this shoot in California in 1998 and was most impressed. The trappers looked as if they had earned their money at the end of the day, though.

Modern Sporting

by Mike Barnes

SO JUST HOW did Sporting shooting get to where it is now? As clay shooting has developed into very much a sport in its own right, rather than a means of practising for something else (pheasants, partridges etc), so Sporting has become the dominant force. This is the discipline that accounts for as much as 80% or more of all clays shot.

So why is it so popular and when did that popularity start to take a grip?

We can turn the clock back to 1960. While the British Open Sporting Championship was first held in 1925, some thirty-five years later there was clearly a feeling afoot that there was sufficient following to support an English Open, which was duly held for the very first time at Beverley & DGC (which changed its name to East Yorkshire GC the following year). Won by Ted Peacock, who went on to develop a clay target manufacturing business, we don't know how many actually entered.

What is clear is that the entries were thin, with only 35 and 34 taking part at the same venue in the following two years. However from then on it began to creep forward and pass the 100 mark in 1970, when the late David Carpenter won against 110 entries. Within three years its entry had shot up to 212, then at Somerleyton, Suffolk, went up to 363 in 1977 (won by Paddy Howe) and 418 in 1978 (won by Wally Sykes) and 529 in 1979 (won by Brian Wells). Sporting had arrived.

That same year the British Open attracted a reord 810 participants, and a winning score of 92 from Brian Hebditch. It was the first and only time that Holland & Holland had staged the event—up until that point it had been hosted by West London Shooting Ground and, thereafter, with the exception of 1982 and 1986 (West London), it has travelled the country.

Howe, Sykes, Wells and Hebditch meanwhile were dominant shots of that period and this really was the start proper of Sporting shooting as we know it today. They were the Faulds, Digweed and Husthwaite of the period.

This was a time when there was big promotion for the sport. Motor racing ace Jackie Stewart exercised considerable influence through his involvement with his sponsors Eley.

Big sponsorship programmes, notably the Eley Extravaganza which saw events taking place across Europe and a final with an extraordinary prize list, topped by a six-wheeled Range Rover Carmichael, along with half a dozen Land Rovers, Rolex watches galore and a star-studded celebrity occasion with royalty and film stars (Sean Connery and Robert Stack) playing a full part.

The final from North Wales Shooting School was broadcast on prime time BBC TV Grandstand. While it can't lay credit for the boom in the sport, it caught the essence of the time and must have helped. Gamebore launched a rival promotion and there were lots of big sponsored competitions taking place. Wally Sykes won no fewer than three cars in a year—BMW, Opel and Ford Fiesta. It seems unthinkable now, but it happened.

Part of Eley's promotion was the Side-by-Side championship which took place with a series of qualifiers at country fairs around the country. Here clay shooting was placed in front of thousands of people. They could watch; they could have a go. There was no stigma about guns at the time.

Sporting was perfect. A course could be set up which, with a little thought, could cater for a wide range of abilities and also for a big number of people. Similarly, during this period, a lot of village fetes would also feature a clay shoot. In the early days, DTL was the clay shoot of choice at these events but Sporting was always going to prove more popular, for two reasons: it was more likely to appeal to the rough/game shooter and, with three or four stands running simultaneously, it was possible to accommodate many more punters. Incredibly, many small shoots at this time were offering £100 high gun prizes. Some even gave away guns.

This exposure, along with a blossoming club growth, produced an expansion of the sport previously unseen. The 1982 British Open Sporting Championship attracted 1,039 entries to West London. Ten years earlier, there were just 444 at the same venue when Joe Wheater won the last of his record eight British titles.

I had joined *Sporting Gun* soon after its launch in 1978, became its editor a year later and saw the boom take place at first hand. The appeal of Sporting to both organiser and sponsors alike was obvious. It attracted a wide audience and, for participants, the Sporting challenge was then just as it is now: ongoing. Every course is different. Yes, you may be taking part in a competition but it is the challenge of the targets which appeals the most. To hit some targets on a particularly difficult stand is always a thrill and, in Sporting, you can beat a top shot, if only over the targets on that particular stand.

At the magazine we were closely involved with the big Eley promotions. We followed them with the launch of Winchester Clubman and the Browning Masters, both hugely popular and appealing to entirely different audiences. We then joined forces with GMK and Saab for a big Easter Sporting championship.

We sponsored the first Chatsworth Country Fair clay shoot—a forty-bird Sporting competition which was brilliantly laid out by Jim Neville—and we offered a Perazzi for high gun. We had more than 1,000 entries in two days. It was incredible.

Sporting had by now really taken a grip. We ran cruises to Esbjerg Gun Club in Denmark, taking parties of more than 100. *Shooting Magazine*, meanwhile, ran the Winchester Knockout and there were several other one-off sponsorships.

Winchester was a big noise at the time. It had pioneered the introduction of multi-chokes with the Winchester 101 Winchoke. It was an easy gun to shoot and caught on spectacularly. Along with Trap 100 and Trap 200 cartridges, Winchester had a winning formula. It had also signed the right man to use its new gun, in none other than AJ Smith, the charismatic Hampshire farmer— once a GB Olympic Trap team member but now at Sporting with a vengeance. With his new gun, he took all before him, including the World FITASC Sporting Championship.

AJ was also something of a pioneer. He was really the first prominent Sporting shooter to favour 32in barrels and tight chokes, the latter giving him his nickname 'Smoker!' This of course is a barrel length/choke combination now favoured by practically all top Sporting shooters.

Barry Simpson, meanwhile, flew the flag for Beretta, winning the British twice, firstly as an 18 year-old, the European FITASC and the World FITASC when it was held in the UK for the first time. Barry, AJ, Paddy and John Bidwell, who won the World FITASC three times, are all still shooting to a high standard and representing GB in veterans classes, as well as winning shoots outright.

Looking back it was a lot of fun, but many of the shoots were, by today's standards, somewhat primitive. All traps were manual and often subject to great variation of target flightline. Nevertheless, some of the course setters were excellent. Somerleyton hosted the English Open for nine years and these were tremendous shoots.

Mike Reynolds at Mid Norfolk held the British Open on nine occasions achieving a record entry of 1,493 in 1990, topped the following year by John Bidwell's High Lodge (at his old Henham Park ground) with 1,560. That figure has not been topped—not because of a decline in interest but largely due to the huge volume of shoots which are now held. The boom in the sport during the

Wally Sykes receives a gun from Peter Page. Sykes was once asked why he shot competitively. 'For the love of cars,' he replied. He won three cars in a year

1980s might have suggested that there were lots of grounds—but 100 birders were not commonplace.

The British was a big occasion, as it still is, but now there are lots of large shoots and travel has become more of an issue.

Of course, it hasn't all been plain sailing. There was a dip in the early 1980s when the Hungerford tragedy occurred and then appalling events in Dunblane coincided with a sharp dip in the economy. Up until that point, the latter part of the 1980s had seen a huge increase in the use of Sporting clays for corporate entertainment. This was excellent for the shooting grounds and, in many instances, also good for the sport, introducing a host of newcomers.

It was during this period that a new talent emerged. George Digweed, an athletic 22-year-old butcher's son from Hastings, was high gun in the Home International Skeet Championship in 1986. The following year he won the EEC FITASC. Then, in 1989, he really cracked it by winning the ICI World Sporting, a win that opened the floodgates. In 1989, he won no fewer than six titles—British Open, English Open, SAAB, World Professional, World Sporting Jubilee and UK FITASC. Incredible—and he has never stopped winning since, amassing no fewer than 14 world titles.

George has gone from Miroku, to Parker Hale, to Beretta, to Kemen to Perazzi. The one constant factor has been his ability to shoot brilliantly. And he has stuck to Kent ammunition throughout (though Kent was absorbed into Gamebore). It should also be mentioned that, in 1991, he set an English Skeet record which will never be broken. He won the British Open at Kingsferry with 100 straight, plus 375 straight in the shoot-off!

As we moved into the 1990s, Sporting went through a transition. Grounds started to become more sophisticated in what they had to offer. West Midlands Shooting Ground at Hodnet led the way with a fabulous clubhouse and neatly presented grounds and shooting stations. America took Sporting on board. I remember bringing a party of influential founder members of American Sporting Clays over to see Sporting at first hand in the UK. We visited Mid Norfolk, Pennsport, finished at the British Open and then the following year returned to shoot the Beretta World at Apsley.

The Americans were hugely enthusiastic about the sport, which was in its infancy over there. Golf with guns was how they were describing it. Very apt, this was, too.

From the English perspective, with an increase of automatic traps and, later, Claymate, the presentation of targets was indeed becoming much more consistent—and in a manner that was comparable to what could be expected at golf. Shooting schools and clubs have been busy trying to catch up with other facilities. Now there are many grounds with first class clubhouses and excellent presentation in every way. The interest in Sporting targets grows unabated.

When I left *Sporting Gun* I spent three years with Gunmark (now GMK) where we also came up with a new discipline. In conjunction with Mike Reynolds at Mid-Norfolk, we dreamt up Super Sporting. It was intended as a half-way house between English and FITASC in which there was greater target variety than English Sporting but at a much reduced cost from FITASC. These were good shoots but the discipline never caught on a in a big way—again due to cost and the fact that it is slower to shoot, therefore limiting on numbers. But some grounds do still stage Super Sporting competitions from time to time and an annual event at High Lodge is popular. Also during this period at GMK we ran sponsorships with Saab, Ford and Mitsubishi.

Nowadays, it is much more difficult to secure sponsors from outside the sport and the CPSA did well to enjoy the support of Embassy for so long before the tobacco advertising ban put an end to the relationship. Potential sponsors are now being attacked from so many directions, particularly with the dramatic growth in satellite channels—and of course there is some sensitivity about guns. We all know that it's nonsense and that not only are handguns banned, but shotgun certificate holders simply do not commit crime. But it's often hard to get this through to a potential sponsor unless they have first hand experience of the sport.

The CPSA, however, does a good job, a fact reflected by its recent growth in membership to 25,000 and its ambitions not only to grow the sport, but to attract grass roots shooters with a special Clubman Package. Meanwhile, on the competition front, it has staged some excellent events, where the overall standards of performance are higher than ever.

George Digweed remains a huge presence in the game and again won the 2005 English Sporting World Championship in the USA. But the man of the year was undoubtedly Richard Faulds, who first started to turn heads as a fourteen year old. As a junior he won everything—British and English, World and European—and, as a senior, has truly hit the heights following his fifth place in the 1996 Atlanta Olympics with a Double Trap gold medal in Sydney in 2002.

In 2005, the twenty-eight-year-old left hander used his Beretta DT10 and Express Supreme ammunition to devastating effect to win an unrivalled hat-trick of Sporting titles—the British, plus World and European FITASC.

There are others too—in fact too many to mention. The sport is buoyant and the choice of grounds and quality of targets has improved beyond recognition. And though there is no standardisation in the difficulty of targets, shooters tend to go to the grounds which offer the type of targets that they favour.

These are good reasons to believe that Sporting could well become more popular than ever. Its appeal is enduring to all people of all ages—it's a great sport for couples, excellent for youngsters and big for what is now termed the

Wilf Harris Junior (left) and Alan Poskitt, deep in discussion in 1954. Alan is one of few shooters to have honours as a junior, a senior and a veteran

Shooting at Southern Counties, or Blandford as it was known then. Pictured are the competitors at the Dorset Olympic Trench Championship on 11-12 September 1964

grey market: those with more time on their hands. Sporting clay shooting really is a sport for all.

Sporting/Skeet/Trap hybrids

Riverside Skeet uses a Trap-style, five-position firing line with a trap positioned at either end, throwing birds forwards so that they cross at a point about 25 yards ahead of position 3 (centre). The individuals on the line fire at single targets (before doubles are introduced). There is, however, a back-up system so that, if the first gun misses, the next may fire and so on down the line while the target is still in the air. The basic concept is amusing, but backed-up shooting—save at two or three man flushes—seems to encourage the wrong approach unless the second firer is very experienced. It certainly compounds the problems of safety on the firing line.

Modern Skeet is Skeet with vertically oscillating traps. Modern Skeet originated in the US with Ken Gagnon's wonderfully named Quack Sporting Clays. Ken, who for many years worked for the NSSA, wanted to create a game that was less predictable than conventional Skeet and cheaper than Sporting Clays. He has also done something similar on a Trap field—placing an oscillator under a standard trap—to create an ABT-like discipline called Modern Trap, but at far less cost than buying a dedicated 'wobble' trap.

Giant Skeet or **High Tower Skeet** is Skeet-style shooting with birds launched from abnormally high and widely spaced trap houses. Essentially, it is Skeet with two high towers and great for those with the resources who enjoy long crossers.

Andy Castle offered a discipline along these lines at his West London Sporting Targets Club. It used a straight firing line rather than a semi-circle. Two singles and a simultaneous double were shot from each position with a round consisting of twenty targets. The towers were placed about 50 yards apart. The 'low' tower was positioned forward and to the left of station 1; the 'high' tower was positioned to the right and rear of station 5. This created an exceptionally challenging shoot with many long-range targets.

Doc Adams is a game that uses a trap or a combined Skeet and trap field, but only makes use of one forward firing trap-style trap. Shooters fire at single trap birds as for DTL or ATA trap—but they shoot from the Skeet stations 1-7 or spots marked out in imitation of them.

Skrap uses Skeet positions too, but makes use of both Skeet high and low birds and a central trap. It is especially challenging, as birds may fly out of any one of the three traps. To work fairly, the puller must make sure by one means or another that the distribution of hard and easy shots is similar for each participant. A fixed order can also be used, but this is not quite so interesting.

Skratch or **Last Man Standing** is another great game. It has a special charm and drama to it. Each shooter starts with a box of twenty-five shells and no more. Conditions are similar for Doc Adams / Skeet positions, but Trap birds. The excitement mounts because you may not leave station 1 until you have broken your bird. It might take one shell or half a dozen or more. It is quite an achievement to get to station 7. Then the tension really builds.

If two or more shooters make it, they then go backwards through the stations 6, 5, 4, 3, 2, 1 until the winner is determined. You may handicap this event by removing one or more cartridges from the better shooters' boxes. A little thought can really make this an evenly-matched contest.

Crazy Quail, a Sporting game seen in the US in the 1980s, was shot as a mini-competition or as part of a Sporting layout. Its novel feature was a rotating trap in a pit. This moved a full 360 degrees. The shooter stood 16-27 yards in front of this and engaged the unpredictable targets. Handicaps could be created by distance. There was a prohibition on incoming targets.

Whirlybird was a similar shoot without the pit that used to be offered as a pool shoot in the UK. The trap, powered by a starter motor, had two arms, spinning round and released two targets anywhere in a 360 degree 'arc'. The angle of release was completely random.

For **Rabbit Run**, you stand on a suitably reinforced trap house and engage Trap-style targets which have been adjusted to skim the ground. I have never seen it in England and anyone trying it should make quite sure about the security of the trap house roof. A rigid, but removable, cage would also make sense; otherwise, someone losing his or her balance could fall over the edge with a loaded gun. The idea could be modified by standing to one side of the trap house.

Properly constructed with safe steps and a good side rail, a platform stand is an asset to any Sporting clays course, especially if the trap underneath the shooting platform has the facility to throw unpredictably angling targets or targets in differing directions.

SUB—and the meaning of the name is lost in the mists of time—was a kind of compact Sporting shoot involving a single 'Altemus' ball-joint trap devised by Abercrombie & Fitch at its British-style Long Island Shooting School in the 1930s. It could throw single birds, doubles, triples or coveys. Its angle could be 'quickly swung to any angle or elevation'. A diagram entitled 'Preferred set-up for Altemus trap with six shooting positions' appears in *Shooting Psychology* by Lawrence B Smith.[126] It is especially interesting because it is a proto-version of Sporting that appeared in the United States before the Second World War.

Other forms of clayshooting

Star Shot was invented by David Maxwell. Many readers will have seen it on television some years ago and it still appears at some country fairs. Star Shot involves a large tubular grid rather like a massively enlarged section of a dart board. Clays must be broken in specific zones. The hardest zones are the lowest. Star Shot requires its own technique and is easier with a short, open-choked gun—ideally something like a Skeet gun but with a Trap stock. It was created to make clayshooting more television friendly and had a brief success.

Eurotrap was invented by Mrs Rhian Hughes. It involves coloured targets and two people firing side-by-side on a raised platform. Like Star Shot, it was devised to give clayshooting more spectator appeal. You shoot as a team but one shooter is designated 'red', the other 'white'. Clays are thrown from traps underneath the platform upon which the shooters stand. They may be red, white or blue. On each release of targets, both guns may fire. You can shoot your own colour (one point) and the blue clays (six points) but only after you have shot any of your own colour which are in the air. Some targets are of the flash type and score ten bonus points. There is a penalty if you shoot your partner's colour. A round consists of forty birds.

Tom Bryer (left) and Chris Gladwin of ATS with their Gnats. Picture courtesy: James Marchington

PDQ Twister is marketed by Michael Murphy & Sons in the USA. It is designed around a specialist trap, which combines two target launchers and an oscillator. There are five shooting stations set out in an arrowhead formation. Singles, simultaneous, following and report pairs are thrown.

Among novelty shoots, the **Red Baron Shoot** in the USA is a game in which the target is a surprisingly tough radio-controlled plane. It is derived from the drones used by the military to train gunners. Its equivalent in the UK is **Gnat**, developed by John Cavendish and John Green. Each Gnat has 'flash pods' offering a spectacular witness to hits. It is free-flying and was developed principally for corporate events and charity fundraising. It offers a real challenge and can do things that no clay or live bird could. It can be brought in at great speed and brought to a sudden halt just as all the guns are swinging past. The Gnat usually carries up to twelve flash pods. Each is about 1½in in diameter and, if struck, explodes with a bright flash. John Cavendish

PDQ Twister

says: 'We developed this concept because the planes will take an awful lot of flack before they break. To maintain interest and to keep scoring simple, a visual reference is needed. We usually conduct the shoot rather like a flush, with four shooters in cages. The plane is flown in a series of five passes, each squad of four gets the same number of passes and, in so far as conditions permit, the same profiles. The aircraft is launched from a trailer by catapult. No 6 shot is the largest allowed and there is a bonus if the plane crashes.'[127]

Turkeys, kettles and parrots

ANOTHER US shotgun game—and one in which there has been a resurgence of interest and some development—is the Turkey Shoot at a static paper target. Similar events were once popular on the Pennine moors in Britain, too, where they were known as 'kettle' shoots because the prize was typically a copper kettle. Modern Turkey Shoots in the USA are organised with classes for 'stock' and outrageously modified 'outlaw guns'. There are limits concerning barrel length and choke and ranges are 50-100ft depending on event and local custom. The renewed interest in this sort of competition is probably connected with the modern interest in super-choked shotguns for turkey hunting, a major sport in the USA with millions participating.

The usual aim usual of the modern Turkey Shoot is to obliterate a spot on a paper target—not unlike the shooting games sometimes seen at fairs and carnivals—or to achieve the highest pellet count in a small area on a target. Turkey shoots may, however, have begun with tethered birds behind logs which offered an occasional head shot to festively minded gunners. The Royal Company of Archers in Scotland, whose records date to 1676, used to have an annual goose shoot along somewhat similar lines.

Old records of the Company inform:

> They went to the butts… where a living goose was fixed a convenient distance from the north but and nothing but her head in view. The same was shot through by the captain-general (Viscount Tarbet), the arrow entering the left eye and going out a little behind the right eye, about four inches quite through, so as she never moved after she received the shot.[128]

Balfour goes on to write:

> This cruel sport, in which the unfortunate bird was buried in turf, the head only being left out, continued to be practised for many years, as it is only about 1764 that the item of 'half a crown for a goose ' disappears from the treasurer's accounts. The competition is still kept up, but the prize is now a medal and the goose's head is represented by a small glass globe of about an inch in diameter placed in the centre of the buttmark, which is a circular piece of cardboard four inches across.[129]

The above is not only interesting to historians of the Turkey Shoot, but also to glass ball enthusiasts. It appears to put that target in use in a marksmanship context well before Messrs Portlock, Paine and Bogardus.

The Kettle Shoot of Northern England, like the more recent Turkey Shoot, involved shooting with a shotgun at a square or rectangle of paper, the object being to plaster it with as many pellets as possible to win the kettle prize. *The Encyclopaedia of Sport*, a work of 1912, states quite credibly:

> One of the chief features of many village feast sports held in the remote dales… the Kettle Shoot, is, in all probability, a modernised survival of the ancient sport of 'Shooting the popinjay'… Almost everybody in the hamlet enters for the shoot—young, old, gaffer or gammer, halt or blind—for, the law insisting that nobody shall actually fire at the target without possessing a gun license, much of the shooting is done by deputy, marksmen of repute firing a dozen times as representative of a dozen different entrants. On the village green or in some convenient field and backed by a speculative and appreciate 'gallery', the shooters quickly follow one another at the firing line and discharge their pieces loaded for them by the officials of the sports… After each shot the appointed marker hurries to the target… counts the pellet marks in it and replaces it with a new one… Eventually the marksman who has put the most pellet marks into the envelope is declared the winner of the kettle.[130]

Miniature clayshooting

Mo-Skeeto is an older novelty shoot using specially modified .22 rimfire shotguns. I have seen a single-shot bolt action and a pump action repeater in contemporary illustrations. Based on information in an article in *Guns Magazine*, May 2003, by Holt Bodinson, it seems that the Royal Canadian Air Force may have used the Mo-Skeeto system to train Second World War flyers. Mo-Skeeto miniature clays were designed for use up to about 50ft. In the Mo-Skeeto version of Skeet, the high and low houses were placed 60ft apart with special Mo-Skeeto traps adjusted to throw targets 66ft.

The tiny Targo target

Mossberg Targo was another pre-Second World War miniature clay-shooting game. The essential piece of equipment was a Mossberg Targo barrel-mounted mini-trap. This could be fitted to any .22 or .410, although a dedicated Mossberg .22 gun was also offered, its 20in barrel could be fitted either with a Targo smoothbore tube or a Targo rifle adaptor (a rifled extension piece fitted in much the same way as a sound moderator by screwing on to a thread at the muzzles). The whole package weighed 5½lb. The firing procedure was to load the trap first, then the gun and to release the bird by means of a supplementary trigger just in front of the fore-end. The birds had an intended range of up to 40ft. A pistol-like Targo hand trap was also available.

Crossman marketed a diminutive clayshooting outfit in the early 1960s. Most unusually, it made use of a .38 CO2 powerlet-powered smoothbore airgun intended for use with a charge of fifty-five no 8 shot. It was called the **1100 Trapmaster** and had a 28in barrel, a plastic stock and a diecast alloy action. The Crossman outfit also included a foot-release trap, re-usable, rimmed, plastic cartridges (closed at both

Trapmaster CO2 shotgun

ends with wads) and a re-usable plastic 'clay' shaped in the normal way but with an outer rim that breaks away. Sadly, many of the Crossman powerlet shotguns were rebarrelled as rifles. Meantime, I might note the comment of someone Stateside who noted that the guns lacked power but were the 'cat's pyjamas for shooting bees'.

The American gun writer Holt Bodinson has re-discovered an entirely new 'Mini' shooting system. It was manufactured by the Sports Ammo Company of Minneapolis, Minnesota and required the use of a conventional 20-bore. The sporting package consisted of mini shot shells, a mini trap and mini clays. The shells were .410 bore internally and could be powered by primer alone, or a very small (1 grain) charge of propellant. Their cases were made from a fluted alloy casting and offered ultra-low recoil. The clays were made of plastic had a yellow dome and a detachable black skirt. The idea of the Mini system, apparently, was to provide a means of instructing novices not only in elementary short-range clayshooting

A pair of Wingo guns

but also in reloading. Wingo was a sophisticated indoor recreation devised by Olin Winchester in the late 1960s. The idea was to offer an exciting shooting sports alternative to ten-pin bowling. The range consisted of eighteen galleries, each with its own 50ft range and elevated shooting station and each with its own automated refrigeration system to manufacture the targets, which were hollow balls of ice, 1/10in thick and 2 5/8in in diameter. Plastic had been tried in the early stages of development. Positioned pneumatically, the targets were launched by compressed air from one of five 'launch ports'. There were three speeds of target: slow at 50fps, medium at 55 and fast at 60. Wingo was designed as a team sport. The opposing team programmed the electronic targeting console to try and outsmart the shooter at the firing point. You could also program the electronic controller for individual shooting.

The gun used in Wingo was based on a Webley & Scott-made, Greener-style Martini, similar to those used for normal .22 target shooting. However, the Wingo gun was made in .20, so that normal .22 rimfire ammunition could not be inserted in the chamber. There was also a clever safety system: an electronic tether was attached to the muzzle of the gun, which could only be fired while pointing downrange after the target had been launched. The sighting system was also most interesting. It consisted of a Weaver 'Quick-Point' red dot unit mounted like a telescopic sight above the action. Winchester clearly poured a lot of money into the project and there were extensive trials with Winchester employees. A Wingo centre was actually opened in San Diego, California. It did not last, but it sounds as if it could have been a lot more fun than bowling.

Part III
The Olympics

'The most important thing in the Olympic Games is not
to win but to take part, just as the most important thing
in life is not the triumph but the struggle.'[131]

The Olympics

THE STORY of Olympic shooting begins in the late nineteenth century when the French nobleman, Baron Pierre de Coubertin (1863-1937), was inspired to revive the Games first staged in Ancient Greece in 776BC. These had lasted more than 1,000 years and were terminated by a ban imposed by the Christian Emperor Theodosius in 392AD. It has been suggested that de Coubertin's motivation for his great project was profound sorrow over his country's defeat in the Franco-Prussian war. As he was only eight when the conflict finished, this may be overstating it. But, the Baron certainly appears to have seen sport as a means of rejuvenating his war-torn and revolution-battered nation. He noted that athletics was honoured more in Britain and the United States than in France. His own nation, he believed, had become too obsessed with the intellect.

In search of his sporting grail, de Coubertin travelled widely. He was especially impressed with the way sport was organised in English schools and clubs and spent much time making notes of our practices. He used this material when building his modern Olympic movement in the 1890s. To the traditional track and field events of ancient Greece, he added many others including shooting. It may be relevant that he was a former national champion pistol shot, but it is also notable that shooting was then at the height of fashion.

The first new Games were held in Athens in 1896 with rifle and pistol shooting on the programme but without shotgunnery as far as we can tell. Shooting would go on to become one of the most popular of all Olympic events with regard to the number of participants and disciplines represented. It was absent only in the 1904 and 1928 Games (save for the pentathlon). Shotgunnery would be introduced in 1900 and has been seen in most of the Olympics since (the exceptions being 1904, 1928, 1932, 1936 and 1948). Shotgun events consisted of Trap shooting until 1968, when Skeet was introduced. Sporting is still not recognised as an Olympic discipline, more is the pity.

1896 Athens

THE QUEEN of Greece literally fired the first shot at these games—her son Crown Prince Constantine having persuaded rich Greeks abroad to help underwrite the great cost of staging the large, international event. As far as we can tell from existing records, the shooting competition was restricted to rifle and pistol marksmanship—although it is possible that there was some sort of live pigeon or inanimate target match running parallel to the other recorded competitions.

Sidney Merlin, who would become a stalwart of British Olympic shotgun shooting in later Olympiads, competed in one of the rifle events but was not in the prizes. He was an interesting character. Born in the Piraeus district of Athens in 1856, the son of the Vice Consul, Merlin married Zaira Theotokis, daughter of the Greek Prime Minister and lived until 1952. His well-established family even had an Athenian street named after them. We will hear more of the Merlin family.

1900 Paris

CLAY PIGEON shooting made its debut at the Paris Olympics of 1900. Confusion reigned at an event that appears to have been little more than an adjunct to the Great Paris Exposition of the same year. Paris 1900 and St Louis 1904 (the venue for another great exhibition) are sometimes referred to as the 'farcical' Games. In the case of Paris, even the 'Olympic' designation appears largely retrospective. The words Olympics or Olympiad do not appear to feature in the contemporary advertising. Indeed many competitors only discovered later that they had been competing in a major international event.

Baron Pierre de Coubertin

However history may choose to name them—and there is debate about what is now considered an Olympic event and what is not—there appear to have been no less than thirty-five shooting matches held over a period of several months in or around Paris. The status of the shotgun events seems especially clouded. There were two live pigeon shooting contests and a clay event of which we can be certain. The latter match, now recognised as an Olympic contest, was held at Le Stand de L'Ile Seguin at Billancourt on 15-17 July 1900.

It was a twenty-bird trap competition with one shot only allowed per bird. There were thirty-one entries. The competition was won by the Frenchman Roger de Barbarin (who shot 17 ex 20), with G Guyot second (also on 17) and Comte Justinien de Clary coming third (on another 17). Indeed, the first six places all went to French competitors. Pure coincidence, no doubt. There is no record of how, or if, a shoot-off was conducted. Sidney Merlin (Great Britain) was seventh equal (with six others) on 12. Comte de Clary became a member of the International Olympic Committee (IOC) in later life and was Commissioner General in charge of the 1924 Olympics in Paris. Merlin would go on to compete with a shotgun again in 1906 and with more success at the 'interim' Games in Athens.

As for the disputed live pigeon events at Paris in 1900. It appears that the first major competition—Le Grand Prix Centenaire (the centenary grand prix)—took place at the Cercle de Bois de Boulogne on 19-20 June 1900. Shooting took place from the 27m line. Donald Mackintosh of Australia grassed 22 birds ex 25, Santiago Pidal (the Marqués de Villaviciosa), was second for Spain on 21 and Edgar Murphy of the USA was third on 19.

Le Grand Prix de L'Exposition Universelle ran on 25-27 June and appears to have been a much larger pigeon shooting event with no less than eighty-five competitors. It also took place at the famous Cercle de Bois de Boulogne. Shooters shot from the 27m line. Each shot at one bird in each round. Two rounds were shot in each of the first two days. Shooters were eliminated when they missed two birds. There were 300 birds killed and a first prize of 20,000 francs—a vast sum for the day but less than *Le Grand Prix du Casino* at Monte Carlo. When only four competitors remained, they decided to share the loot. The final results were: Leon de Lunden (Belgium) on 21; Maurice Fauré (France) on 20; and, third equal Crittenden Robinson (USA) and Donald Mackintosh (Australia) on 18. The best placed Britain was J Banwell who was seventh. The irrepressible Sidney Merlin was half way down the field on thirty-seventh equal.

1904 St Louis

THE 1904 the Olympics went to Saint Louis after the burghers of Chicago, the original choice, agreed a change of venue. The St Louis Games were no more true to the Olympic ideal than those at Paris and, once again, became a sideshow to a grand and essentially commercial exposition—this one, ostensibly at least, celebrating the purchase of Louisiana. The show covered 1,200 acres, had exhibitors from more than sixty countries and no less than 1,500 buildings and seventy-five miles of roads. These 'Olympics' had few foreign competitors, in spite of the many foreign businesses represented.

As far as documentary records suggest, there was no competitive shooting competition, but there was at least one interesting shooting event. Winchester's trick-shooter, Ad Topperwein is reported to have smashed 3,507 2¼in diameter aerial 'composition' targets without a miss—I presume with a rifle. This was a new world record. The ice cream cone, the hot-dog, the hamburger and peanut butter are all reputed to have made their debut at St Louis as well.

1906 Athens

IN 1906, the Olympics returned to Athens and the original, rather purer ideals. The Greeks had, in fact, hoped to keep Athens as the permanent venue after the 1896 Games. This did not transpire, probably because the International Olympic Committee wanted to retain control. It is notable, though, that Athens has hosted more modern Games than any other city (1896, 1906 and 2004). The 1906 event has been called the 'intercalated' or 'interim' Games because it broke the ancient (and now re-established) four-year cycle. It was also notable as a celebration of the first ten years of the modern Olympics.

These Games, though generally credited as important for re-establishing the Olympic ideals, have never been officially recognised by the International Olympic Committee. They were, nevertheless, the first Games to have truly representative national teams. They introduced national flag-raising at the medal ceremony and they also introduced the concept of an Olympic village in which all competitors stayed in a spirit of sporting fraternity. Bearing in mind all the tacky commercialism and confusion of Paris (1900) and St Louis, it is remarkable that the 1906 'Olympics' have not been properly recognised. Perhaps it is because we have returned to commercialism.

There were two clay target matches in Athens. Records are not complete, but there appears to have been a single barrel Trap event and a 'two shot' or 'double shot' competition. The former was a thirty-bird event with four traps at 16m. Fifteen birds were sent from the 'lower' traps and fifteen from the 'higher' traps. There was a restriction on bore size—no larger than 12-bore—a maximum shot payload of 32 grams, a maximum case length of 65mm and a maximum shot size of 6. The double shot event was ten pairs for a possible of twenty. Shooters were 14m from the traps for this. All birds were thrown from the higher traps. Stipulations for calibre, payload, case length and shot size were the same as the single bird event. Great Britain won both events.

Gerald Merlin, a relation of Sidney, took top honours in the 'single shot' event with Greek Cypriot Ioannis Peridis in second and Sidney Merlin winning third. The 'double shot' event had Merlins taking first and third again, but with Sidney first and Gerald third—which seems a very satisfactory family arrangement. Anastasios Metaxas of Greece was the runner up. Gerald, for the record, was significantly younger than his kinsman, Sidney. The former was born in 1884 (also in Piraeus) dying in India in 1945.

At the time of the Athens games, Gerald and Sidney were aged twenty-two and fifty respectively. Their exact familial relation is unclear, but it would be a fair bet that Gerald was Sidney's nephew.

Anastasios Metaxas at the 1908 London Games

1908 London

THE 1908 Games—the first really successful modern Olympiad—were held in London after Mount Vesuvius in Italy erupted and Britain offered to host the Games at short notice. Rome, the city originally designated, had set aside a considerable budget for the shooting events to be held at the Poligono di Tor di Quinto. In an official document, Le Projet Financier de la IV Olympiade Rome, which was published in 1905 and reprinted in *Olympism: Selected Writings* by de Coubertin, the Baron noted:

> Clay pigeon... will replace live shooting which is too expensive and necessarily involves cash prizes. The idea should be to copy the very simple and very comprehensive installation at the Malden School of Shooting near London—nothing could be easier. We do know that the very inexpensive equipment used there makes it possible to imitate the flight of a sequence of widely differing game birds.

This sounds as if some sort of Sporting competition was being considered for Rome, which is most interesting if that interpretation is correct. The competition that finally took place in England was, however, more conventional. It was what we would now call Olympic Trench or Trap. The British National Rifle Association organised the rifle and pistol shooting at Bisley and the Clay Bird Shooting Association, the forerunner of the CPSA, was delegated the organisation responsible for clayshooting under the chair of Lord Westbury.

The venue selected for the meeting (which eventually took place on 8-11 July) was the Uxendon Shooting School of Charles Lancaster, also known as the North Western Shooting School. The week after the games, the sixteenth Annual Championships of the Clay Bird Shooting Association were scheduled to take place on the same ground. To meet the transportation needs, a new Metropolitan line station was built between Wembley Park and Harrow which set passengers off opposite the club. This was opened with some pomp and circumstance in May. Mr J Newton Hayley, a member of the ten-man clay bird committee chaired by Westbury, invited VIP visitors to lunch at the club grounds and witness 'an exhibition of shooting from the tower and from the ground traps and examined the new trench in the course of construction for the Olympic Meeting'.[132]

A great deal of effort went into all preparations, but the heavens were not co-operative. The Official Report noted that 'wretched weather conditions prevailed'. Poor light meant the black clays would be difficult to see so the organisers daubed them with white paint 'giving them a magpie appearance'. There was drama almost immediately, too. After the first day of shooting, there was a three-way tie between British shooters Charles Palmer, Richard Hutton and John Postans. The Canadians lodged an objection about the scores and were allowed to shoot again. John Postans withdrew and did not shoot in the remainder of the competition. The average score in the final stages was 65 per cent which prompted The Field to suggest that the limit on pellet payload should be increased to 1½oz and the second barrel dispensed with altogether (as it had proved worse than useless to most competitors).

Walter Ewing (Canada) shot 27 in the re-shoot using an American Lefever gun with Winchester factory-loaded 'Leader' shells (some small comfort to the US contingent whose shooters did not otherwise feature in the prizes). As well as the gold medal on a final score of 72 ex 80, Ewing was also awarded Lord Westbury's Cup, as the outstanding shooter in the games. Another Canadian, George Beattie was second on 60 and Alexander Maunder (UK) took the bronze on 57 after an exciting shoot-off with Anastasios Metaxas, the Greek Cypriot runner-up of the 'double-shot' event of 1906. It was reported as one of the highlights of a disappointing meeting.

Three countries and four teams took part in the team event (the United

Kingdom A and B, Canada and the United States) and as many as eight (the UK, Canada, Greece, Finland, Sweden, Holland, France and the United States) appear to have been involved in the individual competition. The fact that the host nation fielded two teams is some indication of the more relaxed attitude taken to such events before the First World War. There was no stopping the six-man British A squad captained by FW Moore, the man who had also set up the first international between England, Scotland and Ireland in 1895.

In spite of dreadful conditions Moore's team of himself, P Easte, A Maunder, O Plamer, JF Pike and JM Postans, set up a lead on the first day of competition that was never subsequently headed. The Canadians staged a late rally on the third and final day but Britain's bronze medallist Alexander Maunder broke forty birds, two more than the individual champion, Walter Ewing. That turned out to be the margin of victory. *Sporting Life* of 13 July 1908 reported:

> The result was looked upon as a foregone conclusion but, contrary to expectation, the issue remained in doubt till the last few shots. Canada shot with great nerve and determination and slowly but surely decreased their opponent's lead... the excitement grew intense...
> In striking contrast to the dearth of spectators on the previous days, the picturesque enclosure at Uxendon presented quite an animated scene.

The final score was United Kingdom 407 and Canada 405. The concluding comments on the 1908 Olympics should, however, be left to *The Field*:

> A shooter who knows himself to be a fairly good shot on the average, not to say brilliant on occasions, hates to see his score on the 50 or 60 per cent level. In almost all classes of shooting a collapse of form is overwhelming when once it begins. If the number of competitors is large enough for only the successful ones to be named, others who fall by the wayside remain in welcome obscurity. The figures of a published score are, unfortunately, more permanent than the explanations as to why they are so low.

1912 Stockholm

THERE WAS particular royal interest in the shooting events at this Olympiad. The president of the Clay Bird and Running Deer Committee was Captain Fredrik Bjorkenstam, master of the hounds to His Majesty King Gustav V. This time, the Americans, who had had poor luck in Britain in 1908, dominated the clayshooting. They won both the individual and team competitions at the Rasundra range. James R Graham (USA) took the championship.

After the first round, there had been a three-way tie with Graham, fellow American Edward Gleason (a surgeon from Cape Cod) and the German nobleman Franz, Baron von Zedlitz und Leipe. The Baron fell away in the second round to leave Graham and Gleason to tussle for the lead. In the final round Graham again posted the best score, 49, which gave him a total score of 96. He eventually won by 2 points from the German Alfred Göldel Bronikoven (94). Could there be a connection to the H Goeldel who would did so well in the CBSA championships at the Middlesex Gun Club in 1913? Could they be the same person—which I suspect? A is easily miss-transcribed as H, 'ö' is properly replaced by oe if the typeface offers no suitable German accent.

Third place went to a Russian, Harry Blau (91). Britain's Harold Humby led a pack of five shooters who tied for fourth place with a combined total of 88. They were awarded diplomas of merit for their efforts.

The team event also went to the USA. Graham again posted the best individual score and received good support from Charles Billings (later Mayor of Oceanside, New Jersey), Hendrikson Hall and Gleason. Their total of 532 was 21 points clear of the second-placed 'Great Britain and Ireland' team (511). The Germans, who came third, included Baron von Zedlitz und Leipe and Count

England's top shooters in the late 1920s: none of them able to compete following the 1925 ruling. Among them are Charles Lucas (front, left) and Wilf Harris Senior (third from the right at the back)

von Bernstorff-Gyldensteen (510). Graham, the pre-eminent amateur of his day, turned professional after the Games.

1916 Games cancelled

AN OLYMPIAD had been planned for 1916 in Berlin, the Germans having previously withdrawn a bid for 1908 and refused an offer for the games in 1912. The 1916 Olympics did not take place due to the First World War (which, of course, broke out in June 1914). Games scheduled for 1940 and 1944 were also cancelled. In the days of the original Olympics, it is notable that war stopped for the Games; not so for the industrialised mass murder that war became in the twentieth century.

1920 Antwerp

THE OLYMPICS and clayshooting returned in 1920 at Antwerp. The Americans continued their dominance, winning most events including both team and individual clay competitions. The six-man team match was conducted over ninety targets, two men up. The first eighty targets were presented from a known trap but at unknown angle, the final ten from an unknown trap at unknown angles. Gun position was optional and two shots could be fired at each target. The individual event was similar, but with one man up only. The members of the winning 1920 US squad (scoring 547 ex 600 in total were) were: Jay Clark Jr (84); Forest W McNeir (93); Horace R Bonser (93); Mark P Arie (94); Frank S Wright (89) and Frank M Troeh (94). The Belgians were runners up on a combined score of 503 and Sweden third on 500. In the individual event, the first three places were taken by the US: gold for Mark Arie on 95, silver for Troeh on 93 and bronze for Wright on 87.

The US team had trained believing a gun-down (off the shoulder) rule would be enforced, so it was an especially good result for them. On previous trips, moreover, they had been allowed to practise on board ship during the transatlantic crossing. This was a concession not granted to the 1920 Olympic team (reportedly due to a prohibition on ammunition carriage imposed by the shipping company). It did not seem to cramp their style much. The Americans stopped off in the UK en route to Antwerp and went to the British Clay Pigeon Shooting Championships for pre-Olympic practice, where—to quote the official US NRA history *Olympic Shooting*[133]: 'won about everything possible and set a number of new records'.

Colonel Jim Crossman, author of the last mentioned work relates another interesting but possibly apocryphal story:

> [At the time] the English birds had the reputation of being very hard and the Americans soon found the reputation was well deserved… the team paid a visit to the clay bird factory, where they gave the plant operator some lessons in how to make breakable birds. To the infinite delight of the English, birds from that plant immediately became vastly improved.

We have so much for which to be grateful.

1924 Paris

IN 1924 the Olympics was held once again in Paris. The shooting programme was somewhat reduced, although there was a team and individual trap event for shotgunners. The US won the team prize again, captained by the soon-to-be famous Fred Etchen from Kansas. Etchen also managed to make a name for himself in England in 1924, confirming the reputation of US trapshooters in Britain that had begun with Bogardus and Carver. He travelled over from Paris to win the British Open with a perfect 200 ex 200. Nothing close to it had ever been posted. *Shooting Times* looked back on 3 January 1925 in a review of 1924:

> The visit of the American and Canadian teams en route to the Olympic Games at Paris infused additional interest in clay target shooting in the Metropolis during the past year. Both of them were treated right royally by the London clubs and right royally did they shoot. Never before have such a fine exhibition of shooting and a test of endurance been witnessed as when at the Waltham Abbey Mr Etchens [sic] of America succeeded in defeating Mr Montgomery of Canada at the 200th attempt in a sequence of kills which to the lay mind must have been seen to be credited.

The son of a market hunter, Etchen was one of the all time greats. Apart from the successes already noted, he won no less than seventeen Kansas state titles over a fourteen-year period and helped form the American Trap Shooting Association. He had himself once been helped on the competition circuit by Frank Butler and his diminutive but eagle-eyed wife, Annie Oakley. A lifelong enthusiast and most famous in later years as an instructor, Etchen wrote the book *How to be an Expert at Trap Shooting* (later updated as *Common Sense Shotgun Shooting*). Chris Cradock regarded this as one of the best clay books ever written. Fred's son, Rudy, also became a famous trap shot and taught clayshooting to pilots as a Naval Petty Officer Gunnery Instructor in Second World War. His grandson, Joel, a friend of mine, is no mean performer either—twice Pennsylvania state doubles champion. Joel owns a successful gun shop in Western Pennsylvania. Even younger Etchens—Rebecca and Alex—are still winning competitions. Four generations of shooting talent so far and no doubt there will be more to come.

Back at the 1924 Olympics, as far as individual events were concerned, the Europeans reasserted themselves.

Gold went to Hungary's Gyula Halasy on 98 after a ten-bird shoot-off with the Finn CW Huber. An American, Frank Hughes, was one behind on 97.

Rudy Etchen

1925 politics

ALTHOUGH IT was not an Olympic year, 1925 was a significant year in the history of the IOC. At 63, de Coubertin decided it was time to resign as President of the IOC and, at the week-long conference, the question of amateurism in sport was much discussed. This had profound consequences for shooting. Because prize money was sometimes offered at shooting events, the sport was removed from the programme of the 1928 games in Amsterdam. A delegation from the UIT, newly recognised by the IOC as responsible for the rules in shooting, came to plead its case. But the UIT was then only concerned with rifle and pistol shooting. When the decision was taken to restore shooting for the Xth Olympiad in Los Angeles in the summer of 1932, the events were for pistol and rifle only. Nor did clayshooting appear in the Berlin Olympiad in 1936 (although there was a parallel World Shooting Championships). Nor was it restored at the austere London games of 1948, though there was a parallel exhibition championship at Bisley. The shotgun and clay bird finally made their official return in 1952.

1952 Helsinki

THE CLAY events were staged just outside Helsinki at the Huopalahti range and became the focus of much attention when seventeen-year-old George Genereaux of Canada—who had won the silver medal in the World Championship in Oslo in 1951 aged sixteen—shot 95 and 97 (192 total) to be crowned Olympic champion and establish a new Olympic record. It was Canada's first gold medal since 1932 and the circumstances surrounding it were dramatic. Genereaux had trailed in third place after the first day but his second day performance proved decisive. The much more experienced Swedish shooter, Knud Holmqvist, lost the gold medal in the last round by a single point on his twenty-fourth bird having shot twenty-three straight (finishing 1 point behind the young Canadian on 191). Hans Liljedahl, another Swede, took bronze (190 ex 200). The best British placing at Helsinki was Enoch Jenkins, making a return to Olympic competition at the age of fifty-nine after competing in 1920 and 1924. He finished fourteenth. There was no US entry to the clay events, though Huelet L Benner won gold in free pistol.

Genereaux's success was remarkable because the teenager had only five year's shooting experience and used a single barrel pump-action gun. He went on to become a professor of medicine and died in 1989 at the age of fifty-five. He suffered with rheumatoid arthritis all his life, including his time as a world-class shooting competitor.

Shortly before his death, Dr Genereaux made some touching comments about the Olympic experience to Trap shooting historian Jimmy Robinson (as quoted by Richard Hamilton on the ATA Hall of Fame website): 'All in all it was a tremendous experience and one that I am only beginning to appreciate. In a man's lifetime, he is given good days and some bad days; there is no doubt that those two days were the most exciting and rewarding that I will ever see.'

A notable feature of the Helsinki Olympics was that the form of clay competition was beginning to become more standardised. The trap event was held over two days with two sets of a hundred birds to be shot. Gun position was optional but all, or nearly all, competitors shot pre-mounted. It is better suited to Trap shooting (the arguments for Sporting and Skeet are more complex) and allowed more time for a second shot. Birds could be broken on the first or second shot and still scored. Twenty-five bird strings became the standard number (previously it had been ten, fifteen or twenty).

1956 Melbourne

THE DUKE of Edinburgh opened the 1956 Olympic Games on behalf of the Queen in Melbourne. It was the first time the Olympics had visited the Southern Hemisphere. It was also a Games in which the USSR dominated in many events, not least in shooting.

The Soviets did not have it their own way in the clay competitions, however. Although the basic organisation of modern Olympic Trap events had been determined at Helsinki, the format of the Trap championship in Melbourne was changed to include three rounds—two of seventy-five birds and one of fifty.

Italian Galliano Rossini set a new Olympic record under the new format with 195 ex 200.

He finished a full 5 points clear of Poland's Adam Smelczynski (190). Alessandro Ciceri of Italy (188/24) beat off the challenge of two Soviets in a shoot-off for the bronze medals.

The achievements of the top shooters were all the more impressive because of the extreme heat. The British Olympic Association report noted:

At RAAF Laverton... the shooters had no protection at all over the firing stands at such ranges. For records to be broken therefore under such adverse conditions shows almost superhuman endeavour.

Joe Wheater, the great British shooter, came only eighteenth but was the highest-scoring Briton. The BOA report opined another reason for our relatively poor performance:

Undoubtedly the reason for their low scores, compared with their excellent achievements in Britain, is that over here the automatic type of trap is used whereas the foremost continental nations use the manually-operated and electrically-released type which projects the clay bird at a very much higher velocity... there is little chance of Britain being able to hold her own with the leading nations until this handicap is removed.[134]

Enoch Jenkins in 1948. He competed in the 1920, 1924 and 1952 Olympics for Great Britain

Soon-to-be winner Major Hans Aesnaes of Norway (left) and ST Rimmer of Britain at Bisley in July 1948. Clayshooting was an 'exhibition' sport at the Olympics

1960 Rome

IN 1960 the Olympics went to Rome. The Italians had waited more than half a century to stage them after the eruption of Vesuvius had robbed them of the opportunity in 1908. Many of the events were held in spectacular settings.

The clay pigeon shooters had one of the shortest journeys—to the range at Lazio, less than a mile from the Olympic village.

Facilities there left something to be desired, though. It had originally been laid out for live pigeon shooting but, as British team manager GW Cafferata observed: 'It was poorly sited for a clay pigeon range, on the side of a hill which made shooting extremely difficult in the prevailing windy conditions.'

Nevertheless, Romanian Ion Dumitrescu took the Trap Gold with 192. Defending champion Rossini couldn't deliver the triumph the home crowd wanted but he did win silver on 191. Sergey Kalinin of the USSR just edged out 2nd Lt James Clark III of the United States Army for the bronze medal. Britain's Joe Wheater—no less of a phenomenon than George Digweed in his day—managed 188, which was an improvement on his Melbourne performance and allowed him to take fifth.

Baron C Palmstierna of Sweden (left) and Charles Lucas of Britain at Bisley in 1948

The Japanese shooting team, which visited the South of England for the International Olympic Trench Championship in March 1964

1964 Tokyo

THE XIVTH modern Olympiad in Japan set out—optimistically considering the prevailing international mood of cold war and MAD (Mutually Assured Destruction)—to symbolise the dawning of a new era of peace and co-operation.

The Olympic flame was lit by a runner born the day the atomic bomb had first fallen. The Games themselves were superbly organised. The shooting was impressive too.

At the Tokorozawa range, the Italian Ennio Mattarelli shot a superb 198, 4 points clear of the Soviet competitor Pavel Senichev who took silver.

In his turn, Senichev (actually a Latvian) won a three-way shoot-off (194/25) beating William C Morris III of the United States (194/24) and Lliano Rossi of Italy. Just behind them was the reigning Olympic champion Dumitrescu of Romania.

Seventh place went to 38-year-old Bob Braithwaite, a vet from Lancashire. His Tokyo experience would soon prove most valuable.

1968 Mexico City

CONDITIONS WERE difficult for the majority of competitors at Mexico City in 1968—certainly for those born at sea level. Nevertheless, Bob Braithwaite, put his experience in Tokyo to good use. He also demonstrated that champions do not let an early setback put them off. He missed twice in his first thirteen shots, but recovered to finish the first day at the Campo Militar range on an excellent 98 (shooting 87 straight after his initial yips). He tied with six others on this score behind the veteran Pole Smelczynski.

The next day Braithwaite achieved perfect form when he needed it most. He shot 100 straight—a rare feat at Olympic Trap—finishing on a magnificent 198. This gave Britain her first gold in any shooting discipline since 1924. A three-way shoot-off decided the places. The American Thomas Garrigus edged out Kurt Czekalla of the GDR (East Germany) for silver. Both men shot 196, then a perfect 25. On the second 25, Garrigus went straight again (196/25/25), Czekalla missed two targets (195/25/23).

Bob Braithwaite (centre), soon after winning in Mexico

Bob was a fearsome competitor in his day winning, in addition to Olympic gold, the British Open Grand Prix in Olympic Trench in 1965, 1967, 1968 and 1970. His great rival was Joe Wheater who had won the European OT event in 1959 and took top honours in the British Open event in 1964 and 1969.

Skeet gained Olympic status in 1968. It had only taken Trap shooting twenty years or so to get on to the programme, but the Skeeters had had to wait more than fifty. The contest was held over 200 targets and, like the Trap event, was a two-day marathon. Petrov of the USSR, Italian Romano Garagnani and the West German Konrad Wirnhier were all tied on the excellent score of 198. A shoot-off decided the medals. Soviet Yevgeny Petrov smashed all twenty-five birds. Romano Garagnani of Italy and Konny Wirnhier of Germany both missed one. So a second shoot-off was necessary. This time it was the Italian who took the silver, recording a 25 straight (198/24/25) and leaving world champion Wirnhier to content himself with bronze (198/24/23). His time would come.

Mexico 1968 was also an especially significant Games for women. The Olympic flame had been lit by a woman for the first time and women had at last been allowed to compete in shooting and alongside the men. Skeet shooter Nuria Oriz from Mexico took her place in the competition with fifty-one men and finished a creditable fourteenth. Some still regard this situation as superior to the one that pertains now where there are separate competitions for male and female shooters. This arguably sexist division appears to have been brought about by the success of Zhang Shan of China who beat the men in 1992 with an extraordinary 200 ex 200.

1972 Munich

THE ILL-FATED Munich Olympics of 1972 were much disrupted by the murderous attack on Israeli athletes by hooded Palestinian 'Black September' terrorists. Two of the Israelis were killed at the beginning of the drama and eleven more held hostage. Later, nine of the Israeli hostages would die during an abortive rescue attempt together with a German policeman. Five of the eight terrorists were eventually killed too.

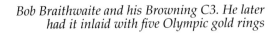
Bob Braithwaite and his Browning C3. He later had it inlaid with five Olympic gold rings

A terrible shadow was cast over the Games. Rather than cancel the Olympiad as some suggested, the IOC announced a day of mourning to be followed by a resumption of competition. The impact of the atrocity was not unlike 9/11 and was amplified by the unrestrained media coverage (as terrorism has so often been aided since).

The Games should have been remembered for something other than a dreadful act of barbarity. They were cutting edge in many ways, not least for the excellent technical facilities at the Hochbruch shooting ranges. The shooting events attracted huge crowds with tickets for the finals even finding their way on to the black market. AJ Palmer observed in the *British Official Report*: 'Shooting must now be regarded as a major spectator sport.'

Britain's Bob Braithwaite was not in Munich to defend his Trap title; he just failed to qualify. The Olympic laurels and his record passed on to the forty-one year-old Italian Angelo Scalzone, a hotel owner and beach concessionaire. He missed only once in 200 shots, a remarkable performance under extreme pressure at a difficult discipline. Corsican Michel Carrega (representing France), the defending world champion, equalled Braithwaite's 1968 score of 198 to take the silver and Italy's Silvano Basagni with 195 made it a Mediterranean hattrick.

Britain's Joe Neville from Matlock in Derbyshire was close to a medal in the Skeet, but a 21 ex 25 in his fifth string sabotaged his efforts. Neville finished on 194. Just one more clay would have got him into the medal shoot-off for gold. To the delight of the large gallery, it was the home shooter Konny Wirnhier who shot 25 straight to take the Olympic champion's title from world record holder Yevgeny Petrov. The Soviet competitor ended with silver and Michel Buckheim of the GDR took bronze. Wirnhier, who became a greatly respected shooting coach and gun designer, worked until his death at the Munich Olympic range.

1976 Montreal

THE 1976 Olympics were another politically-troubled Games. Canada refused to allow the nationalist Chinese (Taiwan) team to compete as 'China'. A compromise was proposed and rejected. The débâcle caused other nations to threaten to withdraw (including the USA). Mainland China would not make her Olympic debut until the 1980 Winter Olympics and 1984 Summer Olympics.

The shooting at the somewhat compromised 1976 games took place at

The GB Olympic Skeet team in 1979 (l-r): Chris Jary, Wally Sykes, Mark Billington, Fred 'Duggie' Duggans, Neville Pryce-Jones, Steve Murton, Chrissie Alexander, Paul Bentley, unidentified and Barry Simpson

L'Acadie, 20 miles from the Quebec capital. Unfortunately the weather did not equal the pleasant surroundings. The Trap competition was most severely affected by atmospheric conditions—as it often has at Olympic events, (and there may be a moral here for coaches). Sgt Donald Haldemann (1948-2003), then a 28-year-old machinist and gunsmith in the US Army, eventually took gold on a total of 190, using a gun with a stock of his own design. He shot 72 ex 75 on his first round, then 71 ex 75 and, on day three, 47 ex 50. He became the third American to win the individual Olympic title. His score would have only been good enough for eleventh place in Munich, but it was a remarkable performance under the terrible conditions prevailing. Armando Silva Marques of Portugal gained silver (189) after a shoot-off with Italy's Ubaldese Baldi.

When considering the results of any clay competition retrospectively, shooting must always be judged on conditions and target severity rather than simply on scores achieved.

In spite of the weather, the Skeet event produced a magnificent competition. Czechoslovakia's Josef Panacek took the gold on countback after a thrilling encounter with the Dutchman Eric Swinkels. Both men equalled the Olympic record but, although Swinkels had shot a perfect 75 when winds gusted up to 30mph, it was the Czech who took gold after shooting 50 to Swinkels's 49 on the final day. Pole, Wieslaw Gawlikowski, took bronze on 196. Britain's Joe Neville shot a reasonable 191, but it was only good enough for twenty-second place.

Colonel Jim Crossman has made some interesting comments concerning the poor US performance at Skeet at the1976 Games. He was adjutant of the 1968 Olympic team. Some of them might be applied to the British experience of Skeet and Trap at the Olympics too:

> Why don't we do better at [Olympic] Skeet? After all, the game was invented here. As a matter of fact we do very well—in the US game. At the 1975 US Championship, there were twenty-two people who tied with 250 straight, plus innumerable hundreds with .410 and 28 and 20-gauge guns. The cause of our downfall in the international game goes back to the 1950s, when the United States Skeet Association moved away from the original field training concept of Skeet. They dropped the mandatory low-gun position and dropped the indeterminate delay in throwing the bird. The result has been a tremendous number of straight

scores of 100, 200, or more. But when we come up against the international people, we usually get our tails whipped. With a new attitude of co-operation between the Skeet people and the NRA and with some strong promotion of the international game, we might pull out of this depression, but it will take time.[135]

1980 Moscow

FRATERNAL SPIRIT was not especially apparent in 1980 either. The Cold War was at its most dangerous height. Following the Soviet invasion of Afghanistan, the Americans led a boycott of the Moscow games.

I was then a young Army officer patrolling the Inner German Border and was well aware of the ensuing global tension and its potential consequences. We were told that we had a life expectancy of less than thirty minutes in the event of war. Clayshooting, by happenstance, was one way of ignoring this unhappy prospect and it was aided by an almost unlimited supply of 12-bore cartridges 'for vermin destruction' from the Regimental Quartermaster.

In Britain the sporting federations—such as the International Board of the CPSA—voted individually whether or not to go to Moscow. Along with such sports as hockey and equestrianism, shooting decided to stay away. Eighteen teams from other nations chose to go but not to use their national colours. The boycott of Moscow still arouses strong feelings among some athletes. Peter Croft—who was selected for Moscow as a British trapshooter and was the reigning European Champion in 1980—is still upset. He recently told me: 'At the time Margaret Thatcher was asking us to sacrifice our Olympic dreams, we were increasing our trade with the USSR.'

It is true that the Games became so politicised that, four years later, political journalists nearly outnumbered the newspapers' sports writers.

The absence of the Americans and many Brits in the USSR in 1980, made it likely that most of the shooting events would be dominated by the Eastern Bloc. The inevitable did not happen on the clay ranges though. Thirty-three shooters competed in the Trap competition and the Italian Luciano Giovanetti dominated the competition with a strong 198 to take the gold medal from the Soviet competitor Rustam Yambulatov and the East German, Jorg Damme. Giovanetti would retain his title four years later in the Californian sunshine.

In the Skeet, the Dane Hans Kjeld Rasmussen did not drop a shot until the fifth series. Lars-Göran Carlsson of Sweden and Roberto Castrillo of Cuba stayed with him, though all finishing their 200 targets on 196. They all straighted the next twenty-five birds too. Only on the next string of twenty-five was the final order settled. Gold went to Ramussen 196/25/25, silver to Carlson 196/25/24 and bronze to Castrillo 196/25/23. Denmark was one of the eighteen states that had elected not to use their national colours. In the medal ceremony, the Olympic flag was hoisted instead of the Danish one and the Olympic Hymn played instead of the national anthem.

1984 Los Angeles

THE USSR (and thirteen other states) boycotted the 1984 Los Angeles Olympics, mainly in a tit-for-tat retaliation for the US-led action against the 1980 Moscow Olympics. Ironically, this aided the Americans in many ways, not least in the results table. They ended the LA Olympics—in which more than 140 nations took part—with more than three times as many medals as any other nation (174 to West Germany's fifty-nine and Romania's fifty-three). The Games were commercially successful too—turning a profit of more than US$200 million.

The Soviets may well have noted with grim smugness that the decadent imperialists had even sought private sponsorship for the Olympic torch run at

US$3,000 per km (the 1984 games were the first since 1896 to be funded without major home government aid). You do not have to be a communist, however, to note that Games in recent years have been horribly commercialised. Perhaps it is a funding necessity, but it is a pity—as is all the corruption and payola that has been associated with the bids by rival cities in recent decades.

The shooting events at LA were held at the Prado range complex in San Bernadino County near Los Angeles. There was, apparently, significant opposition to the shooting sports by the local organising authorities—not something that is usually associated with the United States. This was resolved by the IOC.

In the Trap shooting, reigning champion Giovanetti had to beat Peru's Francisco Boza and American soldier Dan Carlisle in a shoot-off on 192 to secure his second gold medal. Four-time world champion Michel Carraga (France) was silver medallist in 1972 but he could not finish his career quite as he might have liked; he finished just outside the medals in fifth.

There was joy for the exuberant home crowd when Matthew Dryke won the Skeet gold for the USA with an Olympic record of 198 ex 200. Ole Riber Rasmussen—no close relation to Hans Kjeld who won skeet gold in 1980—had to settle for the silver on 196, a score shared with bronze medallist, Luca Scribani Rossi of Italy. At least Rasmussen straighted his twenty-five birds.

1988 Seoul

IN SEOUL in 1988, Dan Carlisle, now one of America's best known shooting coaches, joined a select club of multi-discipline Olympian shotgunners. A trap bronze medallist in LA in 1984 he just missed out on another bronze, finishing fourth in 1988; but he was also, most unusually, selected for the Skeet event where he finished ninth. The gold medallist was Axel Wegner of the GDR on 222, with Alfonso de Iruarrizaga of Chile on 221 taking silver and Jorge Guardiola of Spain the bronze on 220.

A feature of the Seoul Olympics was a twenty-five bird shoot-off in both Skeet and Trap events. After the 1984 Olympics, UIT (the International Shooting Union) came under intense pressure from the IOC to find a means of making the shooting sports more appealing to spectators and television. Their solution was to include a final in both Skeet and Trap. To get to it, you would have to pass an ordeal of fire, which involved 150 targets over two days (seventy-five per day). On the third day the top twenty-four would shoot another fifty birds to decide who the top six were. They would then go forward to the twenty-five bird shoot-off and this score would be added to their first 200 (giving the total ex 225). To add to the visual drama, flash clays would be used. If the final shoot-off was tied, it would all move on to 'sudden death'.

Other significant changes had been introduced for Seoul. Places for the shooting events were awarded by a quota system and by means of a minimum qualifying score. The IOC wanted, allegedly, wanted to improve standards and reduce the number of competitors. Before the Seoul Olympics, competing nations had been allowed to enter two shooters in both the Trap and Skeet event. The new system demanded that they send their competitors to designated events—world cups, and continental and world championships—before the games to achieve the required minimum scores. Let me let Peter Croft, who has suffered these rules, explain. He wrote in 1990:

> …Now, each country must attempt to win places for their shooters by competing in specified events in the run-up to the Games… Each individual shooter can only win one place for his country and each country can win a maximum of three places. It is important to note that the shooter wins the Olympic place for his country not for himself. This new arrangement severely curtailed the number of entrants at the Seoul Olympics. Many of the stronger

Ian Peel made his first appearance for Britain at the 1988 Olympics and won silver twelve years later

shooting countries ended up with three shooters, where some of the smaller ones didn't get to shoot at all. All this is somewhat contrary to the Olympic ethos. Great Britain, unfortunately, only managed to win one place, at Olympic Trap. Fortunately, there is a system of 'wild cards' given at the discretion of the President of UIT, which can give places to those countries that come very close to getting a quota place… Under this system, Great Britain received a place in Skeet. So our team in the 1988 Olympics was reduced to half strength by the imposition of these new rules.[136]

Ian Peel managed to win the quota place at Seoul. He gained it at the 1986 World Championship in Suhl, East Germany, with a score of 196 (for eighth place). He told me: 'It was exciting to be there but daunting to be a small fish in a very big pond. To be honest the occasion got to me. I was very keen to be part of it, to see a lot of sports, to see a lot of people. I ended twenty-fifth equal on 142 ex 150.'

Ian would prove that he could do much, much, better in 2000. The gold medal at Seoul went to the Dmitri Monakov, a Ukranian representing the USSR. By the next Olympiad, neither the GDR nor the USSR would exist.

1992 Barcelona

IF THE Barcelona Olympics represented the beginning of a new world order, it was also the end of an era—the last mixed competition in Olympic Skeet. Twenty-four year-old Zhang Shan of China outshot all the men, equalled the world record and set a new Olympic record with an extraordinary 200 ex 200. This took her to the new style final where she managed 23 ex 25. She was the first woman to beat the men in any shooting event at the Games. The Peruvian Juan Jorge Giha Yarur and Bruno Mario Rossetti of Italy took the silver and bronze medals respectively in the Skeet at Barcelona, both on 222. Diane 'Pinky' Le Grelle was the first British woman to make the open Skeet competition at an Olympic Games but it was not to be an especially successful Olympiad for her; she finished fifty-ninth out of sixty.

The Chinese woman's amazing success did not seem to please the men much. Female competitors were subsequently banned from taking part in Olympic Trap and Skeet events—an act of blatant sexism it would appear and one which might have been more discussed at the time had a freer spirit of discussion prevailed within Olympic organisations. The ban took effect in the 1996 Games. Women's Double Trap was brought in as something of a sop in 1996 and women's Skeet and Trap were introduced for 2000 and 2004. Among her other shooting credits, Zhang won the 1989 World Clay-target Championships—first Skeet individual and team—and the 1990 World Championship. The official website of the Chinese Olympic Committee notes of Zhang that she proved women could perform as well or better than men and must stand as a great inspiration to all shooters:

> She created a sensation in Barcelona by scoring 200 hits to equal the world record…
> She is the first and the last woman champion in this mixed event at the Olympic Games,

as after the Barcelona Games, Skeet shooting was competed separately by men and women contestants. Made a comeback in 1997 when the IOC decided to re-include this event at the Olympic Games. Earned China's first ticket in shooting to Sydney 2000 by winning the World Cup held in Cairo in 1998.[137]

The Czech shooter Petr Hrdlicka took the Trap title in Barcelona with an Olympic record 219. He beat Kazumi Watanabe of Japan in a shoot-off. Marco Venturini of Italy won the bronze (218) after another shoot-off for that medal too. In eleventh place was the twenty-year-old Australian Michael Diamond, an athlete whose star was about to ascend. Britain's Kevin Gill shot OT and finished twenty-second in his debut games.

Kim Rhode with a clutch of Olympic medals

1996 Atlanta

FOR THE centennial Games in 1996 in Atlanta, the Wolf Creek Shooting Complex outside the city staged the events at its state-of-the-art centre, 21 miles from the Olympic village. The clay range saw its busiest programme since before the First World War. In the men's Trap competition it was Australian John Maxwell who looked the best placed along with Germany's Karsten Binrich and the Korean Chul Sung Park. When it came to deciding the medals however, it was another Australian Michael Diamond, who shot a 25 in the final round to give him an Olympic record score of 149. Incredibly it was Australia's first shooting gold since the Paris Olympics of 1900. The Americans Josh Lakatos (147/28) and Lance Bade (147/27) took silver and bronze respectively. Double Trap events for both men and women were introduced in the 1996 Olympics. The seventeen-year-old Californian Kim Rhode shot a superb 141 ex 150 that automatically became an Olympic women's record and showed a remarkable lack of nerve in a young competitor. Close behind was Germany's Susanne Kiermayer (139) and Australia's Deserie Huddleston (also 139) who took silver and bronze respectively after a shoot-off. In men's Double Trap, Russell Mark of Australia shot an Olympic record 189 ex 200 to take the gold medal from the Italian Albano Pera and Bing Zhang of China. Both shot 183 and Pera took the silver after a shoot-off. Writing in the *BOA Official Report*, Peter Nichols noted that:

> …The tension in the final was palpable. Unusually for a shooting competition, the arena was like a bear pit with such volubility from the audience that they repeatedly triggered the acoustic release system, sending clays flying into the air while the competitors were still trying to assemble their thoughts.

Nineteen-year-old Richard Faulds, coached by Ian Coley, presented his Olympic credentials in Atlanta. Already a world junior champion, he had shot magnificently in a preliminary competition but missed six of his first ten clays in the final to see his first chance of Olympic glory disappear into the Georgian sky.

Ennio Falco of Italy took the Skeet championship after a fantastic tussle with Poland's Miroslaw Rzepkowski. Both men were neck and neck in the early stages. Falco with 149 managed to take the gold by one shot. Andrea Benelli made it a superb day for Italy when he beat Ole Rasmussen of Denmark to the bronze. The Official Report reflected on a highly successful competition:

Richard Faulds, who won gold for Britain in 2000

The first event of its type to sell out in the United States with standing room only crowds at six of the eight finals. Overflowing crowds for the eight-day competition set US records at all shooting events.[138]

As well as Richard Faulds (DT), the British Team in Atlanta consisted of Kevin Gill (OT and DT) and Peter Boden (OT).

2000 Sydney

SYDNEY'S OLYMPICS in 2000 earned the accolade 'best ever' from retiring IOC president Jan Antonio Samaranch and with good reason—not least for British clayshooting fans. They were blessed with magnificent facilities and plenty of sunshine. The television pictures that went around the world were of a great spectacle—but it was not quite as smooth as it looked. The clayshooters had to contend with difficult conditions: referring to their Cecil Park venue one shooter, Canadian George Leary, noted frankly 'It's a bitch of a range'. Michael Diamond, the great Australian Trap shot, commented that he had never experienced tougher conditions. All the more reason for the Sydney *Daily Telegraph* to proclaim him as '25 Carat Diamond' after he retained his gold medal. The enthusiastic copy read:

> The Goulbourn Hot shot became the first Australian to win two consecutive shooting gold medals. It was the day when determination soared through all barriers, Diamond blitzed the field to become arguably the greatest clay pigeon shooter of all time...

Diamond was inspired by his father Con, who coached him when he won in Atlanta but was not alive to see his success on home ground. Michael told the Australian newspaper: 'He didn't teach me for twenty-five years to just walk out there and fail. It's my first major competition without him so this is for him. I just wish he could have been here.'

Diamond certainly played the Olympic crowd expertly, at one point holding a finger to his lips to silence their screams of delight so that other competitors could concentrate. He shot better and faster as he closed in on his goal of becoming the second man to win back-to-back Olympic Trap titles. The images of a beaming Australian prime minister John Howard congratulating Diamond went around the world.

My favourite Diamond story however, was published in the *Sydney Morning Herald*. When asked what he thought about at the moment a clay is first presented he noted: 'Always the same thing... holy shit—there it goes and it looks like an aspirin! I better get it.'[139]

Ian Peel took second place behind Diamond. A textile colourist from Blackburn, Lancashire, by day, he is a world-class shooter when time allows. Ian qualified for the final 4 points behind Diamond but couldn't make up the deficit. He doggedly held on to his silver medal despite the strong challenge of Giovanni Pellielo of Italy.

In an age of professionalism, Ian Peel is a true embodiment of the old-style Olympic amateur spirit. Within hours of the medal ceremony he was on a flight back to Britain to resume his day job. It is also interesting to note that he was one of few capable of putting Diamond under real pressure. He exposed a hitherto unknown weakness in the Australian during the 2000 World Cup. Peel won it after Diamond missed four of the final eleven targets. He was, apparently, nervous at performing for the first time before a big home-town audience. 'I thought I was going to have a heart attack,' Diamond said at the time. 'I was green to the pressure.'[140]

Australia's Olympic trapshooters became household names in their homeland. Russell Mark, the defending Double Trap champion and state politician even got his own TV and radio shows. It is a sharp and sad contrast to the experiences of Britain's Double Trap gold medallist at Sydney, Richard Faulds, who can still walk down any street in Britain unnoticed. However, as the *BOA Olympic Report* noted:

> British shooting had to deal with an avalanche of negative publicity and legislation that might have threatened the existence of sport in this country. Faulds and Peel at last reversed that trend and provided some good news

Faulds and Mark are friends and trained together. In Sydney, the Olympic spirit was allegedly maintained by an AUS$10 side bet on the outcome of the competition. In the final dramatic shoot-off, it was Faulds who held steady, breaking three clays to Mark's two. It was Britain's first shooting gold in any discipline since 1988 and the first on the clay range for thirty-two years.

'Mark was generous beyond ten dollars in defeat,' said the official report. The present writer's memory was seeing Richard on TV saying, 'Someone slap me, I must be dreaming!' I was intrigued to read a day or two later in one of the British tabloids (admittedly not always the most reliable of sources), that Richard had trained to be the 'ice-man' by drinking numerous ice-cold drinks and being driven around in limousines with the air-conditioning made as cold as possible. If true, this 'method acting' worked.

In the women's Double Trap, the still young Kim Rhode took bronze on 139 behind Deborah Gelisio of Italy on 144 and Sweden's winner Pia Hansen on an excellent 148. Lithuania's Daina Gudzineviciuté won the women's Trap event with 93, just holding off the challenge of Delphine Racinet of France on 92 and Gao E [sic] of China on 90.

Back in ninth place was the 50-year-old Olympic veteran, Dr Susan Nattrass from, appropriately enough, Medicine Hat in Alberta, Canada. Nattrass, attending her fourth Olympiad, was one of the trailblazers for female competitors in the shooting sports. This Games was vindication of her long campaign to get more events for female shooters. Her own record was impressive. She had begun competing in 1971, qualified for Montreal 1976 and became the first woman trapshooter to compete with the men. In 1990 she had also become the first woman to compete in a shotgun event at a Commonwealth Games.

The *Toronto Globe & Mail* of 23 August 2000 quoted her as saying: 'These Olympics are so special because I worked so hard to get a separate women's event. I'm like a proud mother. I'm so excited for everyone. I'm so pleased it happened.'

'We've come a long way but there's still a long way to go. We can't give up the battle. At the Olympics in our event there are only twelve women spots compared to about forty for the men. We're still second class citizens but we're up from fourth class.'

In the men's Skeet competition, Mikola Milchev broke all 150 clays to set a new World and Olympic record on the way to winning gold for the Ukraine. The Azerbaijan shooter Zemfira Meftakhetdinova won the women's Skeet with a 98 from the Russian Svetlana Demina on 95 and Hungarian Diana Igaly on 93.

As well as Richard Faulds and Ian Peel, the British team included Peter Boden, one of the great stalwarts of British international Trap shooting in the modern era and, for Skeet, Drew Harvey and John Davison.

2004 Athens

THE 2004 Athens shooting events were staged at the purpose-built Markopolo centre, close to Athens international airport. There was much concern in the

Ed Ling, who represented Britain in Athens in 2004 at the age of just 21

build up to the Games that these facilities would not be ready. With the pre-Olympic test event a few days away, the by then retired Russell Mark branded the complex 'a disgrace'. Defending Olympic champion Michael Diamond missed the trials after becoming involved in a court case—he was acquitted and won selection after a hastily arranged shoot-out with Nathan Cassells to take the final Olympic place. He refused to comment on suggestions that the Greeks had invited him to take advantage of his Greek ancestry to switch teams.

His preparation was thus less relaxed than it might have been, though his problems seemed slight compared with American Bret Erickson, who collapsed and was rushed to hospital for emergency heart surgery just over a month before the Games began. Fitted with a pacemaker, he was delighted to take his place in the USA team assuring everyone his doctor had advised him to go to the Olympics. In the circumstances, his thirteenth place in the Double Trap, equal with Richard Faulds on 130 ex 150, was a scarcely credible achievement. Former squash champion Ahmed Almaktoum (UAE) shot 144, which he followed up with 45 (for a 189 total) in the final to take gold from Indian Rajyavardhan Singh Rathore (179).

Why did Richard Faulds only manage thirteenth place? First, and it is easily forgotten, merely to get even that far in an Olympic championship is impressive. He had to contend—in his own words as reported in the CPSA's *Pull!* magazine in October 2004—with the problem of expectation:

> The pressure was something that I can't really describe—until you have won an Olympic gold medal for yourself, you will never know. Undoubtedly this had an effect on my performance and this was true of many defending champions from Sydney, not just in

Bret Erickson, who competed with a pacemaker in 2004

shooting but across all sports.

While others struggled with high winds, Alexei Alipov took gold in the men's Trap competition with an outstanding 149—tying with the Olympic record established by Michael Diamond at Sydney in 2000. The silver medallist was Italy's Giovanni Pellielo, who trailed Alipov by 3 points. Australian Adam Vella took bronze on 145. Al Maktoum stamped his authority on the Games by being placed fourth at the single bird event too. Twice a gold medallist, Diamond failed to reach the finals after qualifying in eighth place, a fate not unlike that of Richard Faulds. Ian Peel's international swansong ended in a share of nineteenth place on a solid 116 ex 125. Twenty-one year-old Ed Ling, one of the youngest, was back in twenty-seventh place on 113 ex 125. It was a creditable conclusion to his first Olympics after a glittering career as a junior.

Suzie Balogh, another premier league Australian shooter, took the gold in woman's Trap with a total score of 88. The windy conditions made balance difficult for all shooters, especially the diminutive Spaniard Maria Quintanal. She finished with silver on 84 but might have done better on a less windswept day. Bronze went to Bo Na Lee of Korea on 83. A generation on from her first Olympic appearance, Susan Nattrass again produced a top ten finish and Sarah Gibbins (GB), soon to be married to fellow British international Mike Wixey, had a share of ninth place in distinguished company of Pia Hansen, women's Double Trap champion from 2000.

Eight years after her first gold medal in Double Trap, Kim Rhode stood on top of the medal rostrum once again. With the event due to be removed from the Olympic programme for Beijing in 2008, she was the first and last gold medallist. She had had a tough struggle with the South Korean Lee Bo Na. Both women were tied at 110 entering the final. Rhode finished with 146, one shot ahead of the Korean. She will now concentrate on Trap and Skeet for Beijing 2008.

Hungarian Diana Igaly took gold in the women's Skeet at the age of thirty-nine, after what her coach described as 'seven year's hard labour'. Her score was 97 ex 100 after a perfect series in the final. Wei Ning of China took the silver on 93 after a shoot-off with Zemfira Meftakhetdinova of Azerbaijan. Russell Mark's American-born wife Lauryn was competing in the Olympics for Australia at Skeet after switching nationalities. She just missed out on a medal.

The men's Skeet provided a thrilling finale with a dramatic shoot-off for gold won by the Italian Andrea Benelli (149/5) who promptly announced his retirement. 'These last few years have been a sacrifice,' he said. The second-placed Markko Kempainen of Finland (149/4) was not even top of his national rankings and astounded by taking silver after equalling the Olympic record with 125/125 in the first round. Cuban Juan Miguel Rodriguez took the Skeet bronze (147/10) after a three man shoot-off. Britain's Skeet rookie, Richard Brickell, could not repeat his good showing in the pre Olympic test event finishing only thirty-fourth on 115 ex 125.

Considering the number of British shotgunners and the level of preparation, Athens 2004 was a bit disappointing. It is sad, though, that this relatively poor performance has led to a partial withdrawal of funding. Britain still has some of the best shotgunners in the world. They need to be nurtured.

The future of clayshooting

CLAYSHOOTING IN the twenty-first century is growing again. This is, of course, great news. The general decline in the number of British shooters and the pressure that they have been put under by successive governments, both Conservative and Labour, is not. We may anticipate more restrictive and pointless legislation on firearms and shooting. It is the nature of the nanny state, which is opposed to expressions of individual liberty. Nor is it especially cheering to note that, as far as shotgunning is concerned, the threat of non-toxic shot looms large. It is probably only a matter of a few years before lead is banned for clays and general gameshooting, just as it has been for wildfowling and for shooting over Sites of Special Scientific Interest.

This is especially bad news because the problems of lead shot have been over-stated and because the replacements for it are expensive. The cheapest, steel (actually soft iron) has severe ballistic limitations. It is just about adequate for Skeet and first barrel use in Trap. Steel has severe deficiencies for all birds at long range. Because the shot is so hard, it also changes the feel of recoil. It is typically a sharper experience firing steel than the equivalent lead load—and it affects the choice of choke constriction. Steel requires less choke than lead to achieve a similar pattern. In some guns, there is a safety issue: choke for steel should be limited to a 20 thou—'half'—constriction.

Many shoots today are also suffering persecution on noise grounds. This is likely to get worse as our society becomes increasingly urbanised with more brownfield and greenfield sites being developed. Clay shoots are directly threatened by new housing developments. I know of several grounds that have been sold off to build estates in recent years—the owners feeling it was time to take the money and run. Land is becoming a scarce commodity in our over-populated world. Finding land suited to shooting—ie not too close to housing—is extremely difficult. The capital costs of developing a shooting ground have increased disproportionately as a result. You would not get much change from £1 million if you tried to open a medium-sized commercial facility in the UK today if you could find a site where you could overcome planning and noise issues.

As clayshooting requires more and more capital to be conducted professionally, there is also an increase in pressure on smaller shooting businesses and clubs. This is because of the factors already discussed and because there are fewer landowners willing to accommodate small operations for modest rents. Everyone knows and counts the cost today. Even the Ministry of Defence, which in previous years used to do much to encourage civilian shooting by offering shooting clubs land and use of ranges at peppercorn rates, has now taken the view that clubs must pay 'market rates'.

All things considered, it is a tough new world and it is essential to be realistic if we are to secure a future. It can be done—

Miss Betty Grosvenor and her mother Mrs Ida Grosvenor at West London Shooting School in July 1949 at the Sporting Ladies' Championship

that is the good news—but it will take hard work and vision. Clayshooting is the most politically correct of all the shooting sports. Our relatively unobjectionable status bodes well for our future provided we don't get smug.

Clayshooting is intrinsically exciting. It appeals to modern man and modern woman. But too many ignore the evident threats on the horizon in my opinion. After tragedies like Hungerford, Dunblane and Columbine, we could—in the worst scenario—be just one such incident away from non-existence.

There is much work to be done. After years of failing, we are beginning to get over the message that it is criminals with illegal guns that are the real danger to the risk-obsessed public. There is more co-operation than there used to be between organisations. We are beginning to shout more loudly for our rights. If clayshooting is to prosper, though, we must explain the true nature of our sport to a wider audience. We know it is no more than 'golf with guns' and rather safer than fishing, or football. With the partial success of a nominal hunt ban in Britain, the considerable resources of the 'anti' lobby are already turned on shooting. Driven gameshooting is the obvious first target. If it went, clayshooting would soon follow.

The most sensible strategy must be to defend the gates of Rome forward of the walls. There is safety in numbers and a corresponding danger in decline. If shooting is to last for future generations, we must go on a dynamic recruiting drive. It is in the interests of all the major associations and commercial interests to do this, just as it was in the interests of the arms and ammunition companies to form the American Shooting Association in 1890 and the Inanimate Bird Shooting Association in 1893. The potential recruits are there; we just have to reach them. If each of us brought just one more person into the sport, much of the work would be done. If we don't, we only have ourselves to blame for the consequence: evil prospers when good men and women do nothing.

Another identifiable issue is cost. Clayshooting can be expensive, especially to those who aspire to the highest levels. To succeed in competition today you must shoot much more than in years past. Entering the sport has also become more expensive. This is a particular concern for young people. It has been addressed to a degree at game fairs, where subsidised shooting is sometimes on offer. There needs to be more. Shooting grounds and clubs could help the under-twenty-ones with special rates. Some suggest a 50 per cent reduction for under-sixteens (assuming that they do not fall victim to some crass new law) and 25 per cent for under-twenty-ones on clays, with cartridges at cost plus handling. It would reap great rewards in the long-term. There needs to be a massive, properly co-ordinated, national campaign to get more people shooting clays. We need to make more use of local radio and papers and we need more out-of-the-closet celebrity endorsement.

Women are coming into the sport in ever-increasing numbers and female shooters should be encouraged by the fact that they can so much more easily than other sports beat men. Manufacturers would be well advised to create products better suited to their female clients, such as options of higher, shorter, stocks on popular guns. Many women feel hard done by on the prize front too. As with young people, more should be done to encourage female shooters. There is also a need to attract more older shooters of both sexes on to the layouts. Shooting can be pursued longer than almost any other sport and may be started in late middle age with excellent results. I frequently have men in their late forties or early fifties asking if it is too late to start shooting competitively. Of course it isn't.

In the US, clayshooting is not only a mainstream sport, it is a true family affair. It could and should be in the UK too. At the Grand, for example, they frequently celebrate the fact that pre-teens and octogenarians take part.

There is a need for more investment in first class facilities in Britain to attract new shooters and for our shooters to get the practice they need to succeed at the international level. As far as coaching and instruction are concerned, there is a need for more general competence. Shooting has not kept up with the times—fishing, golf and tennis are streets ahead on the instructional front. There is too much variation in the quality of instruction in both Britain and the United States. While 'corporate days' have introduced significant numbers of new shooters, tuition must be of a consistent professional standard to ensure we project a positive image and to get novices off to the right start. Organisers of corporate events are sometimes tempted to bring in amateurs or demi-professionals to cut costs. There are consequently some abysmally poor days (if judged by the standard of the teaching offered) as well as some truly excellent ones. There are, meantime, too many partially trained instructors. I have been involved in the training of dozens of instructors myself but I would make the point that it takes much more than a badge and a three-day course to create a competent instructor.

Although 'centres of excellence' are to be welcomed, there are disadvantages to excessive commercialisation of shooting. Smaller, amateur clubs are dying out because of all the problems mentioned and a dearth of members willing to roll up their sleeves. The old-style clubs offered a good atmosphere, a cheap introduction to the sport and economical practice. There are still some out there. As I write this, I have a happy memory of a round of Skeet at a small club in rural Pennsylvania that cost me US$3 (£1.50 or so at current exchange rates). Long may it thrive. The United States also provides good models of how large, modern clubs may be created on a sophisticated co-operative model.

Reasonably priced practice at good quality targets is a big issue when you consider our international performance. With so many people shooting shotguns in the UK, we really should do better at the Olympics and Commonwealth Games than we have done. Braithwaite, Peel and Faulds have been honourable exceptions. The problem, as Col Crossman pointed out in the US context some years ago, is that we practise the wrong games—or they play the wrong ones at the Olympics.

If we are to succeed in the international disciplines, more of us must shoot them more often. Many of us would love to see Sporting get to the Olympics in some form. We need, meantime, more Olympic Trap and Double Trap layouts nationwide and more of us need to practise the tougher Olympic version of Skeet. There are people out there with talent but many of them give up on the international disciplines because of cost or distance and because they do not see immediate results. These are problems that can be addressed.

A thriving, competitive market for leisure provides an opportunity to promote high standards at new luxury venues. As I write this, it has just been announced that a new company—Clayhouse—has been formed to open twenty new major shooting grounds in the UK. The idea is to run them like golf clubs. I know the people involved and they have the talent and drive required. They may well pull it off. To a degree, there is little doubt that this will be our future—bigger grounds, regional centres, with better facilities. It will help with raising standards, but it is important to keep the amateur clubs going as well. The two things are not mutually exclusive. They complement each other.

Finally, let us consider technology. Readers may have noted the omission of 'laser shooting' from this book. It was deliberate. I am no fan—at least as far as the outdoor game is concerned. It may be quiet, but there is no requirement for forward allowance and it is consequently nothing like real shooting. Lasers can be a useful gun-fitting aid, however. And, some of the indoor computer-based 'clayshooting' simulators are

High tech shooting simulator

Competitions for side by sides only are increasingly popular. This pic shows Atkin Grant & Lang's Ken Duglan (left) and Mike Yardley after Mike won the 2004 British Side by Side Championship. He used a non-rebounding lock Lang hammer gun of 1870s vintage to win the main event. The event was held at Broomhillls Shooting Ground, home of Atkin Grant & Lang

highly enjoyable. These have a role as entertainment and, in some forms, may be useful for training too. The best are surprisingly realistic, certainly as far as the simulation of Trap shooting is concerned.

I do not see most of our guns changing much in the next 25 years, though I note the radical new offerings from Beretta and Browning—the UGB25 Xcel semi-automatic and the Cynergy with interest. It is possible that bore sizes might be reduced one day—with less payload, less noise and a greater challenge relative to range. Sound moderators could be forced on us—but, let us hope not.

Compressed air (as once tried in Crossman's small bore shotgun) or something else as yet unknown might replace conventional propellants. Consumable cartridges were once used in rifles but rejected. It is not beyond the bounds of imagination, though, to conceive of a consumable shotgun cartridge, perhaps combined with electric detonation. The composition of our targets will certainly change in the years to come. Petroleum-based products in the mix cannot have that long a future. The future is green and friendly. The ice target, made on range, certainly seems an idea worth revisiting, especially for large commercial facilities.

Whatever the future brings, it is hard to imagine a substitute for the primal thrill of seeing a moving target shot in mid-air, nor should we—in my very biased opinion—be especially inclined to find one. If generations to come lose the opportunity to experience the pleasure of a clay bird breaking first hand, if they are restricted to a virtual shooting gallery (and a virtual life), their spirits will be the poorer. Meantime, these really are the golden years. *Vive le Ball-Trap mes amis.* Long live clayshooting.

Appendices

Useful addresses

Shooting Periodicals

Target Sports
Lawrence House
Morrell Street
Leamington Spa
Warwickshire CV32 5SZ
Tel: (01926) 339808
wes@blazepublishing.co.uk

Sporting Shooter
Archant
Wendens Ambo
Essex CB11 4GB
Tel: (01799) 544200
news@sportingshooter.co.uk
www.sportingshooter.co.uk

The Field
King's Reach Tower
Stamford Street, London SE1 9LS
Tel: (020) 7261 5198
Fax: (020) 7261 5358
Sarah_Fitzpatrick@ipcmedia.com
www.thefield.co.uk

Shooting Times
King's Reach Tower
Stamford Street, London SE1 9LS
Tel: (020) 7261 6190
Fax: (020) 7261 7179
steditorial@ipcmedia.com
www.shootingtimes.co.uk

Clay Shooting
Thruxton Down House
Thruxton Down, Andover
Hants SP11 8PR
Tel: (01264) 889533
Fax: (01264) 889622
info@clayshooting.com
www.clay-shooting.com

Shooting consultancy

Michael Yardley
Tel. 07860 401068
yardleypen@aol.com

Holland & Holland
Ducks Hill Road
Northwood
Middlesex HA6 2SS
Tel. (01923) 825349
Fax. (01923) 836266
steve.denny@hollandandholland.com
www.hollandandholland.com

James Purdey & Son Ltd
Audley House
57-58 South Audley Street
London W1K 2ED
Tel: (020) 7499 1801
Fax: (020) 7355 3297
enquiries@james-purdey.co.uk
www.purdey.com

EJ Churchill
Park Lane
Lane End
High Wycombe
Bucks HP14 3NS
Tel: (01494) 883227
Fax: (01494) 883733
shootingground@ejchurchill.com
www.ejchurchill.com

West London Shooting School
Sharvel Lane
West End Road
Northolt
Middlesex
UB5 6RA
Tel: 07000 12 20 12
Fax: (020) 8842 1493
www.shootingschool.co.uk
info@shootingschool.co.uk

For a full listing of UK gunshops, visit
www.gundealer.net

Shooting organisations

The British Association for Shooting
and Conservation (BASC)
Marford Mill
Rossett
Wrexham
Clwyd
LL12 0HL
Tel: (01244) 573000
Fax: (01244) 573001
enquiries@basc.org.uk
www.basc.org.uk

The Muzzle Loaders' Association of
Great Britain
PO Box 339
Saint Helier
Channel Islands
Jersey JE4 9YQ
Tel: (01534) 733194
Fax: (01534) 733194
www.mlagb.com

National Rifle Association
Bisley National Shooting Centre
Brookwood
Surrey GU24 0PB
Tel: (01483) 797777
Fax: (01483)797285
info@nra.org.uk
www.nsc-bisley.co.uk

Clay Pigeon Shooting Association
Edmonton House
Bisley Camp
Brookwood
Woking
Surrey
GU24 0NP
Tel: (01483) 485400
Fax: (01483) 485410
info@cpsa.co.uk

BICTSF
address and contact details as CPSA

Irish CPSA
Joe Wade (secretary)
Tel: (00 353) 6733146

Ulster CPSA
Jan Daley
33 Ballyculter Road
Downpatrick
Co Down BT30 7BL
Norther Ireland
Tel/fax: (028) 4461 2104
secretary@upcsa.freeserve.co.uk
www.ucpsa.com

Scottish Clay Target Association
Ricky Wright
40 Cranwell Drive
Wideopen
Newcastle NE13 6AS
Tel: (0191) 236 3855
Fax: (0191) 236 5326
scta.secretary@talk21.com
www.scta.co.uk

Welsh Clay Target Shooting
Association
Steve Ball
Mid Wales Shooting School
Ffinnant Farm,
Trefeglwys
Caersws SY17 5QY
Tel: (01686) 430583
steve@wctsa.fslife.co.uk
www.wctsa.co.uk

Amateur Trap Shooting Association
601 W National Road,
Vandalia
Ohio 45377, USA
Tel: (00 1) 937 898 4638
Fax: (00 1) 937 898 5472
www.shoot.ata.com

National Skeet Shooting Association
(NSSA)
5931 Roft Road
San Antonio
Texas 78253, USA
Tel: (00 1) 210 688 3371
Fax: (00 1) 210 688 3014
www.nssa-nsca.com

National Sporting Clays Association
(NSCA)
address and contact details as NSSA

National Rifle Association (NRA)
11250 Waples Mill Road
Fairfax
Virginia 22030, USA
Tel: (00 1) 800 NRA 3888
www.nra.org

ISSF (formerly UIT)
Bavariering 21
D-80336 Munich, Germany
Tel: (00 49) 89 5443550
Fax: (00 49) 89 5435544
munich@issf-shooting.org
www.issf-shooting.org

FITASC (*Fédération Internationale de Tir
aux Armes Sportives de Chasse*)
10 rue de Lisbonne
Paris 75008
France
Tel: (00 33) 1 42 93 40 53
Fax: (00 33) 1 42 93 58 22
fitasc@wanadoo.fr
www.fitasc.com

USA Shooting
Olympic Training Center
One Olympic Plaza
Colorado Springs
Colorado 80909-5762
Tel: (001) 719 578 4883

Royal Armouries Museum
Armouries Drive
Leeds LS10 1LT
Tel: (0113) 220 1999
Fax. (0113) 220 1934
enquiries@armouries.org.uk
www.royalarmouries.org

Imperial War Museum
Lambeth Road
London SE1 6HZ
Tel: (020) 7416 5320
Fax. (020) 7416 5374
photos@iwm.org.uk
www.iwm.org.uk

John Cavendish (Gnats)
Hall Farm
Farringdon, Alton
Hampshire GU34 3DT
Tel: (01420) 588275
Fax: (01420) 587055
www.e-vents.co.uk

American ZZ
171 Spring Hill Road
Trumbull
Connecticut 06611
Tel: (00 1) 203 261 1058
Fax: (00 1) 203 452 9359

Kenneth Gagnon
Quack Sporting Clays Inc
4 Ann & Hope Way
PO Box 98
Cumberland RI 02864
Tel: (00 1) 401 723 8202
Fax: (001) 401 722 5910

Proof houses

The Worshipful Gunmakers'
Company
48 Commercial Road
London EC1 1LP
Tel: (020) 7481 2695
Fax: (020) 7480 5102
gunmakers@btconnect.com

Guardians of the Birmingham Proof
House
Gun Barrel Proof House
Banbury Street
Birmingham B5 5RH
Tel: (0121) 643 3860
Fax. (0121) 643 7872
info@gunproof.com
www.gunproof.com

Shooting book dealers

Tideline books
PO Box 4
Rhyl
Clwyd LL18 1AG
Tel: (01745) 354919
Fax: (01745) 356919
sales@tidelinebooks.co.uk
www.tidelinebooks.co.uk

Coch-y-Bonddu Books (Paul Morgan)
Machynlleth
Powys SY20 8DJ
Tel: (01654) 702837
Fax: (01654) 702857
orders@anglebooks.com
www.anglebooks.com

Shooting Books (strong on
clayshooting)
The Thatches
Teffont Magna
Salisbury SP3 5QT
Tel/Fax: (01722) 716052
sales@shootingbooks.co.uk
www.shootingbooks.co.uk

David AH Grayling
Verdun House
Shap, Penrith
Cumbria CA10 3NG
Tel/fax: (01931) 716746
Graylingbook@fsbdial.co.uk
www.davidgraylingbooks.co.uk

Hereward Books
17 High Street
Haddenham
Ely
Cambridgeshire CB6 3XA
Tel: (01353) 740821
Fax: (01353) 741721
sales@herewardbooks.co.uk
www.herewardbooks.co.uk

Tony Read
Home Farm Books
Home Farm
44 Evesham Road
Cookhill
Alcester
Warwickshire B49 5LJ
Tel: (01789) 763115
Fax: (01789) 766086
readbk@globalnet.co.uk

ABEBooks.com
www.abebooks.com

UK clubs and grounds

SOUTH-EAST

Bedfordshire

Sporting Targets, near Riseley
Ten shooting ranges, three high
towers, tuition, gun shop
Tel: (01234) 708893
www.sportingtargets.co.uk

Berkshire

Four Counties CTC
near Newbury
Sporting, DTL, FITASC, tuition
Tel: (01635) 201657
www.fourcountiesctc.co.uk

Buckinghamshire

EJ Churchill Shooting Ground
(West Wycombe SS), High Wycombe
Sporting, high tower, Skeet, DTL,
tuition, gunshop. Tel: (01494) 883227
www.ejchurchill.com or www.wwsg.
org.uk

Hornet Shooting Ground
near Long Crendon
Sporting, FITASC.
Tel: (01494) 883715
www.adventure001.com/hornet

Oxford Gun Co Gun Club
near Oakley
Sporting, Skeet, have-a-go days,
tuition, corporate
Tel: (01844) 238308

Valley View International
Shooting Ground
near Amersham
Sporting, Skeet, tuition, corporate
Tel: 07860 575055

Hampshire

Cavendish Sporting
near Bentley. Tuition
Tel: (01420) 588275
Fareham Clay Target Club
Skeet, Sporting, ABT, tuition
Tel: (01329) 315185
www.farehamctc.org.uk

Frobury Farm Sporting Club
near Newbury
Sporting, Skeet, tuition, gun shop
Tel: (01635) 297122 www.frobury.co.uk

Lains Shooting School
near Andover
Skeet, practice, tuition
Tel: (01246) 889467 or 07768 632567
www.lainsshootingschool.co.uk

Romsey Clay Pigeon Club
Sporting. Tel: (023) 8069 4623

Test Valley Clay Pigeon Club
near Basingstoke
Sporting, Skeet
Tel: (0118) 981 9202

Three Counties
near Hook. Sporting. Tuition
Contact Paul Beecher on 07739 556790
www.beechershooting.co.uk

Waller's Ash
near Winchester
Skeet, DTL, Sporting
Tel: (01962) 774248

Hertfordshire

Broomhills Shooting Ground
Markyate. Tuition, gunshop
Tel: (01582) 842280
www.broomhills.co.uk

Lea Valley Shooting Assn
near Hertford. Tuition
Tel: (01992) 553693
www.lvsa.org.uk

Nuthampstead SG
Sporting, DTL, OTr, tuition, shop
Tel: (01763) 848172
www.nuthampsteadshootingground.
co.uk

Park Street & District GC
Tel: (01923) 677294

Isle of Wight

Isle of Wight Gun Club
near Godshill.
Sporting, Skeet, DTL, ABT.
Tel: (01983) 567330

Kent

Abbey Shooting Detling SG.
Skeet, Sporting.
Tel: (01580) 752074

Greenfields Shooting Ground
near Canterbury.
Practice, tuition, have-a-go days.
Tel: (01227) 713222
www.greenfieldsshooting.co.uk

Dartford Clay Shooting Club
Sporting, Skeet, OTr, Compact.
Tel: (01322) 311001
www.dartfordcsc.co.uk

Invicta ZZ
off A21 between Tonbridge and
Tunbridge Wells.
Helice (ZZ) only. Canteen serves full
English breakfast until the cook goes
to shoot. Reg shoots only.
Tel: (01580) 892542

Kent Gun Club
near Dartford.
Trap, DTL, ADT, ZZ. Free tuition to
beginners.
Tel: (01883) 340248

Kingsferry Gun Club
Kingsferry Bridge.
Skeet, Sportrap. Non-lead shot only.
Tel: (01795) 877037

Martin Gorse Wood CPC
near Dover.
Sporting.
Tel: (01304) 212319

Springfield Clay Pigeon Club
Sandwich. Skeet, Sporting, DTL.
Tel: (01843) 863265

West Kent Shooting School
near Tunbridge Wells.
Sporting, Skeet, Ball Trap, high
pheasant flush & Compact.
Tel: (01892) 834306
www.wkss.demon.co.uk

London

A1 Shooting Ground
near Rowley Green.
OTr, DTL, Sporting, tuition.
Tel: (020) 8441 9986
www.a1sg.freeserve.co.uk

West London Shooting School
Northolt. 100 traps, 8 towers, tuition,
restaurant, corporate.
Tel: (020) 8845 1377
www.shootingschool.co.uk

Surrey

Bisley Gun Club
near Brookwood. DTL. CPSA
competitions held 1st & 3rd Saturday
of month. Tel: (01737) 242332
www.bisleygunclub.org.uk

Bisley Shooting Ground
near Brookwood, Woking.
Sporting (inc towers) tuition &
practice, corporate. Gun shop. Open
7 days. Booking essential.
Tel: (01483) 797017
www.bisleyshooting.co.uk

Caterham Clays
off Caterham bypass.
Sporting. Tel: (01883) 622656

Gatwick Clay Shooting School
Skeet, SKD, DTL, Sporting
Tel: (01306) 884863.

Horne Clay Pigeon Club
100 Sporting shoots held at Court
Farm, Chaldon, near Caterham;
Gatton Bottom, Merstham, near
Reigate; and Godstone Vineyard,
Godstone. Tel: (01342) 842986
www.clayandcountry.f2s.com

National Clay Shooting Centre
Bisley.
Four OTr layouts, Skeet, OSkeet, ABT,
Double Trap.
Tel: (01483) 797666
www.nsc-clays.co.uk

The Star Gun Club
near Chessington.
Sporting. Tel: (020) 8898 3129

Sussex

Lower Lodge SG
Billingshurst.
Skeet, Sporting & DTL. Tuition by
appointment. Tel: (01403) 823380
www.clay-shooting-grounds.co.uk

Northall Clay Pigeon Club
Sporting, Compact, ABT, D/T, Skeet,
tuition, corporate. Tel: (01825) 791783

Southdown Sporting Gun Club
near Worthing.
Sporting, Skeet, FITASC, Sportrap,
DTL, ABT, tuition.
Tel: (01903) 877555 or (01903) 750244
www.southdownsgc.co.uk

EAST ANGLIA

Cambridgeshire

Country Pursuits
between Chittering and Stretham.
Sporting, Sportrap.
Tel: (01353) 669300

Gransden Airfield SG
Sporting, OSkeet, FITASC, tower.
Tel: (01767) 627663
www.gransdenshootingground.co.uk

Haddon Lodge Shooting Ground
near Peterborough.
Sporting incl tower, tuition.
Tel: (01733) 240119
www.haddon-lodge.co.uk

Essex

Braintree Shooting Ground
Sporting, Skeet, DTL, tuition.
Tel: (01376) 343900

Bush Hill Clay Club
near Billericay. Sporting.
Tel: (01277) 220974

Clacton Gun Club
Little Clacton. Esp, Skeet, DTL.
Tel: (01255) 673146

Colchester Garrison Clay
Pigeon Club Sporting.
Tel: (01206) 330712
Essex Shooting Ground
near Harlow. Sporting, FITASC,
Skeet, OSkeet, ABT, tuition.
Tel: 07836 504726

Mayland & District Gun Club
ESK, DTL, compact.
Tel: (01268) 470 323

Orion Gun Club
near Brentwood.
Sporting, Skeet, DTL.
Tel: 07000 486258
www.gunclub.co.uk

Parkford Shooting Centre
Sporting, Skeet, DTL, practice.
Tel: (01255) 820230

Southend Gun Club
near Rochford
Sporting, Skeet, OSkeet DTL.
Tel: (01702) 219395

Three Acres Sporting Clays
Leaden Roding.
Sporting, pool.
Tel: 07768 742117

Waltham Abbey SG
Sporting, tuition. Tel: 07768 742117
www.claypigeonshoot.co.uk

Spellbrook CSC
50 bird Sporting, tuition
Tel: (01279) 419427
www.spellbrookclays.co.uk

Norfolk

Mid Norfolk Shooting School
Taverham, near Norwich.
Tuition, corporate.
Tel: (01603) 860436
www.midnorfolkshootingschool.com

Suffolk

Badwell Ash GC
near Bury St Edmunds.
Sporting, Skeet, DTL, ABT.
Tel: (01359) 259547

Barrow Heath Gun Club
near Newmarket. Sporting.
Tel: (01322) 405226

High Lodge Shooting School
near Saxmundham.
Practice, tuition, corporate. Skeet, SkD,
DTL, Sporting. Tel: (01986) 784347
www.highlodge.co.uk

Lakenheath Clay Target Club
Between Mildenhall and Brandon.
Skeet, DTL, Sportrap, gun room,
tuition, restaurant. Tel: (01638) 533353
www.lctc.co.uk

NORTH-WEST

Cheshire

Catton Hall Shooting Ground
near Frodsham.
Practice, tuition, corporate.
Tel: (01928) 788295

Holmes Chapel Shooting Ground
Tel: (01477) 532165

Middle Farm Clay Shoot
Bredbury. Tel: (0161) 4302492

North Wales Shooting School
near Chester. Sporting, Skeet, OSkeet,
FITASC, tuition, practice.
Tel: (01244) 812219

Cumbria

Penrith & District Gun Club
DTL, Sporting, tuition.
Tel: (01539) 624402

Isle of Man

Ayre Clay Pigeon Club
Blue Point, at north end of island.
Skeet, DTL, ABT, Double-Trap, UT,
OT and Sporting. Clubhouse with

refreshments. Shoot fixtures every
Sunday and practice available Weds
evenings May-August.
Tel: (01624) 880744
www.bluepointshooting.co.uk

Lancashire

A6 Clay Target Centre
Westhoughton, near Bolton.
ABT, DTL, Skeet, Sportrap, tuition,
restaurant. Tel: (01942) 843578
www.a6ctc.co.uk

Blackpool Gun Club
near Kirkham Preston.
Sporting. Tel: 07730 409415

Kelbrook Shooting School
near Foulridge. Tel: (01282) 861632

Worsley Clay Shooting Club
Sporting, Skeet, tuition, clubhouse.
Tel: (01704) 566554
www.worsley-claysportsclub.com

SOUTH-WEST

Cornwall

Cart Ridge Shooting Club
East of A38 between Landrake &
Tideford.
Sporting, tuition.
Tel: (01752) 851262

County Gun Club
Tel: (01579) 363301

North Cornwall Gun Club
near North Petherwin.
DTL, tuition by appointment.
Tel: (01566) 785550

Trax and Trails Countryside Activity
Centre, Tamar Valley.
Tuition for groups and individuals.
Tel: (01579) 384714
www.traxandtrails.co.uk

Devon

Ashcombe Shooting Ground
near Dawlish. Sporting.
Tel: (01626) 866766

Axminster Gun Club
DTL, tuition.
Tel: (01404) 881588

Bradford Shooting Ground
Sporting, Skeet, DTL, ABT.
Tel: (01409) 281341

Culm Vale Gun Club
near Cullompton.
Sporting.
Tel: (01460) 234245

Four Seasons Gun Club near Ottery
St Mary.
Sporting, DTL.
Tel: (01395) 271335

Newnham Park SG
near Plymouth.
Sporting, Skeet, ABT, DTL, Sportrap,
tuition.
Tel: (01752) 343456
www.newnham.co.uk

Shalden Shooting School
near Shillingford.
Sporting.
Tel: (01398) 331021
www.shaldenshootingschool.co.uk

South West Shooting School
Lynton Cross. Sporting, Compact.
Tel: (01271) 862545

Dorset

Purbeck Shooting School
near Poole.
Sporting, Skeet, OSkeet, FITASC,
Sportrap.
Tel: (01929) 405101
www.shooting.uk.com

Southern Counties Shooting
Sporting, Skeet, OSkeet, FITASC,
Sportrap, DTL, ABT, tower.
Tel: (01935) 83625
www.southern-counties.com

Gloucestershire

Chatcombe Estate Shooting School
near Cheltenham.
Sporting, FITASC, OT, gunshop.
Tel: (01242) 870391

Cotswold Clay Pigeon Club
Fosse Way, near Stow.
Sporting, pool. Tel: (01451) 821431
Gloucester Clay Shooting Club
on the A38 between Tewkesbury &
Gloucester. Skeet, OSkeet.
Tel: (01242) 573501

Hollow Fosse Shooting Ground
near Cirencester & Fossebridge.
Sporting, Pro Sport, practice, tuition &
corporate.
Tel: (01285) 654849 or 07810 228503

Longridge Shooting Ground
Bromsberrow Heath, Ledbury.
Tel: (07971) 447138

Mork Clay Club
near St Briavels.
Sporting. Tel: (01594) 530102

Stroud & District Clay Shooting Club
near Bisley. Skeet, OSkeet, DTL.
Tel: (01453) 764443

Somerset

Cheddar Valley Trap & Skeet Club
near Wells & Glastonbury.
Sporting, Skeet, OSkeet, OTr, tutition.
Tel: (01749) 871055
www.cheddarshooting.co.uk

Mendip Shooting Ground
near Wells.
Sporting, Skeet, DTL, ABT, clubhouse,
gunshop. Tel: (01749) 673471

Podimore Shooting Ground
Ilchester. Sporting, FITASC, Sportrap.
Tel: (01935) 862510
www.podimore-shooting.co.uk

Shipham Sporting Clays
near Clevedon.
Sporting, tuition, practice.
Tel: (01275) 877851

Wiltshire

Barbury Shooting School
near Swindon.
Skeet, Compact, tuition, corporate.
Tel: (01793) 530564 or 07732 684442
www.barburyshootingschool.com

Cadley Clay Shooting Ground
near Marlborough.
Sporting, practice, tutition, corporate.
Tel: (01672) 512052
www.cadleyclays.co.uk

Urchfont Clay Pigeon Club
near Devizes.
DTL, Sporting.
Tel: (01380) 721218

Wood Farm Clay Shooting Club
near Warminster.
Skeet, DTL, Sporting.
Tel: (01747) 860471

Wylye Valley Shooting Ground
Sporting.
Tel: (01458) 273077

MIDLANDS

Derbyshire

Bakewell & Wirksworth Clay Pigeon
Club
near Brassington.
Sporting.
Tel: (01629) 814395

Darley Dale Clay Pigeon Shooting
Club
near Brassington.
Sporting.
Tel: (01629) 733161

Doveridge Clay Shooting Club
near Doveridge.
Skeet, DTL, Sporting.
Tel: (01889) 565986

Lowes Lane Shooting Ground
near Swadlincote.
Sporting, Skeet, DTL, high tower,
flush, tuition.
Tel: (01332) 866800

Ockbrook Sporting Clays
near Derby.
Tel: (01773) 714731

Yeaveley Estate
near Ashbourne.
Sporting, Tuition by appt.
Tel: (01335) 330247

Hereford & Worcester

Longridge Shooting Ground
off M50 at J2.
Tel: 07971 447138

South Worcester SG
near Upton-upon-Severn.
DTL, Sporting, Practice, tuition.
Tel: (01684) 310605
www.swsg.co.uk

Worcestershire Gun Club
near IIIey.
DTL, Sporting.
Tel: (01384) 891 358 or 07836 225580

Wyre Forest Guns
near Button Oak.
Sporting.
Tel: (01299) 403730

Leicestershire

Bagworth Miners Clay Pigeon Club
near Coalville.
DTL, Sporting, ABT.
Tel: (01530) 260816

Grange Farm Sporting Clays
near Desford.
Sporting, Skeet, OSkeet, DTL, ABT.
Tel: (01455) 822208

Hoton Clay Club
Tel: (01509) 560288

Kegworth Shooting Ground
Signposted from j24 off M1.
Sporting.
Tel: (01509) 235420 or 07973 111650

Kibworth Shooting Ground
off A6 Kibworth to Market
Harborough road.
Sporting, Skeet, DTL, ABT.
Tel: (0116) 279 3160/6001

Market Harborough & District SC
Sporting, Skeet, OSkeet, DTL.
Tel: (01858) 463698

Normanton Shooting Ground
near Thurlaston.
Sporting, ABT, DT
Tel: (01455) 888210

Lincolnshire

Ancholme Valley Clay Target Club
Kirton Lindsey Airfield.
ESK, SKD, DTL, ABT, Sporting
Tel: (01777) 818362
www.ancholme-valley-ctc.org.uk

Crowland Gun Club
between Spalding and Peterborough.
Skeet, SKD, DTL, Sporting.
Tel: (01780) 720 260

Grimsthorpe Estate Shooting Ground
near Edenham. Sporting.
Tel: (01778) 591128

Lincolnshire Shooting Ground
Sutton Bridge.
Sporting, Skeet, ABT, Sportrap, tower,
tuition, restaurant, corporate.
Tel: (01406) 359300 or (01945) 700622
www.lincolnshireshootingground.
co.uk

Pinewood Shooting Ground
near Gainsborough.
Sporting, Skeet, DTL, OT, D/T,
Compact.
Tel: (01427) 628900.
www.pinewood-sg.fsnet.co.uk

Sinclairs Shooting Ground
Whaplode Drove, near Holbeach.
Skeet, Sporting, Compact, ABT &
DTL. Open Weds-Sun, all year round.
Tel: (01406) 540362.

Nottinghamshire

Cockett Farm Shooting Ground
near Mansfield.
Sporting, Skeet, STr, White Gold,
tuition.
Tel: (01623) 882244
www.cockettfarm.com

Nottingham & District Gun Club
DTL, Skeet, OSkeet.
Tel: (0115) 927 3492

Oxton Shooting School
Sporting, Skeet, Compact, Sportrap,
ABT, DTL, FITASC, tuition, shop.
Tel: (01623) 882523.
www.netconnected.com/oxton

Stilehollow Shooting School
near Mansfield.
Sporting, Skeet, DTL, ABT, tower,
tuition.
Tel: (01623) 823930
www.stilehollow.com
Northampton

Northampton Shooting Ground
Skeet, DTL, ABT, tuition.
Tel: (01604) 642252
www.northamptonshootingground.
co.uk

Shropshire

Bridgnorth & District Gun Club
near Wolverhampton.
DTL.
Tel: (01562) 883092

West Midlands Shooting Ground
Sporting, Skeet, ABT, Compact,
FITASC, ABT, gun room.
Tel: (01939) 200644
www.wmsg.co.uk

Staffordshire

Cross Gun Club
near Kinver.
DTL, ABT, Sporting.
Tel: (01384) 873017

Garlands Shooting Ground
Tamworth. Sporting, OT, DTL, Skeet.
Tel: (01827) 383300

Kingsley Moor Shooting Ground
near Alton Towers.
Sporting. Tel: (01782) 550371

Leek & District Gun Club
Sporting. Tel: (01538) 386127

Quarnford Shooting Ground
near Leek. Sporting.
Tel: (01298) 22204

Ranton Clay Target Club
DTL, ABT, Sporting.
Tel: (01782) 611775.

Shugborough Shooting School
Sporting, FITASC, High Skeet, DTL.
Tel: (01889) 881391

Wergs Gun Club
near Essington. Sporting, Skeet.
Tel: (01922) 476508

Warwickshire

Barby Sporting Club
near Rugby. Sporting, Skeet, DTL,
Compact, tuition. Tel: (01788) 891873
www.barbysporting.com

Honesberie Shooting Ground
Sporting, tuition. Tel: (01327) 260302
www.honesberieshooting.co.uk

Rugby & District Trap Club
ABT. Tel: (01788) 573257

Wedgnock Shooting Ground
Sporting, Skeet, DTL, Sportrap.
Tel: (01926) 491948
www.adventuresport.co.uk

YORKSHIRE & NORTH EAST

Co Durham

Spennymoor & District Clay Pigeon
Club. Sporting, Skeet, ABT, DTL.
Tel: (0191) 3772412
www.keithbutterwick.com/
spennymoor

East Yorkshire

East Yorkshire Gun Club
near Beverley.
Skeet, OSkeet, SKd, DTL, ABT, UTR,
Sporting. Tel: (01964) 551134

Humberside Shooting Ground
near Beverley. Skeet, DTL, ABT,
Compact, White Gold.
Tel: (01964) 544357
www.pthorn.co.uk/shootingground

North Wolds Gun Club
Sporting, DTL, tuition.
Tel: (01759) 368314

North Yorkshire

Coniston Shooting Ground
near Skipton.
Tel: 07831 399860

Knaresborough & District Gun Club
Sporting, Skeet, DTL, ABT.
Tel: (01423) 561174.
North of England CTC
near Rufforth.
Sporting, Skeet, OSkeet, DTL, ABT.
Tel: (01904) 738120.

North Yorkshire Shooting School
near Thirsk. Tel: (01845) 537269
www.northyorkshireshootingschool.
com

Thimbleby Shooting Ground
near Osmotherley.
Sporting, Sportrap, tuition, corporate.
Tel: (01642) 351725 (evenings)
Mob: 07776 223609

Northumberland

Bywell Shooting Ground
near Felton.
Skeet, DTL, ABT, tower, shop.
Tel: (01670) 787827
www.bywellshootingground.com

Steve Smith Shooting Ground
near Dinnington.
Sporting, DTL, Skeet, ABT, tuition,
gunshop.
Tel: (01661) 822444
www.stevesmiths.co.uk

South Yorkshire

Fox House Clay Sports
Sporting, tuition, corporate.
Tel: (0114) 2663822 or 07976 5211369

Sycamore Shooting Grounds
Sporting, DTL, D/R, tuition,
corporate.
Tel: (0114) 272 4602

West Yorkshire

Batley & District Gun Club
near Morley.
Sporting
Tel: (0113) 2631920

Emley Clayshoot
50 Sporting every 2nd Sunday. Tuition
available.
Tel: (01924) 277965

Holmfirth Shooting School
near Huddersfield.
Skeet, DTL, ABT, Compact, tuition.
Tel: (01484) 685464
www.holmfirth-shooting-school.8m.
com

WALES

Crynant Shooting Ground
Port Talbot, South Wales.
Sporting, Skeet, OSkeet, DTL, ABT,
tuition, corporate.
Tel: (01639) 881185
www.eurotrap.co.uk

Dovey Valley Shooting Ground
Llanwrin, Machynlleth, Powys.
Sporting, Skeet, DTL, simulated game,
practice, tuition, corporate.
Tel: (01650) 511252
www.doveyvalley.co.uk

Griffin-Lloyd Shooting Ground
Mid-Wales, Welsh Marches.
Sporting, ABT, OT, tuition.
Tel: (01547) 550634
www.griffinlloyd.co.uk

Llandegla Shooting Ground
North Wales.
DTL, ABT, Skeet, Compact, clubhouse.
Tel: 07971 413 891

Mid Wales Shooting Centre
near Llanidloes.
DTL, ABT.
Tel: (01686) 430215

North Wales Shooting School
Sealand, near Chester.
DTL, OT.
Tel: (01244) 812219

South Wales 2000,
near Newbridge.
Sporting, Skeet, OT, ABT, DTL, tuition,
clubhouse.
Tel: (01495) 201182
www.southwales2000.com

Treetops Shooting Ground
near Newport—5 mins from j28 M4.
Sporting, tuition.
Tel: (01633) 681197

Woodland Park Shooting Ground
Brecon.
Sporting, tuition, corporate.
Tel: 078111 89413
www.wpshoot.co.uk

SCOTLAND

Auchterhouse Country Sports
Burnhead Farm,
Auchterhouse,
by Dundee.
Sporting, FITASC, Skeet, DTL,
Compact, ABT, tuition. .
Tel: (01382) 320476
www.treemac.co.uk

Arran Gun Club
Isle of Arran,
near Altnaharra
Tel: (01549) 411245

Braidwood Sporting Clays
Braidwood
Midlem, Selkirk
Borders TD7 4QD
Tel: (01835) 870280
Mob: 07771 798342
Fax: (01835) 870280
jim@braidwoodsc.co.uk
www.braidwoodsc.co.uk
Championship standard clay pigeon
shooting ground. Practice, corporate
events, stag and hen dos. No gunshop.
Contact: James Black

Bute Clay Target Club
Kingarth. Tel: (01700) 500274

Cairndow Clay Target Club
Argyll. DTL
Tel: (01499) 600201
Carlisle & District Gun Club
near Wigton.
Tel: (01697) 331452

Central Scotland Shooting School,
near Falkirk. OSK, DTL, ABT.
Tel: (01324) 851672

Clay Target Shooting School
Houston,
Renfrewshire—3 miles from Glasgow
airport. Sporting.
Tel: (01505) 873547

Cluny Clays
Fife. Sporting, Skeet, DTL, Compact,
flush, tuition, restaurant.
Tel: (01592) 720374
www.clunyclays.com

Cortachy Gun Club
near Egnomoss. DTL, practice.
Tel: (01307) 860239

Dalvennan Country Sports
near Kirkmichael.
DTL, ABT, Sporting, Skeet, gun shop,
tuition. Tel: (01292) 531134

Drummond Shooting Ground
Drummond Castle Estate.
Tel: (01764) 681262

Dunoon & District Gun Club
Tel: (01369) 704362

Duns & District Gun Club
near Cockburnspath, off the A1.
Sporting usually last Sunday of
month. Tel: (01361) 883500

Falkirk & District Sporting CC
Tel: (01236) 726159

Glendaruel Gun Club
Tel: (01369) 820217

Harris Gun Club
near Urgha. Tel: (01859) 502141

Highland Deephaven CPC
near Evanton. Tel: (01349) 864315

Isle Of Jura
near Craighouse. Tel: (01496) 820396

Kingscliff Shooting Lodge
Aberdeenshire.
Sporting, Skeet, DTL, ABT, FITASC.
Tel: (01651) 806375

Kippen Gun Club
near Stirling. Tel: (01786) 465125

Kirkcubright Gun Club
near Gibbhill. Tel: (01557) 330447

Knapdale Gun Club
near Achnamara.
Tel: (01546) 606989

Lindertis Woods SG
Sporting, FITASC, tuition.
Tel: (01575) 572501

Loch Ness Gun Club
DTL, Skeet. Tel: (01320) 351295

Lorn Gun Club
Tel: (01631) 564431

Millport Clay Pigeon Assoc.
Tel: (01475) 530367

Monklands & District Gun Club
near Carmichael. Tel: (01555) 840562

North Ayrshire Shooting Ground
near Dalry. Sporting, DTL, Skeet,
tuition. Tel: (01294) 833297

Orkney Clay Pigeon Club
near St Ola. Tel: (01856) 874853

Rothiemurchus SG
Aviemore. Sporting, DTL, tuition.
Tel: (01479) 811272

Scottish Clay Shooting Centre
near Leuchars, Fife. Tel: (01592) 742835

Shandon Country Pursuits Ltd
near Helensburgh.
Sporting, tuition. Tel: (01436) 820838

Shetland Clay Pigeon Club
near Lerwick. ABT, DTL, Skeet.
Tel: (01950) 477381

Strathyre Gun Club
near Comrie.
DTL, tuition. Tel: (01764) 670013

Sunart & Moidart CTC
near Salen. Tel: (01967) 431602

Tarbert Gun Club
DTL, Sporting, tuition.
Tel: (01880) 820482

Thornhill Gun Club
Dumfriesshire.
Sporting, DTL. Tel: (01556) 504124

Taken from *Sporting Shooter* magazine.
For a complete and updated list, see
the magazine

The first formal rules

THE FIRST formal rules for clay pigeon shooting in Britain were published in *The Field* on 14 April 1883. These were also used in the United States in the early days of the sport.

Shooting: The Ranelagh Club Rules for Flying Clay Pigeon Shooting

Edited by H Cholmondeley-Pennell

The objects which have been kept in view in framing the following rules are, firstly, to assimilate clay-pigeon shooting as closely as possible to the conditions of game-shooting in the field; and, secondly, to meet the requirements of match and sweepstakes shooting in which money prizes or bets are involved.

It will be seen that many of the ordinary rules for shooting at the live pigeon are applicable also to clay-pigeon shooting and in this attempt at codification the rules of Hurlingham, the Gun Club, the *Cercle des Patineurs, Cercle du Bois de la Cambre*, the International Gun and Polo Club, as well as Capt Bogardus's extra rules for clay pigeon shooting, as carried out in America, have been carefully collated and selected from, with such additional rules and variations as experience indicates to be desirable. Several of the latter are particularly applicable to trapshooting at the live bird and will be found to provide for contingencies not contemplated in any of the codes of rules already referred to, but which are nevertheless of frequent occurrence in actual shooting.

Finally an attempt has been made to codify and systematise the arrangement of the articles, so as to render them conveniently available for reference,-a desideratum which cannot be considered the strong point of any of the sets of rules already in existence, owing to the 'piece-meal' process by which the parent rules have gradually grown to their present dimensions, younger clubs having again copied from the elder.

In the annexed code the clay pigeon is throughout called for the sake of brevity the 'bird'.
H Cholmondeley-Pennell.
April 10, 1883

Rule 1. Judging. There shall be no appeal from the referee's decision. If, however, the referee does not see the shot, or, from any other cause, is in doubt as to what his decision should be, he shall consult the committee or stewards, or if there be none present, such other competent persons as he may select, not being less than three in number and having no pecuniary or other interest of any kind whatsoever in the referee's decisions, either in regard to bets, stakes, or shooting score. This proviso applies equally to members of the committee or stewards.

Having taken advice in the manner described, the referee shall deliver his judgment, which shall be final, and, for the purposes of such judgment, no bird shall be retrieved, ie brought back for examination subsequent to the shot, under any circumstances, either before or after the referee's decision.

Note—This rule is essential to proper judging in clay pigeon shooting and works thoroughly well in practice. The objection which the editor has occasionally heard made to it—that a bird may be 'chipped,' or perhaps penetrated by a single shot, without being scored 'dead' under Rule 3, is really a strong argument in its favour, as it is evident that live birds so shot would in all probability be only feathered, or slightly wounded and would not fall in bounds if in match shooting, or within fair retrieving distance if in the field. If the rule has a further result of discouraging careless and slovenly shooting and obliges shooters to give their birds the middle of the charge, so as to kill them in a clean and workmanlike manner that will be an additional advantage.

Rule 2. Remarks on the shot. No persons, others than those referred to in the last rule, shall make any remark which may influence the judgment of the referee whilst the shot is under decision.

'Dead,' 'lost,' and 'no birds'
Rule 3. 'Dead' birds. A bird to be scored 'dead' shall be broken in the air; that is, a clearly

perceptible piece must be knocked out of it before it touches the ground.

Rule 4. 'Lost' birds. A bird shall be scored 'lost' if not broken in the air, as per Rule 3 (and if it is not a 'no bird' under other rules.) Shooting at a bird after it has touched the ground does not in any way effect the scoring, which is determined under the preceding rule by the result of the shot whilst the bird was in the air; but if, through his own fault, the shooter does nor fire at any bird until it has touched the ground, it shall be scored 'lost.'

Rule 5. 'No birds.' The coup shall be annulled and the shooter allowed another bird under either of the following contingencies:

A. If two or more birds are sprung instead of one and the shooter does not fire (but if he fires the bird shall be scored).

B. If the shooter stands nearer than his proper distance and makes a shot which would otherwise have been scores 'dead' (but if he stands nearer than his proper distance and misses, the bird shall be scored lost).

C. If the shooter's gun, being properly loaded and cocked, does not go off at all from any cause whatever, excepting through the fault of the shooter (vide also Rule 29, 'mis-fires.')

D. If the shooter carries his gun to his shoulder before saying 'pull,' and makes a shot which would otherwise have been scored 'dead.'

E. If the bird is sprung before, or at any noticeable interval after the shooter calls 'pull,' and he does not fire at it (but if he fires the bird shall be scored.)

F. If the bird does not fly 15 yards from its trap and the shooter does not fire (but if he fires the bird shall be scored).

G. If in the judgment of the referee the shooter is baulked by accident or otherwise.

H. If both barrels go off at once and the bird is killed (but if missed the bird shall be scored 'lost.') See also rule 29, 'mis-fires,' and 'mis-fires' in double rises, rule 33.

Rule 6. Scoring. After each shot, the referee, or scorer acting by his order, shall audibly announce the result 'dead bird,' 'lost bird,' or 'no bird,' as the case may be.

Rule 7. Traps and screens. There shall be five traps set in a semicircle, at a distance of five yards apart and hidden from the shooter by wooden screens; the traps may be partially sunk in the ground, or fixed on a level with the ground. The screen shall be high enough to hide the traps and no more.

Rule 8. Caution to puller. When the shooter is at the mark and prepared to fire, he shall call, 'Are you ready?' and, the puller replying 'Yes,' he shall call, ' Pull. (Vide also Rule 5, 'No birds.')

Rule 9. Carrying the gun to the shoulder. The gun shall not be carried to the shoulder, until the shooter has given the word 'Pull.' Before and at the moment of saying 'Pull,' the butt of the gun must be clearly visible below the arm-pit; otherwise the referee may score the shot 'No bird,' if it is a kill (but if it is missed it shall be scored 'lost').

Rule 10. Accidental delays. In sweepstakes and matches the shooter shall present himself at the mark within two minutes from the last shot, unless in case of accident, or other absolutely unavoidable delay, when the referee shall decide what time is to be allowed.

Rule 11. Number of birds and misses. Unless otherwise specially arranged, all sweepstakes, whether for pools or prizes, shall be decided at an unlimited number of birds; one miss out.

Rule 12. Late entries.

A. No shooter shall enter for pools or prizes shot under Rule 11 after the second round has begun. If previously on the ground and not shooting when called in his proper turn, or not giving his name to the scorer for entry, he shall not be allowed to enter afterwards.

B. But any shooter may enter at the end of any round of pools or sweepstakes, shot under Rules 13 and 14, by accepting the results of all the rounds previously shot and being credited with a number of misses equal to those of the worst score made.

C. Any shooter entering, after three or more previous pools or sweepstakes, with five shooters or more, have been decided, shall be handicapped back one yard further than his regular handicap.

Rule 13. Special number of birds. When it is specially decided to shoot at a fixed number of birds, the number of misses that shall exclude shall be at the same time fixed; and when any shooter has once retired, by reason of such number of misses, he shall not re-enter (except in case of every shooter in the same round missing), even if subsequently all the other shooters should miss likewise. The shooters who are left in longest shall continue 'shoot it out' for the prize or prizes.

Note—This rule obviates frequent inconvenience and the postponement of unfinished events. It cannot be said to be otherwise than fair in principle, as it only operates to definitely exclude a shooter who, out of the sane number of shots, misses oftener than his competitors. At the point, therefore, of his final retirement from the match, he has been actually beaten by those who have not missed as many times as he has; and whether in a subsequent round-that is, having shot at a greater number of birds-they do, or do not, miss, the principle remains the same. To put it in another form: A shooter missing 2 out of 4, shoots worse than one who only misses 2 out of 6; whereas the present rule puts them on a possible equality and often greatly to the detriment of the chance of the shooters who have made the best score. A moment's consideration will show this to be so

Rule 14. When special conditions are fixed under the last rule, it shall also be decided up to the end of what round entries may be made; but no shooter shall be allowed to enter who was on the ground when, or before, the first round finished and who did not then enter, except under Rule 12.

Handicapping and penalties for winning and dividing

Rule 15. The Permanent Handicap of the club is from 10 to 20 yards.

Rule 16. New Members, whose shooting is unknown, shall be handicapped for the first time at 17 yards.

Rule 17. The Temporary Handicap of the club is from 10 to 27 yards; that is to say that although no shooter is to be handicapped at the beginning of the day at a greater distance than 20 yards, he may, by winning or dividing stakes, be put back as far as 27 yards; after which, in the event of his still continuing to win, the other shooters shall all 'go in' the same distance that he would have 'gone back' if he had not been at the maximum distance.

Rule 18. Penalties for Winning or Dividing—When there are less than five shooters, those winning or dividing shall not go back. When there are five shooters or upwards, winners and dividers shall go back according to the following scale:

Winners	Dividers.	
5 shooters and upwards	1 yard	½ yard
10 shooters and upwards	2 yards	1 yards
20 shooters and upwards	3 yards	1½ yards

And so on by one additional yard for every additional ten shooters, subscribing to the pool.

Note—The principle of penalising winners according to the pecuniary value of their winnings would appear to be untenable theoretically and in practise must, of course, be impossible to regulate by general rules, except in cases where the minimum stake is habitually he same. The correct principle seems to be that a winner should be handicapped according to the superiority of skill he has shown and which skill can be approximately gathered only from the number of competitors he has defeated. The question of the stakes does not affect in any way whatever the question of skill and the object of handicapping has always been assumed, at any rate, to be to give every shooter an equal chance upon his proved merits for every event. Further, a shooter who risks £1 in a pool and wins £9 more, wins no more proportionally than if he had risked £5 and won £45 more.

Rule 19. Second and Third prizes. Winners of second, third or fourth prizes shall be temporarily handicapped back according to the number of shooters they have defeated, such number being divided by two, three and four respectively and the penalty being calculated on the result according to the table given for winners in Rule 18.

Rule 20. Saving Stakes. If two or more shooters agree to save stakes and one of them afterwards divides the pool with another person, the shooter or shooters so dividing shall pay the full stake to the non-divider or non-dividers; and a shooter who has the opportunity of dividing and does not do so, shall, for the purpose of saving stakes, be considered to stand in the same position as if he had actually divided.

Stakes and added money—how to be divided

Rule 21. Whenever the entries, carrying a money stake, for any pool or other event, amount to fifteen and upwards, a second prize shall be given out of the net proceeds of the pool (and added money, if any); and third and fourth prizes shall also be given as follows, when there are sufficient entries carrying a money stake:

Above fifteen, second prize 30 per cent of the net proceeds of the pool and added money, if any.

Above twenty-five, second prize 25 per cent, third prize 15 per cent of the net proceeds of the pool and added money, if any.

Above forty, second prize 25 per cent, third prize 15 per cent, fourth prize 10 per cent of the net proceeds of the pool and added money, if any.

Rule 22. 'Optional stakes' in the technical sense of the term, that is stakes of different amounts for the same prize, shall not be allowed; but in all cases of prizes, or added money given out of the club funds, it shall be optional to every shooter to put into the pool or not.

Note—The apportioning of optional stakes and returning of differences to shooters, is more or less inconvenient; and when, as it constantly happens, a shooter who has declared a large stake is left in to shoot it out with a shooter who has declared a small one, the objection in principle is obvious.

Shooters not putting into the pool, as above, shall not participate in any division of the proceeds under Rule 21, except where there is money added by the club, in which case the said added money shall be divided amongst the winners, as per rule 21, irrespective of whether the shooter has put into the pool or not. The stakes put into the pool shall also in like manner be divided amongst those only who have subscribed to the pool.

Rule 23. The minimum stake for pools and sweepstakes, except in case of club prizes as above, shall be ten shillings.

Loading and charges

Rule 24. Powder and Shot. One ounce and a quarter of shot by weight and four drachms and a half by measure (shaken down), of any kind of powder, shall be the maximum charge. No 5 shot is the maximum size allowed.

Rule 25. Wire Cartridges and Concentrators are, on the ground of safety, strictly prohibited; also the admixture of dust, grease, oil, or any other substance with the shot.

Rule 26.- Challenging the Gun. The gun of any shooter at the firing mark may be challenged by any other shooter, when the cartridges shall be at once examined by the referee and if the charges are found correct the challenger shall pay £1 to the shooter. The referee ex othcio may also at any time, when the shooter is at the mark, require him to allow his cartridges to be examined.

If the shooter's cartridges are charged in excess of the limits laid down in Rule 24, or with larger-sized shot, he shall be disqualified and shall forfeit his stake.

Bores of guns and allowances

Rule 27. The Maximum Bore of Gun allowed, except in private matches with special conditions, shall be no 12. Shooters using smaller bores may go in at the rate of half a yard for every size bore less than 12 down to 16, below which no further allowance shall be made.

Rule 28. Muzzle-loaders, on the ground of safety and for the general convenience of the shooters, are prohibited.

Mis-fires

Rule 29. The gun being in all respects properly loaded and cocked, the enalties, &c, for miss-fires shall be as follows:

A. Both barrels. If both barrels misfire the shooter may claim another shot, as per rule 5.

B. First barrel. If the gun misses fire with the first barrel and the shooter fires the second and kills, the shot shall be scored 'dead;' but if fires the second and misses, it shall be scored 'lost;' and if he does not fire the second it shall be 'no bird.'

C. Second barrel. If the gun misses fire with the second barrel the shooter shall be allowed another bird, using the second barrel only. In this case the first barrel shall be loaded without shot, but with a full charge of powder (of the same kind as that used in the cartridge that missed fire) and which blank charge must be fired after the bird is on the wing and the gun has been properly carried to the shoulder in the direction of the bird before the second barrel loaded with shot can be used. If then the shooter kills with the second barrel the bird shall be scored.

See also rules for Double Rise shooting.

Note—These details may appear cumbersome, but they are each and all really necessary in order to prevent unfair advantage being taken of this rule.

Double Rise shooting

Rule 30. What is a Double Rise. Unless at least two birds are in the air at the same time it is not a 'double rise' and if the shooter fires and kills, or fires and missed, whether he fires one barrel only or both and whether at one bird only or at two, the rise shall be scored 'no birds.'

Note—The shooter who has prepared himself for a double rise is naturally baulked if only one bird is sprung, or if one is sprung first and the other so long after that both birds are not in the air at the same time and if he misses either or both he is fairly entitled to have them scored 'no birds.'

Rule 31. If more than two birds are sprung, the shooter may take the rise or not, as he pleases, but if he fires the rise shall be scored.

Rule 32. Short flight. If either bird falls within fifteen yards of its trap without being 'killed,' the rise shall, at the shooters option, be shot over again; but if such bird is duly 'killed' in the air it shall be scored dead and the other bird 'dead' or 'lost,' as the case may be, provided always and in either case that the shooter may at his option claim a fresh rise.

Rule 33. Mis-fires at double rises. If the gun is properly loaded and cocked and the miss-fire, whether with the first or second barrel, or with both barrels, is caused by no fault of the shooter, the rise may be scored 'no birds,' irrespective of kills or misses, unless the shooter elects to abide by the result. If, however, both birds are 'killed' with one barrel in the air they shall be scored 'dead birds'.

Paying for the birds

Rule 34. The price of the birds shall be deducted from the amount of each separate pool or sweepstakes, unless otherwise specially agreed beforehand.

Bets

Rule 35. The committee will not recognise bets or decide any matters arising out of them.

Fines

Rule 36. A fine of ten shillings, to be added to the pool, shall be rigidly exacted for any of the following acts of negligence:

A. Pointing a gun at anyone under any circumstances.

B. Firing off a gun, except when the shooter has been called to shoot and is at the mark.

C. Closing a gun with cartridges in before arriving at the mark, or when in the act of closing it pointing it towards the shooters or spectators.

D. Quitting the mark without extracting a loaded cartridge unfired.

E. Having a loaded gun anywhere on the ground except when at the mark.

Without comparing these rules exhaustively against the ones introduced by the IBSA a decade later. It is interesting to note that the latter body specifically forbade all betting—no doubt as part of a policy of severing ties with the old days of live pigeon shooting.

Annie Oakley writes

LETTER FROM Annie Oakley to Charles Lancaster (HAA Thorn) concerning the guns he has made for her and the visits to his shooting school. The letter was published in the first edition of Lancaster's *The Art of Shooting*, 1889.[141] It is interesting because it confirms that Annie was using 20 and 12-bore guns made by Lancaster. It also makes clear that she went to Lancaster for instruction as well as to give lessons.

New York, 8 December, 1888

Dear Sir,
The four breech-loading hammerless guns you built for me are, in my opinion, as near perfection as it is possible to get them. The pair of 20-bores (weight 5lb 2oz), I have been using now nearly two years. I find them just as tight and sound as when new; I have never had any repairs except having the locks cleaned. The pair of 12-bores (6lb) are as good as the 20s. Since using your guns and receiving a few lessons from you at your splendid private shooting grounds, my shooting in the field has so much improved that now I always make a good score, even at fast and difficult birds. With many thanks for the pains you have taken in making me such perfect fitting and fine shooting guns.
I am, gratefully yours,
(Signed) Annie Oakley,
(Little Sure Shot)

Bogardus writes

LETTER FROM Bogardus to the American *Field* in December 1883:

Twelve years ago I won the title of Champion Pigeon Shot of America. Since then, no one has wrested it from me. Upon going to England, I issued a challenge to the United Kingdom and faced adversaries in eighteen matches, all of which I won. I also won the medal as Champion Shot of the World and in returning to England in 1878 captured a cup there for the same title [though there is no mention of this in *The Field* in London for this accomplishment as far as the present writer is aware].

To give the public a better idea of my claim to champion, I have challenged and beaten Mr Paine, Kleinman, Tinker and King. I have won thousands of dollars on challenges such as to kill 100 pigeons in 100 shots. I issued a challenge in the *Chicago Tribune* to any man in America to shoot a pigeon match for $5,000 and was not accepted. Again, in the *Chicago Tribune*, I challenged any man to shoot prairie chickens against me in the field for one or two weeks and winner to take stakes and all game. None of these challenges were taken, nor was my bet of $100 against $500 I could kill 100 snipes in the field without a miss.

I have made the highest records ever made in the world and general odds are now offered of $100 to $10 that they cannot be equaled by anyone. I accomplished the greatest feat of my life as far as endurance, rapid shooting and accuracy when I broke 5,500 glass balls in seven hours nineteen minutes, shooting at 5,854 and loading my own gun. After this match I was laid up for several days that were most painful.

I could go on ad infinitum to matches I have won and upon which I rest my claim to Champion Shot of the World. As I am fifty years of age, I issued a challenge last October 20 to all in the world, for I was not willing to retire until all who called themselves 'champions' had a chance to capture from me the honors I had won. That challenge has now been published five weeks and since there has been no response, I hereby publicly withdraw with my medals, badges and cups from the championship and leave the field to others with the hope the best man may win the coveted prize which proves there is so much in a name.

In conclusion, let me add that certainly expecting to have my challenge accepted by noted shots, I secured a new W&C Scott & Sons gun for this special match. But as I have not been forced to it in my retiring challenge, it will serve me well in the spring when as a partner of the Hon WF Cody I will go on the road with the Buffalo Bill Wild West Show. I will be accompanied by my four sons, aged eighteen, thirteen, eleven and eight and than whom no better marksmen of their ages live.

I am with respect.
Capt AH Bogardus[142]

Live birds and small loads

TAKEN FROM *The Gun and Its Development*, ninth edition, 1910:[143]

A modern variation of ordinary trapshooting is to use small loads of shot, thus greatly handicapping the shooter and increasing the chances of the bird. This form demands greater skill in wing shooting, perhaps, but does not require so good a gun as when a clever shot is handicapped by being put back—say to thirty yards or beyond. The sport has attained considerable popularity in the North of England and is usually contested at twenty-one yards' rise. The shooter is restricted to the use of one barrel and must no use more than one ½oz of shot, or some other fraction, as 3/8, 5/8 or 7/8oz, may be agreed upon. Usually no 8 shot is chosen and it is rare that even an expert shot, well used to this variety of trapshooting, accounts for more than half the birds. The charge of powder is proportionately reduced with the decreased shot load—2 drams for ¾oz etc. The birds are generally well trained and fetch high prices; they escape unhurt or are killed, few get away wounded, some are trapped a dozen times or more. Up to the present no special gun has been produced for this class of shooting.

Tales of a grandfather

TAKEN FROM *Clay Pigeon Shooting*, May 1928 but relating to a bygone age:

During an International Week [a popular annual institution based around competitions with foreign shooters] at the Gun Club, long, long, ago, the late Mr Dudley Ward—one of the finest specimens of an Englishman whom it has ever been my privilege to see—and a diminutive waiter named Fritz, decided as a result of a heated conversation, to run off a race at 100 yards.

The stakes were deposited and the distance marked out. The tape—a handkerchief—was held up by two brother sportsmen, who immediately the two competitors started to walk to the starting point, moved away, thus increasing the original distance of the race. The waiter was evidently out for 'blood' as he appeared with his trousers turned into socks, his coat off and sleeves turned up.

The race is started—Fritz is leading—with the Englishman in close proximity, when he closed on the waiter, picked him up and carried him right past the tape. Naturally, as first past the post, the waiter claimed victory, until he realised the joke.

Olympic Games results

Men's Trap

Year	Gold (score)	Silver (score)	Bronze (score)
1900	Roger de Barbarin FRA (17)	René Guyot FRA (17)	Comte Justinien de Clary FRA (17)
1904	not held		
1906A	Gerald Merlin GBR (24/4/4)	Ioannis Peridis GRE/CYP (24/4/3)	Sidney Merlin GBR (23)
1906B	Sidney Merlin GBR (15)	Anastasios Metaxas GRE (13)	Gerald Merlin GBR (12)
1908	Walter Ewing CAN (72)	George Beattie CAN (60)	Alexander Maunder GBR & Anastasios Metaxas GRE (57)
1912	James Graham USA (96)	Alfred Göldel GER (94)	Harry Blau RUS (91)
1920	Mark Arie USA (95)	Frank Troeh USA (93)	Frank Wright USA (87)
1924	Gyula Halasy HUN (98/8)	Konrad Huber FIN (98/7)	Frank Hughes USA (97)
1928-48	not held		
1952	George Généreux CAN (192)	Knut Holmqvist SWE (191)	Hans Liljedahl SWE (190)
1956	Galliano Rossini ITA (195)	Adam Smelczynski POL (190)	Alessandro Ciceri ITA (188/24)
1960	Ion Dumitrescu ROM (192)	Galliano Rossini ITA (191)	Sergey Kalinin URS (RUS) (190)
1964	Ennio Mattarelli ITA (198)	Pâvels Senicevs URS (LAT) (194/25)	William Morris USA (194/24)
1968	John "Bob" Braithwaite GBR (198)	Thomas Garrigus USA (196/25/25)	Kurt Czekalla (196/25/23) GDR
1972	Angelo Scalzone ITA (199)	Michel Carrega FRA (198)	Silvano Basagni ITA (195)
1976	Donald Haldeman USA (190)	Armando Marques POR (189)	Ubaldesco Baldi ITA (189)
1980	Luciano Giovannetti ITA (198)	Rustam Yambulatov URS (UZB) (196/24/25)	Jörg Damme GDR (196/24/24)
1984	Luciano Giovannetti ITA (192/23)	Francisco Boza PER USA (192/22)	Dan Carlisle (192/24)
1988	Dmitriy Monakov URS (UKR) (222/8)	Miroslav Bednarík (222/7)	Franz Peeters BEL (219/16)
1992	Petr Hrdlicka TCH (CZE) (219/1)	Kazumi Watanabe JPN (219/0)	Marco Venturini ITA (218/23/9)
1996	Michael Diamond AUS (149)	Joshua Lakatos USA (147/28)	Lance Bade USA (147/27)
2000	Michael Diamond AUS (147)	Ian Peel GBR (142)	Giovanni Pellielo ITA (140)
2004	Aleksey Alipov RUS (149)	Giovanni Pellielo ITA (146)	Adam Vella AUS (145)

A = single shot, B = double shot

Team Trap

Year	Gold (score)	Silver (score)	Bronze (score)
1908	Great Britain & Ireland (407)	Canada (405)	Great Britain & Ireland (372)
1912	United States (532)	GB & Ireland (511)	Germany (510)
1920	United States (547)	Belgium (503)	Sweden (500)
1924	United States (363)	Canada (360)	Finland (360)

Double Trap

Year	Gold (score)	Silver (score)	Bronze (score)
1996	Russell Mark AUS (189)	Albano Pera ITA (183/7)	Zhang Bing CHN (183/6)
2000	Richard Faulds GBR (187/3)	Russell Mark AUS (187/2)	Fehaid Al-Deehani KUW (186)
2004	Ahmed Al-Maktoum UAE (189)	Rajyavardhan Singh Rathore IND (179)	Wang Zheng CHN (178)

Skeet

Year	Gold (score)	Silver (score)	Bronze (score)
1968	Yevgeniy Petrov URS (RUS) (198/25)	Romano Garagnani ITA (198/24/25)	Konrad Wirnhier FRG (198/24/23)
1972	Konrad Wirnhier FRG (195)	Yevgeniy Petrov URS (RUS) (195)	Michael Buchheim GDR (195)
1976	Josef Panacek TCH (CZE) (198)	Eric Swinkels NED (198)	Wieslaw Gawlikowski POL (196)

1980	Hans Kjeld Rasmussen DEN (196/25/25)	Lars-Göran Carlsson SWE (196/25/24)	Roberto Castrillo CUB (196/25/23)
1984	Matt Dryke USA (198)	Ole Riber Rasmussen DEN (196/25)	Luca Scribani Rossi ITA (196/23)
1988	Axel Wegner GDR (222)	Alfonso de Iruarrizaga CHI (221)	Jorge Guardiola ESP (220/24)
1992	Zhang Shan CHN (223)	Juan Giha PER (222/24/3)	Bruno Rossetti ITA (222/24/2/10)
1996	Ennio Falco ITA (149)	Miroslaw Rzepkowski POL (148)	Andrea Benelli ITA (147/6)
2000	Nikolay Milchev UKR (150)	Petr Málek CZE (148)	James Graves USA (147)
2004	Andrea Benelli ITA (149/5)	Marko Kemppainen FIN (149/4)	Juan Miguel Rodríguez CUB (147/10)

Women's Olympic Skeet

Year	Gold (score)	Silver (score)	Bronze (score)
2000	Zemfira Meftakhetdinova AZE (98)	Svetlana Demina RUS (95)	Diana Igaly HUN (93)
2004	Diana Igaly HUN (97)	Ning Wei, CHN (93)	Zemfira Meftakhetdinova AZE (93)

Women's Double Trap

Year	Gold (score)	Silver (score)	Bronze (score)	1996
	Kim Rhode USA (141)	Susanne Kiermayer GER (139)	Deserie Huddleston AUS (139)	
2000	Pia Hansen SWE (148)	Deborah Gelisio ITA (144)	Kim Rhode USA (139)	
2004	Kim Rhode USA (146)	Bo Na Lee KO (145)	E Gao CHN (142)	

Womens Olympic Trap

Year	Gold (score)	Silver (score)	Bronze (score)
2000	Daina Gudzineviciute LIT (93)	Delphine Racinet FRA (92)	E Gao CHN (90)
2004	Suzanne Balogh AUS (88)	Maria Quintanal SPA (84)	Bo Na Lee KO (83)

Womens Skeet

Year	Gold (score)	Silver (score)	Bronze (score)
2000	Zemfira Meftakhetdiniva AZE (98)	Svetlana Demina RUS (95)	Diana Igaly HUN (93)
2004	Diana Igaly HUN S (97)	Ning Wei CHN (93)	Zemfira Meftakhetdiniva AZE (93)

Commonwealth Games results

Men's Trap

Year	Gold (score)	Silver (score)	Bronze (score)
1974	John Primrose CAN (196)	Brian Bailey ENG (193)	Philip Lewis WAL (191)
1978	John Primrose CAN (186)	George Leary CAN (185)	Terry Rumbel AUS (183)
1982	Peter Boden ENG (191)	Terry Rumbel AUS (190)	Peter Croft ENG (190)
1986	Ian Peel ENG (195)	Peter Boden ENG (192)	Roland Phillips WAL (192)
1990	John Maxwell AUS (184)	Kevin Gill EN (183)	Ian Peel ENG (179)
1994	Mansher Singh IND (141)	George Leary CAN (140)	Andreas Angelou CYP (137)
1998	Michael Diamond AUS (144)	Ian Peel ENG (144)	Desmond Coe NZL (141)
2002	Michael Diamond AUS (148)	Adam Vella AUS (146)	Anwer Sultan IND (142)

Trap—Pairs

Year	Gold (score)	Silver (score)	Bronze (score)
1982	Jim Ellis & Terry Rumbel AUS (190)	Peter Croft & Peter Boden ENG (186)	James Young & Martin Girvan SCO (183)
1986	Peter Boden & Ian Peel ENG (185)	Tom Hewitt & Eamon Furphy NIR (183)	Terry Rumbel & Domingo Diaz AUS (183)
1990	Kevin Gill & Ian Peel ENG (181)	Colin Evans & James Birkett-Evans WAL (178)	Russell Mark & John Maxwell AUS (178)
1994	Tom Hewitt & Samuel Allen NIR (188)	Ron Bonotto & George Leary CAN (187)	Bob Borsley & John Grice ENG (186)
1998	Mansher Singh & Manavjit Singh IND (192)	Michael Diamond & Ben Kelley AUS (190)	Bob Borsley & Ian Peel ENG (189)
2002	Michael Diamond & Adam Vella AUS (187)	Christopher Dean & Ian Peel ENG (187)	James Birkett-Evans & Michael Wixey WAL (186)

Double Trap

Year	Gold (score)	Silver (score)	Bronze (score)
2002	Rajyavardhan Singh Rathore IND (191)	Russell Mark AUS (190)	William Chetcuti MLT (189)

Double Trap—Pairs

Year	Gold(score)	Silver (score)	Bronze (score)
2002	Ali Khan Moraad & Rajya-vardhan Singh Rathore IND (184)	Michael Diamond & Russell Mark AUS (184)	John Bellamy & Richard Faulds ENG (182)

Skeet

Year	Gold (score)	Silver (score)	Bronze (score)
1974	Harry Willsie CAN (194)	Joe Neville ENG (191)	Robin Bailey ENG (189)
1978	John Woolley NZL (193)	Paul Bentley ENG (191)	Joe Neville ENG (190)
1982	John Woolley NZL (197)	Ian Hale AUS (196)	Wally Sykes ENG (195)
1986	Nigel Kelly IOM (196)	Joe Neville ENG (195)	Brian Gabriel CAN (195)
1990	Ken Harman ENG (187)	Georgios Sakellis CYP (187)	Andy Austin ENG (184)
1994	Ian Hale AUS (144)	Christos Kourtellas CYP (143)	Andy Austin ENG (143)
1998	Desmond Davies WAL (145)	Joe Trinci CAN (144)	David Cunningham AUS (143)
2002	Clayton Miller CAN (146)	Michael Thomson SCO (145)	Antonis Nicolaides CYP (144)

Skeet—Pairs

Year	Gold (score)	Silver (score)	Bronze (score)
1982	Brian Gabriel & Fred Altmann CAN (191)	Jim Sheffield & Wally Sykes ENG (190)	Alex Crikis & Ian Hale AUS (190)
1986	Joe Neville & Ken Harman ENG (195)	Brian Gabriel & Don Kwasyncia CAN (193)	John Woolley & Jeff Farrell NZL (189)
1990	Ian Marsden & James Dunlop SCO (189)	Andy Austin & Ken Harman ENG (185)	Tim Dodds & John Woolley NZL (183)
1994	Antonis Andreou & Christos Kourtellas CYP (189)	Brian Thomson & Geoffrey Jukes NZL (186)	Michael Thomson & Ian Marsden SCO (186)
1998	Costas Stratis & Antonis Nicolaides CYP (188)	Andy Austin & Drew Harvey ENG (187)	Douglas McCutcheon & Joe Trinci CAN (186)
2002	Christos Kourtellas & Antonis Nicolaides CYP (194)	George Barton & David Cunningham AUS (188)	Richard Brickell & Drew Harvey ENG (188)

British Open Skeet: Chesham Cup winners

1934	Percy Stanbury	1988	Martin Elworthy
1935	JW Hunt	1989	Martin Elworthy
1936	FT Moore	1990	Jim Munday
1937	Percy Stanbury	1991	George Digweed
1938	Percy Stanbury	1992	Mark Vessey
1939	P Jackson	1993	Allen Warren
1947	Percy Stanbury	1994	Alan Coy
1949	Joe Wheater	1995	Peter Dodd
1950	Captain WB Marriot	1996	Martin Elworthy
1951	Joe Wheater	1997	Alan Vesty
1952	Percy Stanbury	1998	Rob Hibbert
1953	Joe Wheater	1999	Neil Faulkner
1954	Joe Wheater	2000	Mike Bradley
1955	D Allingham	2001	Mark Rowbotham
1956	EL Nickols	2002	David Billington
1957	GA Morin	2003	Johnny Walker
1958	Joe Wheater	2004	Alistair Ford
1959	Joe Wheater	2005	Joe Kitson
1960	AJ Steele		
1961	Jim S Edgar		
1962	AJ Steele		
1963	NE Sansome		
1964	Bob Townroe		
1965	NE Sansome		
1966	Bob Townroe		
1967	NE Sansome		
1968	BA Smith		
1969	JR Matthews		
1970	DJ Styles		
1971	Dave Seabrook		
1972	Dave Tilden (USA)		
1973	Trevor Poskitt		
1974	Wally Sykes		
1975	Brian J Wells		
1976	D Ellis (USA)		
1977	G Paget		
1978	Jed Welham		
1979	JM Brazzell		
1980	H Harrop		
1981	Brian Parker		
1982	Barry Simpson		
1983	Jimmy Ling		
1984	Iain MacDonald		
1985	Doug Summerbee		
1986	Peter Theobald		
1987	Martin Elworthy		

Most championships
6 Joe Wheater
5 Percy Stanbury
4 Martin Elworthy
3 NE Sansome
2 AJ Steele, Bob Townroe

English Open Skeet winners

1961	JR Matthews
1962	JP Breckon
1963	Jim Sheffield
1964	Konrad Wirnhier, West Germany
1965	NE Sansome
1966	Colin Sephton
1967	Eric Grantham
1968	Eric Grantham
1969	Dave Seabrook, 97 ex 100
1970	DN Dixon
1971	Dave Seabrook 100 ex 100
1972	Wally Sykes
1973	Doddy Dodd
1974	Jim Sheffield
1975	Jim Sheffield
1976	Jim Sheffield
1977	E Chapman
1978	AG Parr
1979	Peter Billington
1980	Iain MacDonald
1981	Ian Payne
1982	Peter Dodd
1983	Geoff Waite
1984	Peter Theobald
1985	Phillip Thorrold
1986	Martin Reynolds
1987	Andrew Harvison
1988	Andrew Harvison
1989	Mickey Rouse
1990	Martin Elworthy
1991	Johnny Walker
1992	Martin Elworthy
1993	Steve Brightwell
1994	Alistair Ford
1995	Alistair Ford
1996	Mark Vessey
1997	Martin Elworthy
1998	Stevie Taylor
1999	Ray Effamy
2000	Ben Husthwaite
2001	Peter Cook
2002	Nick Coupe
2003	Dave Morgan
2004	Todd Bender
2005	Allen Warren

Most championships
4 Jim Sheffield
3 Martin Elworthy
2 Andrew Harvison, Alistair Ford, Eric Grantham, Dave Seabrook

Dougall Memorial Trophy

To perpetuate the memory of the late Mr ID Dougall, first chairman of the IBSA. Trophy purchased by various members of the association and of the gun and allied trades 1896

Year	Winner
1896	Frank Izzard
1897	A. Bruno
1898	Dr J P Moran
1899	Denis O'Conor
1900	R. Merrill
1901	F F Persse
1902	Denis O'Conor
1903	R Hutton
1904	A Maunder
1905	J F Pike
1906	A Maunder
1907	W E Steers
1908	A W Westover
1909	F W Moore
1910	G H South
1911	W O Chambers
1912	C W Ferguson
1913	M Gernaert
1914	Mr J F Pike
1920	Mark Arie
1921	E Jenkins
1922	W Lee
1923	E Jenkins
1924	F Hughes
1925	F G Horne
1926	Major HR Northover OBE MC
1927	P Stanbury
1928	F G Horne
1929	P Stanbury
1930	P Stanbury
1931	J Westaway
1932	P Stanbury
1933	C Lucas
1934	P Stanbury
1935	W J Sable
1936	T H Hughes
1937	E C Ledger
1938	T H Hughes
1939	L T Field
1946	P Stanbury
1947	W T Jones
1948	No name
1949	P Catterall
1950	E Horlock
1951	H B Pitt
1952	E Fear
1953	J Wheater
1954	W L Harris
1955	E Fear
1956	J Wheater
1957	W Heald
1958	J W Cowen
1959	D T Jones
1960	B W Bailey
1961	B W Bailey
1962	W Heald
1963	S Farrow
1964	B W Bailey
1965	B W Bailey
1966	B W Bailey
1967	B W Bailey
1968	E A Grantham
1969	J W Cook
1970	J G W Sensicle
1971	W J C Reskelly
1972	J A Haynes
1973	I Meadley
1974	D H Wynn
1975	J Young
1976	C A Stewart
1977	No name
1978	No name
1979	K W Milner
1980	A Benson
1981	R J A Fletton
1982	R W Leach
1983	K Bond
1984	G Thickbroom
1985	A B Hebditch
1986	R J A Fletton
1987	D Whyte
1988	P Ainsworth
1989	A V Womble
1990	J Broughton
1991	D J Ball
1992	R J Walsh
1993	P T Bugler
1994	R W Peacock
1995	Joe Walsh, Ire
1996	R Hall
1997	J C Yarwood
1998	J Stafford
1999	J M Bellamy
2000	J Stafford
2001	S Williams
2002	P R Morgan
2003	J Stafford
2004	I D Mullarkey
2005	Nigel Chapman

Percentage cut-off points

THE FOLLOWING are the percentage cut-off points from the CPSA averages year ending 31 October 2004.

Down the Line
Class AA = 95.6 & over
Class A = 92.6-95.5
Class B = 88.9-92.5
Class C = 88.8 & under

Single Barrel
Class AA = 94.3 & over
Class A = 90-94.2
Class B = 84.5-89.9
Class C = 84.4 & under

Double Rise
Class AA = 84.4 & over
Class A = 78.2-84.3
Class B = 68.6-78.4
Class C = 68.5 & under

English Skeet
Class AA = 96.5 & over
Class A = 93.8-96.4
Class B = 90.9-93.7
Class C = 90.8 & under

Skeet Doubles
Class AA = 95.5 & over
Class A = 92.8-95.4
Class B = 88.5-92.7
Class C = 88.4 & under

English Sporting
Class AAA = 85.1 & over
Class AA = 81.1-85
Class A = 73.9-81
Class B = 67.1-73.8
Class C = 67 & under

Sportrap
AAA = 87.4 & over
AA = 81.3-87.3
A = 75.6-81.2
B = 67.3-75.5
C = 67.2 & under

Automatic Ball Trap
Class A = 90 & over
Class B = 85.5-89.9

Class C =80.3-85.4
Class D = 80.2 & under

All Round
Class AA = 87 & over
Class A = 80.8-86.9
Class B = 74.5-80.5
Class C = 74.4 & under

Olympic Trap
Class A = 86.4 & over
Class B = 81.8-86.3
Class C = 75-81.7
Class D = 74.9 & under

Olympic Skeet
Class A = 91.2 & over
Class B = 82.6-91.1
Class C = 77-82.5
Class D = 76.9 & under

Double Trap
Class A = 80.4 & over
Class B = 69.3-80.3
Class C = 60.6-69.2
Class D = 60.5 & under

Universal Trench
Class A = 89.4 & over
Class B = 85.1-89.3
Class C = 80.1-85
Class D = 80 & under

FITASC Sporting
Class A = 80.9 & over
Class B = 74.2-80.8
Class C = 67.3-74.1
Class D = 67.2 & under

Notes and sources

1 *The Field* 18 June 1887
2 *San Diego Union-Tribune*, 19 May 2004
3 p 419, *The Iliad* by Homer, translated by Robert Fitzgerald, Oxford University Press, Oxford 1998
4 John Dryden's translation
5 See chapter XI, Badminton Library's *Archery*, CJ Longmans, Green and Co, London 1894
6 William Blackwood, Prince's Street: and John Murray, Albemarle Street, London, 1816
7 As quoted in Chapter XIII, *Scottish Archery* by J Balfour Paul, 'Lyon King of Arms', Badminton Library's *Archery*, CJ Longmans, Green and Co, London 1894
8 p166, *Modern Shot Guns*, Cassell & Company Limited, London, Paris & Melbourne, 1891
9 p234-5
10 Quoted on p145-147, in Robert Blakey's much later work *Shooting, A New Edition, with Illustrations*, George Routledge, London, 1859
11 Bunny & Gold, Shoe Lane, London, 1802
12 *The Sporting Dictionary and Rural Repository of General Information upon Every Subject Appertaining to the Sports of the Field* by William Taplin, published in 1803 by Vernor & Hood, Longman & Rees, J Scratcherd, J Walker & J Harris, vol 2, p165-167
13 *Shooting Simplified* by Purple Heather (JD Dougall), Alexandra and Shepherd, 1893 third edition 'revised and enlarged'
14 p32
15 p56
16 As reproduced in facsimile on p10 *Holland & Holland* by Donald Dallas
17 p148, *Shooting: A Manual of Practical Information* George Routledge & Sons, the Broadway, Ludgate
18 p226-7, *The Victoria History of the County of Middlesex*, edited by William Page FSA, London 1911
19 ibid
20 p469, ninth edition
21 p167, second revised edition, Cassell & Company, London, Paris & Melbourne, 1891
22 p166-8
23 p156, *Deane's Manual*, 1858
24 Longman, Green, Longman & Roberts
25 p208
26 Hurlingham Club website: www.hurlinghamclub.org.uk
27 p266-7
28 p545-9, *The Gun and Its Development*, third edition, Cassell & Company, London, Paris, New York and Melbourne, 1885
29 p168
30 p168, *Modern Shot Guns*, Cassell & Company Limited, London, Paris and Melbourne, 1891
31 p20
32 p122
33 p452, *The Gun and Its Development*, fifth edition, Cassell & Company, Limited, London, Paris & Melbourne, 1892.
34 p180, *Modern Shot Guns*—the match is also mentioned in other Greener works

35 *Field, Cover and Trap Shooting*, appendix to 1878 edition
36 p344-345, *Shooting: Field and Covert*
37 p20-22, *Holt's Shooting Calendar*, 1882, published, London 1883
38 p2, *Trapshooting: The Patriotic Sport*, revised edition, Sportsman's Review Publishing Company, Cincinnati, Ohio, 1920.
39 p350, *The Complete Shot*, Methuen & Co, London, 1907
40 p553-5, Cassell & Company, London, Paris, New York and Melbourne, 1885
41 p199, *The Dead Shot*, by 'The Marksman', 1866
42 p121, *Experts on Guns and Shooting*, by Teasdale Buckell, 1900
43 issue XXVII *On Target!*
44 p208, *The Dead Shot*, by 'The Marksman', 1866
45 p9, *Holland & Holland*
46 p9
47 p196-197, Walter Winans, *The Art of Revolver Shooting*, GP Putnams Sons London and New York, 1901. This magnificently produced work also includes useful chapters on 'Big gameshooting With The Revolver', 'Shooting From a Bicycle,' 'Shooting in the Dark' and 'Clay-Shooting with the Revolver'. I have once tried clayshooting with a cheap Belgian .410 double hammer pistol and found it to be far harder than anticipated. As with any light small-bore, the essential problem is over-swinging. It might have been easier with Winan's refined Renette, though
48 p91-2, *Modern Shot Guns*, Cassell & Co, London, Paris and Melbourne, 1891
49 p103-4 *Shooting with Game and Gun Room Notes*, published by Cogswell & Harrison, London 1900
50 p168, *Holt's Shooting Calendar*, 1883
51 p471, *The Gun and Its Development*, by WW Greener, ninth edition, 1910
52 *The Victoria History of the County of Middlesex*, p267, Volume II, edited by William Page FSA
53 p394, *Shooting Directory* by RB Thornhill, Longman, Hurst, Rees and Orme, Paternoster-Row, 1804.
54 *Sporting Shooter* magazine, August 2004, p15
55 p183
56 p22-23, *Trapshooting: The Patriotic Sport*, revised edition, 1920
57 First edition, JB Ford & Co, New York, 1874, p414
58 p35-37, *The Art of Shooting*, 1889, printed by McCorquodale & Co. Ltd, The Armoury, Southwark
59 p16, *Trapshooting: The Patriotic Sport*, revised edition, Sportsman's Review Publishing Company, Cincinnati, Ohio, 1920
60 p365-366, *Practical Hints on Shooting*
61 p106-7, *Wingshooting*, published by Rand, McNally& Co, Chicago and New York 1895
62 p562-563, *The Gun and Its Development*, by WW Greener, 1885
63 p51-2 *Trap Shooting: The Patriotic Sport*
64 p417-418, *The Dead Shot*, by 'The Marksman', seventh edition, 1896
65 p8 *On Target!* Winter, 2002-2003, Issue XXI
66 As quoted without date on p84 *'Wild West' Doc Carver: Spirit Gun of the West*
67 *The Field*, 19 April 1879
68 Phaidon, Christie's, Oxford, 1989
69 p150, *The Greener Story*, Quiller Press, 2000.
70 *Powders I Have Used*, Annie Oakley, the Dupont Powder Co, 1914
71 p53, as quoted by Bob Hinman in *The Golden Age of Shotgunning*
72 as quoted in Raymond W Thorp's *'Wild West' Doc Carver: Spirit Gun of the West*, W Foulsham & Co, London, 1957, together with newspaper extract from *The Louisville Commercial*, of 21 February 1883
73 ibid
74 *'Wild West' Doc Carver: Spirit Gun of the West*

75 p134-6, *Holt's Shooting Calendar* 1882
76 p564, *The Gun and Its Development*, by WW Greener, Cassell & Co, London, fifth edition, 1892
77 p564, *The Gun and Its Development*, third edition.
78 See her letter to HA Thorn, p221, *The Illustrated Treatise on The Art of Shooting*, first ed, 1889, printed by McCorquodale Ltd & Co Ltd, The Armoury, Southwalk, by Charles Lancaster aka HA Thorn
79 p171-172
80 p35-37, *The Art of Shooting*, 1889, printed by McCorquodale & Co Ltd, The Armoury, Southwark.
81 p39 *House of Churchill*, Safari Press Inc, Long Beach, California, 2003
82 p418-9, *The Deadshot*, by 'Marksman,' Longmans, Green and Co, London, New York and Bombay, 1896
83 As quoted on p114 of *Shooting with Game and Gun Room Notes*
84 p229-30, *House of Churchill*, Safari Press Inc, Long Beach, California, 2003
85 p228, *The Field*, 5 August 1893
86 Author's collection
87 p228, 5 August 1893
88 p399
89 15 June 1895
90 *The Field* 16 June 1900
91 p398
92 Vol 4, *Rackets to Zebra, Encyclopaedia of Sport*, 1912 second edition, Richard Clay and Sons Ltd, Brunswick Street, Stamford Street SE, and Bungay, Suffolk various contributors
93 p72-3, *A Brief History of the Westley Richards Firm 1813-1913*, by Leslie B Taylor and published by Shakespeare Head Press, Stratford Upon Avon
94 *The Field* 14 July 1914
95 *The Field* 4 July 1914
96 p953
97 p146-147
98 p198-199, Walter Winans, *The Art of Revolver Shooting*, GP Putnams Sons London and New York, 1901
99 p19, *Clay Pigeon Shooting* by FM McFarland, Percival Marshall & Co, London, 1964.
100 p103, *'Wild West' Doc Carver: Spirit Gun of the West*
101 March 1925
102 *Shooting Times*, 3 January 1925
103 p2, August 1929
104 p4
105 10 August 1927
106 Source: Don Masters
107 6 August
108 p81, the 1932 fourth edition
109 p20, *Clay Pigeon Shooting*, Percival Marshall & Co, 1964
110 As quoted on p262 of *The Other Mr Churchill* by MacDonald Hastings.
111 *Bomber Crew*, Channel 4 Television, first UK transmission 29 November 2004
112 p21, *Clay Pigeon Shooting*, Percivall Marshall & Co, London, 1964
113 p21, *Clay Pigeon Shooting*, Percivall Marshall & Co, London, 1964
114 p278-9, *Rifle and Gun*, Macdonald and Evans Ltd, London, 1953
115 With thanks to JA Crawford and PG Whatley from whose work *The History of W&C Scott Gunmakers* this is partly copied
116 p9, *Pull!* magazine, November-December 1999
117 p30-31
118 p1-2
119 Source: Don Masters

120 p3, *Clay Target Shooting*, December 1927
121 p22-23, *Clay Pigeon Shooting*
122 p68, *Handbook on Clay Target Shooting*, Nobel, 1927
123 p5-6, *Trapshooting: The Patriotic Sport*, Revised Edition, Sportsman's Review Publishing Co, Cincinnati, Ohio, 1920
124 p206, *Shotgun Psychology*, Charles Scribner's Sons, New York
125 p64, *Black's Wing and Clay*, 1999
126 Charles Scrivener's & Sons, New York, 1938
127 Interview with author 2003
128 As quoted by J Balfour Paul, chapter XIII Badminton Library: *Archery*, CJ Longmans, Green and Co, London 1894
129 ibid
130 p170, Volume III *Hunting to Racing*
131 Baron de Coubertin, inspired by the Bishop of Philadelphia
132 *The Field* May 23 1908
133 NRA of America, 1978
134 p75, *BOA Report*, 1956
135 p116-7, *Olympic Shooting*
136 p126, *Clay Shooting*, published by Ward Lock, London 1990
137 Official website of the Chinese Olympic Committee
138 p415, *Atlanta Official Report*
139 *Sydney Morning Herald*, 4 September 1998
140 *Time*, 25 September 2000
141 McCorquodale & Co. Ltd, The Armoury, Southwark
142 As quoted by Bob Hinman, p71-2, *The Golden Age of Shotgunning*
143 p481, *The Gun and Its Development*, ninth edition, Cassell & Company, 1910

Index